SURVIVING THE SILENCE

SURVIVING THE SILENCE

Black Women's Stories of Rape

Charlotte Pierce-Baker

W. W. Norton & Company

New York   London

Copyright © 1998 by Charlotte Pierce-Baker

Quote from the forthcoming *In Search of Africa* by Manthia Diawara, Harvard University Press. "The Creation Story," *The Woman Who Fell from the Sky.* Copyright © 1994 by Joy Harjo. Reprinted with permission of W. W. Norton and Company, Inc. "The Hill Has Something to Say" by Rita Dove, copyright 1993, reprinted by permission of the author. This material originally appeared in *Selected Poems.* "Spelling" by Margaret Atwood © 1981, reprinted by permission of the author. This material originally appeared in the poetry collection *True Stories.*

For information about permission to reproduce selections from this book, write to Permissions, W. W. Norton & Company, Inc., 500 Fifth Avenue, New York, NY 10110.

The text of this book is composed in Adobe Garamond with the display set in Corvinus Skyline & Metro Black Two Desktop composition by Roberta Flechner Manufacturing by Quebecor Printing, Fairfield Inc. Book design by Chris Welch

Library of Congress Cataloging-in-Publication Data
Pierce-Baker, Charlotte.
Surviving the silence : Black women's stories of rape /
by Charlotte Pierce-Baker.
p. cm.
Includes bibliographical references (p.   ).
ISBN 0-393-04661-3
1. Rape—United States—Case Studies. 2. Afro-American women—
United States—Crimes against—Case Studies. I. Title.
HV6561.P54   1998
362.883'08996073—dc21   98-14518
CIP

W. W. Norton & Company, Inc., 500 Fifth Avenue, New York, N.Y. 10110
http://www.wwnorton.com

W. W. Norton & Company Ltd., 10 Coptic Street, London WC1A 1PU

1 2 3 4 5 6 7 8 9 0

FOR MY PARENTS, JOSEPH AND WESLYNE,
WHO TAUGHT ME LOVE, PATIENCE, COURAGE

AND . . .
FOR ALL THOSE WHO HAVE TRIED
TO HEAL THEIR SOULS.

It was as if the words were helping her, as if the words repeated again and again could be a substitute for memory, were somehow more than the memory.

—*Gayle Jones,* Corregidora

[The stories] are all we have . . . to fight off illness and death. You don't have anything if you don't have the stories.

—*Leslie Marmon Silko,* Ceremony

CONTENTS

Many of the names in this book have been changed to protect the individuals.

Like an ebony phoenix, each in her own time and
with her own season had a story.

—Gloria Naylor,

The Women of Brewster Place

BEGINNINGS

There was a void . . . an absence . . . a silence. There were no voices. There were no structures of feeling or support. So I went in search of structures and voices—in search of community.

I remember vividly a young black woman I'll call Renee; I met her while on hotline duty. I had been called to a "Code R" at Thomas Jefferson Hospital in Philadelphia, Pennsylvania. (Code R indicates that a rape victim has been admitted to the hospital's emergency room.) I thought she was nineteen or twenty years old. She had cuts, fresh bruises, a look of eerie calm. She was waiting to be examined by a physician and sampled for a "rape kit." As an emergency room crisis volunteer for Women Organized Against Rape in Philadelphia, known as WOAR, my duties were specific:

help the survivor feel comfortable and safe, explain procedures, and tell her about WOAR's services. We were instructed to stress that the rape was not her fault and instructed to help her feel less alone. I asked Renee several questions. No response. She obviously was shaken. But her silence was as solid as stone. It made me desperate with uneasiness. I knew Renee needed immediate attention. But in the emergency room everyone waits her turn.

Renee seemed to resent my presence. I asked if she wanted to be alone, and she answered with an abrupt "No." We sat in silence, staring into our separate spaces. Before long, Renee began to speak without my urging. She was not nineteen or twenty. She was fourteen. Only hours before, she had been raped at school by a fifteen-year-old boy in her neighborhood who was "known for doing things like this." She said, "I am not the first." When I asked if the boy had been caught, suspended, and arrested, Renee answered: "Why would anybody care? Nobody's going to do anything anyway." The boy had cornered Renee in a locker room—raped her while a group of students stood and watched. This fourteen year old had resisted as best she could. But now, alone in the ER—with me and her much older boyfriend—she needed and was asking for help. The rapist would be out of school for two, at the most, three days—perhaps a week. Then back to terrorize. According to Renee, this was a familiar story. Why should she go back to school if no one could keep in check this fifteen-year-old boy or ensure the safety of girls in the school community? I realized with a sudden emptiness that I had no idea what Renee would confront when she returned to school after "telling."

We who have survived must tell our stories for Renee and her classmates.

While I was nervously awaiting my turn on the stand at my own preliminary hearing—after bringing criminal charges against one of the black men who raped me—I saw women come and go. The other women who were there on the day of my hearing happened also to be African American. I waited and listened. (Everyone waits her turn in the courts of criminal justice.) I learned implicitly that a woman's word is not enough, that we, the women harmed by rape, serve merely as witnesses. The rendering of our specific brutalities, as in any other case in court, becomes "The Commonwealth vs. the Defendant." Our names do not appear.

When my turn came, I told my story; and the case was given a date. It would go to trial. At the time, I didn't know to be happy. Just as well, since I also didn't realize that going to trial meant I would be dragged through harsh details time after time after time, until I persuaded a jury that my rape had actually occurred and that the "alleged perpetrator" was, in fact, the man who raped me. There were many women, on that day and others, who were not given a trial date due to "insufficient evidence."

As a woman harmed by rape, I write for those women who never have their day in court—who, like Renee, are never guaranteed the safety of everyday life.

I met many women while training to become a volunteer for WOAR. Some disclosed their rapes for the first time during our training. As they labored through rape awareness videos and case history role playing, the pain of their scars was palpable. They fought to endure in order to bring solace to others. Some were able to remain; several had to leave to do the work of their own souls.

I write for those who could not stay.

There are women who continue to care for families and children, when rape and sexual violence have ripped away all intimacies of family life. Husbands, friends, lovers flee; they cannot bear the strain of disclosures, the effort of healing. These women live alone in their nightmares. They have no mediators for their "tellings."

I write for the women who lie alone in the night.

There is an uncanny silence surrounding the trauma of black rape. I believe I understand the silence of black women who survive. I am a black woman wounded, and because I kept silent for so long, my newly found voice is still emerging. Silences have become important to me. I'm not sure why I refused to tell. But I do know I was intensely afraid of the truth in all its manifestations. I was afraid to be heard.

Though I continued "to function" after being raped, it would be years before I began to integrate the trauma into my life. It would take years to embrace the joy of seeing morning light as anything but the end of yet another fearful night, survived with scant sleep or rest. But once I allowed myself to feel the fury that anyone—especially black men, who shared my skin color—would burglarize my home, steal my possessions, rob my body, and wound my soul, then—and only then—I was able to begin my own internal sorting, grieving, and retrieving.

I write now for those who must make the same journey.

Surviving the Silence is the mapping of a new space. A space in which black women can learn to trust and speak to "one other" and then to "one another" in a sharing recovery of memory, of sanity. In this book of voices are voices that worried my head for so long. Now they are "out." Never again will they be silent.

In *Surviving the Silence* you will meet women who have closeted themselves. In some instances, days of silence became years of undisclosed pain. For other women, survival of trauma remained unheard and sadly unheralded. All the women who have told their stories in these pages have chosen to live in some degree of secrecy, to protect themselves from censure, to stave off family discomfort and worry, or to protect those they have been conditioned to believe are African American "brothers." As I have connected with and come to know these courageous women, I have discovered striking, useful, and productive stories of black survival. Women came forward as I disseminated a "call for interviews" to several Philadelphia agencies. Then, by word of mouth, others heard of my work. Many chose to participate. Slowly, cautiously, women emerged from shadows of silence. I found myself in a world tragically inhabited by more—more than ever I imagined.

While men are not usually incorporated into discussions of rape, they have been allowed place and voice in this book. In the pages that follow, you will hear black men who have nurtured and supported black women surviving rape. These black men labored to understand. They speak with honesty as they attempt to tell other men how to feel, reach out, and connect with women wounded. They speak, I believe, to make our collective black lives better, to acknowledge our wounds and, more precisely, our black woman sorrow. They help us "to tell."

As a researcher and a survivor, my voice joins the voices of other women in this book—women for whom I desperately began searching after my own rapes in 1981. The voices of my mother, my father, and my husband join the book's chorus of witnesses. I have every faith that the force of this book's collective memory will engender a sense of community and renewed possibilities of self-love.

In order to ensure positive beginnings, I ask the reader to be patient, to read only as comfort allows. This is not an easy book, or a soft book. I have tried to tell my story and the stories of my survivor-sisters in ways I feel they must be told: with honesty, humility, and compassion. I profess to have no answers. This book is the story of who I was, who I became for a time, and the way in which I reconstructed my life. It is the story of people I found and refound, and chose to take along with me on my journey toward healing.

In the telling of the other women's stories, I have been protective of privacy (perhaps overly so) and the special relationship I now have with each woman. They gave me their trust. To attempt to explain, analyze, theorize, or interpret their actions would be a betrayal of that trust. If I were to further intrude into their lives with theory or precise interpretations, I would surely compromise their stories. They might flee, be silenced once again.

In our conversations, each woman began a new personal journey toward wholeness. Some have been successful and are working in productive ways. Others still struggle with sharing a deeply painful part of their lives, finding themselves repeatedly trapped in victim behavior. For all women with whom I have conversed, I must listen, without judgment or comment, and pass on their words and wisdom. I know now my role is the ancient one of the storyteller: to open the door and create a medium for survival voices. The storyteller of Native American lore is covered with—attached to—myriad cultural figures. Perhaps she is really only listening. For trauma *must* tell its own story.

Each reader, I hope, will find and take away what she or he needs. Our souls heal on levels, as wounds to flesh heal in layers. I am certain, however, that we can never again wait in silence. We must "tell." We must begin now to talk to one another—woman to woman, woman to man. And since we must, and I make the demand, it is only fair that *I* begin—use my own voice—before others speak. The reader must know how I was *then* in the dark silences and despair of 1981. My voice joins our collective voices, and we shall scratch the surface of our wounds. We shall form community with our stories. We will cast spells with our disclosures. "Spelling," by Margaret Atwood, wondrously captures how the spell of language, the power of stories, can move in the world:

. . . .

A word after a word
after a word is power.

*

At the point where language falls away
from the hot bones, at the point
where the rock breaks open and darkness
flows out of it like blood, at
the melting point of granite
where the bones know
they are hollow & the word
splits and doubles & speaks
the truth & the body
itself becomes a mouth.

*

This is a metaphor.*

———

. . . .

*And so—I write . . . as our words split and double and speak
the truth of bodies wounded.*

*Margaret Atwood, from "Spelling," *True Stories* (Simon & Schuster: New
York, 1981), p. 64.

Among the Mande, there is a traditional song called "Baninde," which means being in the mood to say no to oppression, to refuse categorically, to defy the oppressor. Grior women sing this song to exhort young people to resist injustice the way their forebears did, in order to make the world a better place. The song keeps returning to the refrain, "Ban ye dunya la dyala," or "resistance brings joy to the world." Then come the names of heroes whose resistance transformed Africans' lives for the better. A modern version of the song would go like this: "Say no! Martin Luther King said no! And he brought joy to the world. Say no! Malcolm X said no! And it brought joy to the world. . . . Say no! Black women said no to sexism and racism! And it brought joy to the world."

—Manthia Diawara,
In Search of Africa

Part I

PERSONAL NARRATIVE

To put it simply, we must begin to tell the truth, in groups,
to one another.

—CAROLYN HEILBRUN, *WRITING A WOMAN'S LIFE*

A WOUND
TO THE SOUL

*I just lay there, in the early morning light wondering where God
had been last night.*

—P. J. Gibson, *"Masks, Circles: Healing the Pain"*

On September 6, 1981, the evening of a gorgeous late summer–early fall day, the kind with winds that catch ceiling-high curtains and whip them gently against the window sills, I was raped. Horrors occurred in a house that only hours before rang with the giggles and laughter from my own child and other neighborhood children. My husband and child were in that house. The violations, humiliation, and wounds of that day changed me and the course of my life. It changed all of us.

With the sun high and the breeze in our faces, my husband David (a pseudonym) and I relaxed in conversation at the kitchen table, watching our nine-year-old, passionately playful son, Matthew (a pseudonym),* run in and out of the back door playing "catch me if you can" with his best friends. We scanned the local newspapers for good Labor Day sales. We tore out an ad for a microwave at a super low price, and we planned to buy it the next day. We felt pleased with ourselves for holding out for the right time. A microwave would give our son, Matthew, a sense of independence—he could "cook up a pizza" whenever he wanted. And so we sat and talked, not concerned about dinner, which we always prepared together on weekends. It felt good sitting there enjoying the warm breeze, with no pressing agenda and nothing immediate to worry about. *We never purchased the microwave oven.*

As the light in the sky began to fade and the air to cool, we turned our attention to dinner. There must be something in the freezer we could scare into a decent meal. The freezer was in the basement. As I got halfway down the stairs, a chill swept over me— yet there was no window open. I stopped. I was afraid—but of what? With great haste and determination, I crossed to the other side of the basement, opened the freezer door, snatched out three fancy, gourmet dinners, quickly ran back up the stairs, latched the door, and picked up our conversation where I'd left off. I didn't mention that queer sensation I felt in the basement. I convinced myself that my fears were "childish." *Even today I wonder if things might have been different if I had listened to my instincts. Told my husband of the strange chill in the air. I wonder how long he had been waiting down there?*

We ate dinner and then began Matthew's preparations for his first day of school in fourth grade. The beginning of a new school year signaled, of course, the end of summer. And Matthew was

*During the beginning stages of writing my narrative, I was unable to use my husband's and son's real names in relating the traumas of my story, so I used pseudonyms.

reluctant to return after spending a week with indulgent grand-parents.

As I write this, I remember how the light in the evenings shifted that time of year. The air always had a touch of crisp promise. I now bristle when the light in the sky begins its seasonal changes and I hear the song of geese.

Finally, with clothes laid out, plans made for pickup on Tuesday, David and I discussed what our full schedules would look like for the next couple of weeks. And then, Matt was in bed. Asleep? We could never be sure. Matt was a thinker even as a small child. He would spend hours planning his next super-hero feat to be execut-ed with his best friend, Jimmy. David and I settled down about 11 P.M. for the late news, sleepy and content from the day's relaxation, enjoying the comfort of being home together.

Nodding in and out of the late-night sports coverage on the sofa of our second-floor family room, we both jolted to the sound of a loud crash—no, a blunt thud—like body against wood. We were on our feet in an instant. At that moment I knew the meaning of the word "*non*sense." *We had already locked up. The winds had calmed.* We exchanged glances. David went to the hallway to listen. "Check Matt," he said. I headed for the third floor where our son slept. Perhaps he had fallen out of bed? Without my knowing, David headed for the first floor.

Matt was sound asleep—or pretended to be. But when I returned again to the second floor to make my report to David, he was nowhere to be found. It was now extremely quiet. I called to David. No reply. As my adrenaline pumped, my ears and neck began to burn; I could hear my head pounding. Something was not right; I just knew it. The lower half of my body became too heavy to move. I called to David again. This time, his voice returned. Weird, calm, almost matter-of-fact, he said: "There is someone in the house. Don't do anything. He's got a gun." This only happened in movies. His words couldn't be true. Should I push the alarm panic button?

I suddenly couldn't remember whether it would sound aloud or silently. I couldn't remember anything. I couldn't think. So—I just listened. At that moment my mind went on vacation, my body on automatic pilot. I listened for orders—for directions. Anything to make me move.

In the midst of my mind sorting, I heard a second voice—not my husband's—and then I knew that this—whatever "this" was—was real. Options? Strategies? A plan? *All I could think of was, "I don't want to die."* I heard a voice say: "Get down here, bitch, and open this door." He meant the front door. I could see it from the top of the stairs where I had been standing—where I had been waiting, it seemed, forever. Then I saw him. He had a gun at the base of David's head. With the gun he pushed David along the downstairs hallway as he shouted obscenities at me. He glanced upward from time to time, ordering: "Get down here and open the fucking door."

My mind tried desperately to make sense of chaos. Where had he come from? How did he get in? What had been the loud noise we heard only a few minutes earlier? Did we forget to put on the alarm before coming upstairs? *How thoughtless.* And then I looked to the front door and saw that the red light was illuminated. The alarm *was* on. How *did* he get in? I deliberately, carefully walked down the stairs as ordered—head erect, eyes half closed—feeling with the toe of my sneakers the turn of each step. I was carrying the alarm keys in my hand. As I made my descent, David kept repeating, "Don't do anything. Just come down and do what he says." The voice said: "I'll kill him, bitch, if you try anything." The intruder seemed agitated, and I definitely did not want to make him more nervous. *I remember thinking to myself, "If I walk slowly, it will calm him."* As I approached the bottom of the staircase, I kept my eyes narrowed so I wouldn't fall. I kept repeating slowly, calmly, and (I think) loudly, *the mantra pounded in my head,* "I can't see you. My eyes are closed. I can't see you. I'm coming to open the door. Don't hurt us. I can't see you." *I could see everything.*

When I got to the bottom of the stairs in the hallway, the man pushed David to the floor and put the gun in my back nudging my unwilling body along to the front door. "Open it and the alarm better not go off or I'll blow your brains out," he threatened. When David tried to speak consoling words, the man kicked him twice in the face. "Shut the fuck up," he said. I shakily and hurriedly began to disarm the alarm and open the front door, thinking that the intruder must want to get out after gaining access. *I must get him out as quickly as possible.* Did I think he had gotten into the wrong house? Somehow I managed to delude myself that he had. With quivering fingers I worked assiduously to unlock the two locks. I never screamed. Time slowed, and the instant the door parted from its hinges, it was forced inward, knocking me to the side. I saw another face—the second man. He was much darker of complexion, stocky, with a black knit watchcap covering his hair. He shoved past me into the hallway. It was then that I realized two things: our porch light was not on, and this was not the end.

The mayhem began. Scuffling, shouting, pushing, confusion— orders, obscenities spat in our faces. Do this. Do that. "Stand still, bitch." "Motherfucker if you want to live, you better shut the fuck up." Still Matthew had not appeared. One of the two men asked if there was anyone else in the house. *Should I lie?* Finally, I said our son was sleeping. "Get him down here!" they ordered. "Please," I begged, "please, don't bother our son." They talked over each other. Loud, obscene voices. *Shh-shh-shh . . . you'll wake him.* They rustled about, looking for what was not there. "Where's the money? Where's the safe? They said you had a safe. Where's the safe?" The gun was waving about my face. I said softly, "There *is* no safe." *A safe? And who are "they"?* "There *is* no money." And I got louder, "Take what you see and get out. We don't have anything. We don't keep money in the house." Then one man spoke up again, pointing at me: "Get the boy down here."

They shouted orders to one another. The first guy in the house was clearly in command. One man even called the other by name. *Remember the name. You might need to know it. Remember the name.* I still, to this day, can't be sure of the name I heard that night. But I remember thinking it was such a soft-sounding name for someone so brutal, like Billy or Jimmy or Bobby. It was the name of someone I knew—and liked.

Prompting us with his gun, one of the men told David and me to lie face down in the hallway. Without questioning we immediately did as we were told. David and I couldn't see each other, but I knew my husband was there. I could feel his presence. I gazed upward, and then I saw Matt. He was leaning over the third-floor banister in his two-piece, colorful super-hero pajamas, quietly watching and listening. He said nothing. He just stared. He looked so small. It was eerie. Now I know why in the movies at moments of trauma, filmmakers use slow motion for effect. Our world slowed down to almost stopping. Every gesture, every shift of the eye registered.

As the first man ran up the stairs toward my son, I reached out my hand and said, "Come down, honey. It's okay. Come down and get on the floor here with Mom. It's okay." *What a lie. All of it.* I pleaded with the two men not to hurt him: "He's only a kid." One guy, the thinner one—the one with the gun, the first one to smash through the basement door into our first-floor hallway—met Matt at the top of the stairs. They disappeared for a few moments. *Oh God. Don't let them hurt him.* And then they reappeared—just a couple of minutes later. As they descended the stairs that night, I saw only my son, one step then another step, then another—even though one of the men was at his side. So slow. *Was his hand on my child? Please don't let him touch my child. Not even his arm!* I held Matt's eyes with my own; I didn't want him to be afraid. I knew my own fear. I wanted it to be enough for the two of us. I wanted him to believe—however falsely—that I could protect him, that I could make it all all right. It took forever for him to reach my arms; it felt as if someone or something might snatch him before he made it. When Matt got to the bottom of the stairs, I pulled him to me, brought him to the floor and held him close, whispering comforting sounds—as if my nine-year-old son were a baby. But at that moment, he *was* my baby.

The two men proceeded to search the house. They rummaged through closets and bureaus, boxes and desk drawers. They took the diamond engagement ring and gold wedding band off my second finger, left hand. *It was the most beautiful diamond I'd ever seen. Not big; just right. I remember it caught the laser beam at the museum and sent blue prisms dancing about the walls. I remember the Christmas David gave it to me.* Later they robbed me of the thin gold neck chain I wore—another gift from David. They were ever so careful as they unlatched it. I later learned that they could sell the chain more easily if it were unbroken. They did not take David's wedding band. *Strange.* More shouting, running, frantic movements. *I've not worn a diamond since.*

I now know that I was in shock throughout the trauma of that evening. But I do remember trying with great effort to overcome my chilling fear and to make myself remember everything for later—and then promptly forgetting everything. A self-silencing. It has taken me years to reconstruct situations and sequencing from that night. It has taken me years to learn again how to focus, how to concentrate, how not to let my mind wander. I remember that night making myself try to remember the names I had heard. *I must remember. I must remember everything.* What I did remember well at the end of the evening was the face and shape and feel of the body of the first man. I knew his approximate age from the smoothness of his body against my own. *I remember being surprised. How could such a young man be so cruel?* And I remembered the peculiar smell of the second. That smell lingered in my clothes, on my body, in my hair—a sour mixture of old vomit and cheap dead cigars.

The first man ordered my husband to the second floor with his partner. Matt and I were left on the first floor in the living room. I had no idea what was to happen next. *The mind protects.* I shivered as I crouched on our new, gorgeous, rust-colored velveteen sofa. *We had loved it on sight. We had not bought a new sofa since we were first married fourteen years before.* We had just finished paying for it. And there we sat, Matt and I, huddling for warmth on a pleasant September evening as if we had been abandoned on a tundra. I could feel the almost imperceptible quivering of his slight body next to mine. *He seemed so tiny, so fragile.* My heart pounded for us both.

The first man began to hurl the same questions again. "Where's the money? Where's the safe? Where're the valuables?" There were none, I said, over and over. I told him that I did have silver flatware—a wedding gift—in the dining room. I told him I had "good dishes" (china) and some "good sterling", but that was all. "Take anything. Take it all. Just don't hurt us." And his refrain: "Shut up, bitch." After some time, the second man rejoined his partner on the first floor. They moved hurriedly through the rooms of the dimly lit house searching for loot. David had not returned; he was nowhere in sight. I couldn't even hear him, but my mind did not allow me to think of anything horrible. I knew I had Matthew with me; and if they intended to hurt *him,* they had to hurt me first. I knew I had to get through the next minute, and then the next . . . and then the next.

The two men appeared and stood before Matt and me on the sofa. They exchanged whispered words, snatched a small goat-skin rug from the floor, tossed it behind the sofa and ordered Matt onto the rug: "Lie down, and be quiet." *They were going to take him from me! NO. I wouldn't permit it—somehow. NO. You cannot have him.* At this point I thought we were going to be shot. I held Matthew tightly and possessively as he wiggled about; I wanted him to be in my arms when they killed him. I also knew I did not want him to see *my* death. If we were to die, we would die together. *Perhaps if I hold him, it will hurt less, I thought. He won't be alone.* They were insistent. "Get on the rug." They tried to pull him from me. Matt and I clung.

My mind and body split; my gut knew that something terrible was about to happen. My mind just didn't let the rest of me in on it. But I felt Matt had a chance of surviving if he could get out of that room. He could not be a part of "it," whatever "it" was. Again I gripped him tightly; I lied hysterically, "He's a problem. He'll scream and make noise if he's alone. You don't want that, do you? Someone might hear him yelling. And that would be terrible. The police might come." *Please let someone hear.* I begged them to take Matt upstairs with his father. For whatever reason, they did. *A blessing.* The short, darker man took my son to the second floor. I watched Matt slowly ascend. And then . . . I was totally alone . . . with a stranger in my own home. And then began the humiliations: the groping and raping and shoving, oral penetration, and repeated attempts at sodomy. *And my son might have been there.*

The thin man, the first one to break through our basement door, shoved his gun in my face and threatened: "Take off all your clothes." *I remember exactly what I was wearing that evening. White jeans and a bright aqua tee shirt. I liked the outfit.* "Will you leave us alone, if I do that?" "Yeah," he said. "You promise you won't hurt us?" "Yeah," he repeated. *I believed him.* Undressing quickly, I felt relieved that it would soon all be over. *I only had to undress.* Why ever would I believe someone like this? *I needed to believe.* As I undressed, I remember carefully taking off my sanitary napkin and shoving it under the cushion of the white mock-leather chair in our living room, wondering all the while if the blood would stain the fabric underneath. I've never been sure why I hid the napkin. In trauma, one tends to regress to earlier taboos. *Perhaps to hide the blood.* The gun-wielding first man then said to me, "Now be quiet."

And then on my newly purchased, recently paid for, gorgeous velveteen sofa, I was raped and fondled, handled and humiliated. All with a cocked revolver pounding at my temple. I remember hearing the click of the hammer cocking into place. *Ready.* I've never been sure why it never fired. Tears burned inside as he pushed and manipulated me as if I were a slab of meat. He whispered obscenities, and "Move, bitch, move." He kept warning me, "Don't yell. Don't make a sound. You don't want your husband to know that you are doing this, do you?" *As if it were my choice.* With the gun at my head, I whispered, "No." I promised to be quiet. *I could see the streetlight through the shutters at the living room window. I tranced.* I tried to think of other things. Let my mind drift to other places. I remember the blunt sound of rhythmic thumping as my head repeatedly hit the end of the sofa. And . . . I remember the slicing pain between my legs. Wherever Matt and David were, I didn't want them to know that this was happening in our home. Please—let it end.

But there was a second part to the evening. The short stocky, somewhat older second man reappeared with that awful, sickening odor. The two men exchanged places. The second man had a knife quickly at my throat and held it there as he pushed me to my knees. I knew; and immediately a dizzying wave of nausea engulfed me. *This can't be happening. What will I do now? I'll be killed—I can't do this.* He ordered: "Open your mouth—wide." I did. I retched. *I can't do this. I screamed inside.* "I'm going to throw up," I said. I felt the knife push harder against my throat. "Do it. I *dare* you to throw up." A nightmare's nightmare. Each time I gagged, I was reminded with the tip of the knife. I don't know if he ever ejaculated. At that point I could feel nothing. I *was* nothing. His partner returned aggravated, chiding, "Hurry up. What's taking you so *long*? It's getting late." The corners of my mouth hurt.

I remember it all. But it took many years before I knew that none of it was my fault, that I was not paying for some past sin. That it was all right to be alive.

Afterward, I was told to hurry up and get dressed. "Don't say *anything* to *anyone*." I obeyed quickly, leaving the sanitary napkin under the cushion. My husband was to know nothing. The one man said again, "You wouldn't want your husband to know what you were doing down here, would you?" I only knew that David would go crazy, and I was afraid of what he might try to do. I was then shoved up the stairs where I discovered that Matt and David were together, but tied up—David with heavy cord and Matthew with gift-wrapping yarn, faceup on our king-sized bed. I found out later that the men had told my husband I had been tied up in the next room. David's mind, he told me later, had not let him entertain any thoughts of further violence. Me—they hog-tied with white stereo wire, pulled tight. They put me on the same bed with David and Matt, face *down. Perhaps this position was reserved for the woman of the house.* I said nothing of the downstairs horrors. *I had vowed silence.*

They covered us with the bedspread so that we could no longer see. But since I was lying face down, there was a space at the end of the spread that allowed me to follow the movements of the men about the room. We were all tied up in the main bedroom, and that's where they found our ATM (automatic teller machine) card. And under the press of the revolver at his head David was coerced to give our personal identification number (PIN) to use in the machine. One man kept watch over us while the other left the house in search of money. It was a long time before he returned. When he did—cash in hand—they began to ruthlessly grab at things, swiping the tops of dressers and tables—jewelry, TVs, medicines, radios, whatever was not pinned down. They ripped the stereo from its wall wiring. One emptied a bottle of aspirin into his mouth. They even took clothes, coats, shoes. "What size do you wear?" my husband was asked. They took everything away in boxes and in our suitcases. I remember the sound of dragging cardboard over hardwood floors. I also remember that my two suitcases were yellow. *Gifts from David after an illness.* Later, I only allowed myself to miss things as I looked for them and couldn't find them.

Under the bedspread—I was thankful we had not been separated—David continuously whispered to me and Matthew as the men wildly ran about thrashing through our personal belongings and trashing the bits of our lives. Matt was extremely quiet. (I had no idea that he was planning, as he told me later, in one of his superhero fantasies what he would do when the men left.) David was softly encouraging, "Be calm. Breathe deeply. Think of someplace else." *My hands and feet began to tingle and go numb. The wires were so tight.* "Wiggle your toes and fingers. Keep the blood circulating," he told me. He helped us to pray quietly. With the fear, the heat, and numbness setting in, I began to feel panic. *My first "feelings" since my arrival upstairs.* Whenever the men heard us talking, they pounded the bedspread, not caring what they hit, "Shut the fuck up!" David would stop a few moments, and then begin again his litany of comfort, checking on each of us, not waiting for answers. "Speak to me. How are you feeling? Stay calm. Matt, can you hear me? Keep breathing—deeply." And when he heard our deep, labored breaths, he said, "That's it. That's good." And then he began to pray. I'd never heard David pray aloud. " 'Our Father, who art in Heaven, . . .' " *I can still feel the soothing of his voice.*

I remember the eerie calm that came over the room. I knew the next sound would be a gunshot. I prayed that Matthew be taken away first. That way, he would not for an instant have to deal with the murder of his parents. I knew we were going to die. It was only a matter of the order in which each of us would be killed. Why would they let us live after all they had done? Did they really believe I would not tell my husband I had been raped and sexually abused? Did they really believe we hadn't seen their faces? Even now, thirteen years later, it is difficult to say I was raped and that my husband and child were there. It still hurts so badly. Did they think we would just become another black-on-black statistic? I have no idea why they didn't kill all of us. I have always been amazed.

We all heard what we thought was a final slamming of the front door. After waiting an interminable amount of time, we cautiously emerged from under the bedspread. The house was in darkness. Matt had freed his feet from the soft yarn and was outwardly calm. He dashed downstairs—in super-hero fashion—to get a knife from the kitchen. By the time he returned, David had white wire covering embedded between his front teeth from biting away at the stereo wire on my hands and ankles. With the knife, Matt proudly freed his father's hands, and David sawed through my wires. He then called the police and went from room to room relighting our house. We waited at the front door for their arrival as if we were about to receive guests. When the lights came back on, I remember seeing the *ojo de Dios* ("eye of God") weaving we purchased in New Mexico that dominated our upstairs hallway. I wondered if it had saved us.

The flashing lights of the patrol cars appeared quickly in the silence of the night. Then once again our home was contaminated with more boisterously loud voices and the thud of heavy feet. This time with mostly white male faces and swaggering bodies prying into our personal lives. I remember the glib, "Boy, you sure were lucky." I guess that meant because we were alive. Our home teemed with police and detectives. It reeked of the already stale smells of violence.

When I realized the police squad was about to leave, I thought they should know there had been more than a burglary. With reluctance and trepidation, I pulled David aside and told him—the first time I'd said the words—"They raped me." *I hated doing that. Our home and family had already been violated. And now there was more.* David looked stunned, but immediately reported the news to the police, and their departure was delayed with further questioning. One policeman seemed vaguely amused by this new information. Reaching for the telephone, with an enigmatic smile he commented offhandedly, "Then I guess we'll be needing the Sex Crimes

Unit." David never flinched at my revelation. He merely held my
face with his hand and said, "I loved you before, I love you now, I'll
love you forever." That was it. With a look of "nothingness" on his
face, he turned toward the noise of police leaving.

We left the house also, but our evening continued. I was taken to
Episcopal Hospital for medical treatment and then to police headquarters. Matthew asked to stay with his best friend next door. They
had stories to swap.

*In the weeks immediately following the rapes, I often thought, "Why
didn't someone send me flowers?" For some reason, I had needed flowers—lots of flowers. I kept waiting.*

The "incident of 1981," as we often refer to it, almost cost us the
trust and equilibrium of a son—our only child—and of our marriage. It was a long time before I understood what havoc the rapes
and our silence and silencing had wrought. Since that time in 1981,
I have learned a great deal about the give-and-take of love.

In September 1989—eight years after the rapes—I wrote the following words in my journal:

> . . . I can now feel the smoothing out of the ragged edges, and I
> now have a sense of wholeness and of possibility slowly returning.
> And I am excited (and scared) about what lies before me, now
> that there is a glimmer of light. I don't know what's lurking in the
> darkness of my own creation. I have been silent for so long, I only
> know the sound and feel of fear. I will never forget. And I will
> forever move with a new caution and a restraint of feeling. . . .

AFTERMATH

[The trauma] would teach us over and over of the abidingness, the terrible constancy, that accompanies a wound to the spirit. Though our bodies would heal, our souls had sustained a damage beyond compensation.

—*Pat Conroy,* The Prince of Tides

On the morning after the rapes, my family, except for my father, arrived from Washington, D.C. They tiptoed into the room where I was lying and one by one whispered words of comfort over me, gently kissing my forehead. I was silent. They were furious, hurt, in grief, in disbelief. *I need my father.* But how was he to know? They had all discussed before coming to Philadelphia that one of the four parents should wait at home in case there was an accident on the drive up. One catastrophe was enough. Someone had to be left "to take care of the children." (They still thought of us as "the children.") For reasons only they knew, my father was the one chosen to wait. *I needed my father.*

My body bore bruises, lacerations, and other physical pains, but emotionally I felt absolutely nothing. My spirit was broken. *This must be the way you feel when you're going insane.* The others in the family were fluttering about, making all seem back to normal. *They were pretending.* Close friends arrived. I don't remember talking much with anyone. Matthew enjoyed telling the story of the break-in and how he planned to share the details with his class during "show and tell." *I felt absolutely nothing.* I went somewhere else in my mind; I started fabricating the story I would tell in place of the truth. The next day, I called Women Organized Against Rape (WOAR) asking for help; they referred me to a local organization for crisis therapy. At that time, WOAR was not staffed for therapeutic services. I called my doctor; he was on vacation. I went through all the steps like a first-aid drill. It scared me that I had no emotion. Nothing. Even the bandaged lacerations were beginning not to hurt so much. *I still have the scars.*

The police took me, David, and Bessie, my supportive neighbor-friend, to the hospital the night of the rapes. I felt like a damaged child. The knot of fear in my belly made me quiver and recoil from touch. Still I insisted that I go alone into the examining room. I demanded a female nurse. I remember the doctor in emergency being extremely comforting and gentle. He seemed to understand my fragility. But still he had to handle me. Inside I was hysterical. I did not want to be touched. *Could they hear me screaming inside?* When the two hypodermics of penicillin hit me, I yelled so loudly that Bessie startled everyone as she charged into the room uninvited. I heard the screams, but I didn't know they were mine. They let Bessie stay; I needed her. She tried soothing me. *I was so afraid. I felt I was being tortured all over again.* I couldn't focus. I couldn't think fast enough to follow the smallest command. "Turn on your right side," I was told by the nurse. *I needed time to process the making of any decision.* The evening went on interminably. I was not allowed to shower until after all the examinations. *Evidence.* I felt dirty. I still could smell the putrid odor of the second man. By the time I was allowed to shower it was close to 2 A.M.

After arriving at "the roundhouse" (police headquarters) downtown, I was positioned before a seemingly disinterested, tired, and totally unsympathetic woman, a detective-stenographer who worked for, I think, the Sex Crimes Unit of the police department. She needed to hear the entire story: "Start at the beginning." David sat next to me and quietly held my hand. At this stage, they only wanted *my* statement; David had given his already. I was the one pressing charges for the robbery (valuables taken from one's body), rape, "deviant sexual intercourse" (sodomy and oral rape come under this heading), assault with deadly weapons, conspiracy—fourteen counts in all. I used to be able to repeat the litany of charges. Perhaps it's good that I can no longer do that. I was forced to be explicit about everything. I relived the evening sitting on a hard chair in a dark, drafty police station just a few hours after the horrors had occurred. At that point I joined the ranks of countless women who had recreated their rape events for strangers—almost instant replay. I later understood why this had to be, but at the time I thought it pointless and cruel punishment for something I didn't do. *I am* not *the criminal here.*

When the second ordeal of the evening was finished, I was allowed to go home. *Where was home?* I couldn't go back to that place where the events had been like something from a based-on-a-true-story, made-for-TV movie. I was sure I had read or seen this all before. A police car took us to the home of relatives who lived near our neighborhood. As David and I left police headquarters at the roundhouse, the sun was coming up. I remember the cool morning felt wonderful on my face. My eyes burned. My body was weary. I felt alone. *What will I do now? Is this what it feels like after the funeral services for a loved one?* The city seemed calm.

As the three of us moved our belongings into their home, my uncle and aunt made life comfortable for us. They said we could stay as long as we needed. David, like a hero, went back into our house (just a few blocks away) with one of the detectives to pack clothes and necessities. Each day he faced, alone, the "going back and forth" to fetch whatever it was we needed, returning wearily to our safe space. David and I celebrated our fifteenth wedding anniversary in the wake of trauma and turmoil, four days after the burglary and rapes. On the very evening of our anniversary, interrupting a lavish celebratory dinner prepared by my aunt, a detective from the Sex Crimes Unit arrived to show me mug shots. I was surprised to discover he didn't recognize me in my festive attire. But I remembered him; he was one of the first detectives to arrive on the scene that evening. As he kept glancing at me—I guess to make sure I was the same woman—I flipped through the books of "sides and fronts" in an attempt to identify the perpetrators. No luck. *No celebration.*

From that evening on, there was no peace. Any day at any moment the doorbell might ring, first at my uncle's home and later at ours. So many countless intrusions by the police department and unannounced visits from one detective or another to check out leads and to look at "new shots." I wondered through all of this about the women whose cases had not been considered convincing enough for a possible trial. For some of them, the police had *never* arrived. I knew that our solid middle-class status and my husband's high profile at the university were partial reasons for the attention from police and the positive treatment by the court system. This knowledge sickened me, and at the same time brought comfort. Gradually I learned to swallow the anger. Each time detectives arrived, I became disoriented. Fear rekindled. My focus on the case and caring that it might matter—I faked. I began to create the fiction of a life and a past to account for my now new mode of distanced behavior.

It was now the beginning of a new school year. Matthew was becoming impatient with not being in his own home with familiar games and neighborhood friends. A decision had to be made; we couldn't live indefinitely with my uncle and aunt. *But why not? I feel safe here.* As long as we were with them, I didn't have to be an adult or parent. I was adamant: I would not, could not go back into our house. *My beautiful blue house.* But David had a plan: we could rent an apartment for me to live in until I *could* return. In the meantime, he and Matt would return to the house. *He doesn't understand that I can never return*—never. *How could he not know that?*

How could I tell my husband that emotionally, overnight, I had become a vegetable? I was inside myself—alone. I couldn't explain it to him. I had no words that made sense. I had hurts that were much too sore to touch, hurts that no one would ever reach. I was afraid of being *left* alone. I was incurably afraid of the dark. I felt that I was being punished. *What was it that I did wrong?* This was no short-term trauma; this was forever.

We discussed new strategies for living. Or rather, David talked and made the decisions. My mind was quick to wander, and often participated in an interactive, continuous-loop video of the rape night. A word, a certain glance, a smell, a feeling, the angle of the sun in the sky could transport me into a trance back into that other world of chaos. Sometimes I was revealed by someone's concern at my lack of focus, but at other times I succeeded in my charade of normalcy.

David had spent psychologically taxing days preparing for our reentry. He decided that I must reclaim my home. *It belonged to* me. He returned each day to switch the rooms and furniture about in preparation for my arrival. He stripped the bed on which we had all been held captive. I was never again to see those bedclothes. He junked the sofa on which I had been raped. *My beautiful new, just-paid-for velveteen sofa.* He moved Matt's bedroom from the third floor to the second and made the large second-floor sitting room into our bedroom. David rearranged the first-floor living room where the rapes had occurred, putting my piano in a central location. *The thought of music was impossible.* And so it was only left for me to decide which would be the day to move back home. I cried as I moved from room to room, chanting: "This is *my* home. I won't let them take it from me." In spite of David's efforts, I wondered how I would ever be able to live in a place I now considered penetrable and evil. After the rapes, we stayed nine months in the blue house.

We tried entertaining friends and colleagues. *David never stopped looking for a way to heal us.* Fill the place with warmth and laughter, I imagine he thought. But after the last guest had departed there were always the unbelievably long nights. And sometimes after everyone else was in bed, I spent those nights alone, crouched in a chair with a kitchen knife—or pacing the rooms. The recurrent reel played over and over in my head—sometimes intruding upon ordinary daytime tasks like taking a bath or ironing a blouse. *I felt someone was in the house.* And so I would stop my ironing or get out of the tub and carefully search every room. How long could I remain sane? I tried focusing on the upcoming trial. But each time I talked with the lawyer, it provided more fodder for my anxiety and imagination. A vicious cycle of quasi sanity, anxiety attacks, remembered bodily violence, and threats of death pervaded my life.

Matthew seemed to be the only one functioning, and that was something positive. *But there was no way of knowing for sure.* We worked diligently to keep life normal for Matt. He laughed hard, played intensely, and continued to do well in school. I remained in my graduate program at Temple University—in fact I stayed at the university each day as long as I could. Anything not to go home. Therapy continued, but I seemed stuck. We moved cautiously from day to day and hour to hour. David and I talked little and laughed not at all. And—we learned to fire a revolver.

There were times when I could not travel alone. Certain open, well-lit, peopled streets and areas felt dangerous; a trip to the supermarket was an emotional day. I couldn't travel on buses or elevators—the closeness made me want to bolt. And I did—onto wrong floors and at unknown stops. If I could get one good, hearty laugh during the day, it had been a success. During the night, I was busy keeping watch and taking pills. I always made certain I had tranquilizers close at hand. I forced myself to remain awake to listen for sounds of intrusion. Sleep would have to overtake me. I could never give in. As novelist Pat Conroy writes in *The Prince of Tides*, "rape is a crime against sleep and memory. . . ."* If I heard anything—anything at all—I frantically woke David and insisted that we search the entire house. Sometimes this happened more than once on any given evening—most often with a revolver poised for action.

"To tell or not to tell" became an extremely complex issue. The day after the violence in our home, I had decided I would tell no one of the rape. Gradually my silence grew into a secret. I insisted that if someone were to be told about the rapes, *I* had to be the one to make the disclosure. If David told anyone, he had to tell me who the person was so I would be prepared with a response when next I saw that person. Thus I began to struggle to regain control of my life by trying to control the lives of others. Our son knew intuitively that something more than a burglary had occurred. He had no name for it because I continually denied that anything else had happened. "Did they hurt you, Mom?" he asked, repeatedly. Each time I responded "No," I was guilty of transgressing in ways I had taught him were unacceptable. *I lied repeatedly.* Of all the possible wrongs, I'd taught that not telling the truth was paramount. *I continued to lie.* And so another kind of guilt joined my anger and fear.

I needed time to think about how a mother tells her son that she has been raped. At that time, this is what I felt: how does a mother tell her son that she *let* two men rape her? What would I say to him when he asked, "Didn't you fight?" Matt passionately believed in super-heros, that a good and fair fight wins every time. Wouldn't he

*Pat Conroy, *The Prince of Tides* (Houghton-Mifflin, New York, 1986), p. 483.

wonder why I didn't fight? I was sure I understood his nine-year-old ways of reasoning. And so the lie was set.

While I negotiated my days and nights, David taught classes, wrote proposals, completed household errands, held office hours, researched possibilities for a year of leave from the university, and tried to stay as close to home as possible. He knew I didn't want to be alone after dark. David thought of me first and did not, until years later, get professional help for himself. I believe he thought I might die, or just disintegrate from the intensity of my living. I continued to lie to Matthew, while trying desperately to be a good mother. I never moved very far without my pills. I couldn't be sure when a day would prove too much. I think I stopped touching. I was afraid to get too close; I was afraid to trust my touch with anyone, especially Matt. It's hard to love when you are hating.

Work saved me. I went back to meetings with academic advisors (I was preparing to write my doctoral dissertation), lunched with colleagues, laughed disingenuously at anecdotes I promptly forgot. I told no one of the rape.

I began to notice that my temper flared at the slightest *perceived* injustice toward me or others. The anger I had been swallowing for years was beginning to rebound in often misdirected and overly intense ways. It was unlike me to vent anger. My behavior raised eyebrows. I was no longer "sweet." I was paranoid, constrained in my movements, and preferred staying out to coming home. David did the best he could, but he was suffocating. I felt safe nowhere. He increased his efforts to find a teaching position or fellowship that would take us out of the state. In the meantime, I continued to tell myself, "Forget it happened. Bury it. Get on with your life." But then I would proceed to cry alone in silence, in the darkness of closets and bathrooms where I would retreat when even the daytime grew too burdensome.

Our son continued to demand the truth of me, and I continued to resist. He became overly protective and confrontational with anyone who even seemed to approach me. *He didn't even know why he was protecting me.* When I wasn't being consumed by fear, I obsessed about his welfare. *Would he be irreparably harmed by all of this?* At the time, we were told by professionals that as long as we could handle his reactions to our family trauma, he need not have a therapist—that having a therapist might create a dependence. *Was I really handling it? Were we?*

One morning weeks, after the incident and after we had returned "home," my husband confronted me: "Matt's got to know what happened. I know you want to be the one to tell him, but you're not doing it." David took our son to another part of the house. I paced and cried quietly as I heard their muffled voices. *It was obvious I couldn't handle telling Matt.* Then I heard an animal's wail. Our son sounded as if he had been gutted. *I froze.* As dramatic as it sounds, this signaled the end of my son's innocence, and I feared that he would never be the same. David took Matthew with him into the shower. He bathed and consoled our nine-year-old son. I heard the two of them crying.

"Where's Mom?" It was Matt's voice. Although I'm not sure where the feeling originated, I had been afraid my son would no longer love me after hearing the truth. "Is it true what Dad said? I knew what they had done to you, Mom. I didn't know what to call it." Why had I denied myself the support of this little person? I had believed what society, teachers, nuns, and priests had implied for so long: that if I were raped, it was my fault. *The nuns had said I should die before being raped. That's what the saints did.* My son not only continued to love me, but became a nurturer. He no longer had to protect his mother from the "unknown forces of evil"—whoever and whatever *they* were. He could go back to being a nine year old. I told him that he had been a hero on that evening because he had. I asked for forgiveness for not telling the truth and tried to explain why I had lied. I continue to apologize for not believing in his always unconditional love.

About this time I began to play my piano again—the one David had centered in our new living room. I went back through old pieces I'd learned as a teenager. I began to practice for my own personal concert; music once again filled the blue house. Each day, as I surmounted yet another difficult arpeggio, I took pride in the musical expertise I had enjoyed as a young woman. We began to successfully entertain family and friends around the fireplace—in a room that, before the incident, had not been used except for business people. It had been a kind of way station. Now it resonated with melody and with the voices of our loved ones. We even had a splendid Christmas in this room with all our parents present. I remember a fire nursed into the night and early morning and the growing-up stories our parents told. Matt fell asleep, his head in my father's lap, as my dad told us in graphic detail how as a teenager he had primed tobacco in his native North Carolina. We were all right there next to him in the fields. I don't think our parents ever knew that this room had been the scene of terror.

I tried desperately to get on with my life, but a palpable fear and the lingering smell of violence kept intruding. I tried to incorporate into my daily living the advice given me by some of the women (white and black) whom I met during our ordeal. One older woman, when I told her weeks after the rape that I needed help and someone to talk to, patted me on the head with a stop-sniveling, brace-up attitude and said, "Oh, I've heard much worse. I know women who've gone through much more than *that*. You mustn't be weak." Another well-meaning woman offered in confidence (with the implication that she should not be treading these waters), "Now don't let this affect your private relations with your husband." I was confused by their direct advice and constantly frustrated by the implied admonitions to keep quiet and move on. It proved impossible to monitor the opinions and mind-sets of an entire population and keep myself whole in the process. I sought comfort in the church. It was sometimes a solace, but it was also a reminder that I had *not* behaved "appropriately"—the way the impressionable girl-child had been taught. *I let it happen.* I kept practicing my music.

It was difficult to get in touch with anger, fear, guilt, and pain. Just after the rapes, I remember not being angry. My husband was furious enough for the two of us. He kept pleading, "Get angry. They hurt you. They had no right. They took from you. Stop being so forgiving." The intensity of his rage scared me because I felt nothing. I knew *fear;* it was inside my body. But anger was foreign and disturbing. My one secure place had been taken from me—my home. *If you can get home, you're safe.* And my body was no longer just mine. I had so much to recuperate, to reclaim.

I spent an inordinate amount of time "out of touch" and in disguise. In groups I either laughed or remained quiet. In an instant, I could drift to "other places" in a conversation. Movies dredged up the sore places in my being; songs and music demarcated the same. I approached the world with doubt, caution, and suspicion. Nothing passed me without scrutiny. The pain of others affected me to extremes. And the pain of others for which I felt responsible caused me to weep. I did not understand our responses as humans—or, too often, our non-responses. . . . Still I weep for what I can never change.

GOING PUBLIC

Despite the significant legislative reforms of the 1960s and 1970s, sexual assault crimes remain the most under-reported cases within the criminal justice system.
    —*Linda Fairstein,* Sexual Violence: Our War against Rape

I told my story in a court of law, with the continuous support of friends and the continual urging of my husband. It was not a decision made lightly or without great concern. Telling my story in a courtroom was like giving the world license to judge, analyze, speculate, point fingers.

Before appearing in court to testify, I was "trained" in order to become a credible witness for the prosecution. David and I met with the ADA (assistant district attorney) at least three times a week—it seemed every day—until the trial. Each day we'd pull into the same garage near city hall hoping to get there in time for the "early-bird special rates" and put in another day in the halls of justice. And each day we made our way down the alley street that was the shortcut to the courthouse. David and I shared quick lunches on park benches and the stoops of out-of-the-way delis while we watched the crowds rushing back to downtown corporate desks.

Mark Lipowicz, the ADA on the case, was personable, patient, and thorough. Not at all what I had expected of a prosecuting attorney. He wasn't pushy and never rushed me as I told my story. He always gave me the impression he understood my reticence and fear in recreating the crime night. But that is exactly what I had to learn how to do with clarity and believability—to recreate the crime night in every sordid detail. "You must make the jury believe you. You can't be strong in front of the jury. They expect you to cry, to be upset. They have to feel your pain," he explained. This angered me. I didn't want to cry for the jury. And I didn't want the defendant to see me cry. I didn't want him to know he had succeeded in wounding me so deeply.

During the time we prepared the case, in my effort to recapture all the details, my mind would often be transported to that early fall evening in the blue house. I was both "there" and "not there." It was as if I were moving through the house with a video camera mounted on my forehead, yet feeling all the sensations of being afraid, of being hurt. Virtual reality. I could hear every creak, every moan of the house. I could hear my own breathing . . . hear the cocking of the pistol at my left temple. As I transported myself through the house, I felt a foreign presence—the stillness just before the mayhem.

One evening while at the courthouse late, "rehearsing" for the trial, the details of the rapists' entry into our home, I stopped abruptly. I had been retracing my steps through the house in real time, viewing the interior of the house, pointing out distances and the proximity of rooms, describing the lead-up to the rapes in an effort to bring a jury into the scene with me. Mark Lipowicz was asking questions and taking notes. Suddenly there was a loud crash in the hallway outside his office; someone passing had stumbled or dropped something heavy. *I* heard the crash as another sound, a body hitting against wood. Immediately I was transported back in the blue house. My heart began to race. Another anxiety attack. I *had* to get out. *Grown women don't run!* I could discern from the look on Mark Lipowicz's face that he knew something horrible had just happened. We never talked about it. We took a break, I regrouped, and we continued to prepare for the trial. I still have aural memory of the sounds of intrusion, of heavy body against wood. It still wakes me in the night. And then I walk the rooms until my legs are too heavy to stand.

After countless viewings of mug shots, lineups in prison confines—with pockets emptied and body frisked—almost daily meetings with the ADA, and far too many continuances, a final trial date was set. One perpetrator had been apprehended from a photo taken at an ATM when he used our card that evening. The other man was never located. When our day in court arrived, I allowed no one to come to the trial. No family. No friends. I couldn't bear to see my own pain reflected in their faces. Our friends begged me to allow them to come for support; I consistently refused. I didn't want to see their horror and hurt. *The faces of Matthew and David were enough. It was easier to choose strangers.* Now I know, had I allowed them to assist me, it would have assuaged some of their helplessness. In the courtroom, David and I were separated. By law he was not allowed to be with me since he was also testifying. In the courtroom I pretended as best I could that I was handling life with equanimity. It would be another year and additional trauma before the trial was complete and the verdict pronounced.

For the duration of the trial, Bessie—the neighbor-friend who accompanied us to the hospital the evening of the rape—stayed with me in court. Taking time away from her own work, she met me each morning and was a warm and familiar presence in a sea of anonymous, wide-eyed, curious faces. The courtroom was packed. The guards were armed; they frisked everyone as they arrived. I could not have testified if Bessie had not been sitting in front of me.

I sought out her face and spoke only to her. *How could she listen to such horrendous details for all those weeks?* Sara, a court advocate on staff at WOAR, was at my side before and after testifying, and appeared at court between other clients and trials, if only for a moment of encouragement. It was her strength, and confidence in me, that enabled me to tell my story to strangers day after day. Years after the court procedures and some recovery on my part, I was able to integrate Sara, and later her family, into my ordinary life. But it took time because I didn't want the "tainted" trauma and court parts of my life to intrude on the present I was struggling to construct.

Our friends called regularly to get "caught up" on court proceedings. Our parents called every day. Though appreciative, we stayed to ourselves. But we knew we were never without "safety nets." Our longtime friends, Bill and Ellen, arranged dinners out, remembered our anniversary, included us on Friday-night-end-of-the-week celebrations, and saw to it that we slept and had a few laughs. Rinna and Gary, fellow runners, insisted we maintain our friendship, even though we fought hard to retreat. In fact, Gary and David ran together in the evenings at Valley Green. Even if a 6K or half-marathon race were not eminent, he and other running buddies kept David in shape. Life had some semblance of normalcy.

Just before our court date in the summer of 1982, I discovered on a routine doctor's visit that I had a large suspicious growth on my right ovary that had not been palpable a few months earlier. The results were immediate hospitalization, a continuance of the trial—by the prosecution this time—and a total abdominal hysterectomy, complete with subsequent hot flashes and additional physical pain. Another violation. *Definitely no more children. No time to mourn.* I was lucky though. It wasn't cancerous. Within three weeks of the surgery, I was back on the stand testifying. I moved slowly, sat with pillows around me, and even talked with less verve. Long days with little to do except wait until called to testify.

Between my testimony and that of others, I had distracting conversations with one of the detectives on the case. So gentle, so engaging with me was the same detective who had collared the perpetrator of another crime just prior to arriving at the blue house one evening. He and I sat on the unnecessarily hard benches and talked trivia. I tried to forget the rapes, but I was constantly reminded as cuffed black men were paraded by on their way to courtrooms along the corridor. Whenever my gaze locked in a stare on some particular face, my detective-bodyguard-friend leapt into action, thinking it might be the rapist who got away. I wondered if they'd ever find him. Each day when I left city hall, I saw on the streets the surly, slumped, hands-behind-the-back-defendant's posture on almost every young black man. It would seem they either had been "inside"—or unfortunately had seen enough models to imitate.

The trial took place during one of Philadelphia's dank, humid Julys. My postsurgery hot flashes continued. The courtroom had air-conditioning, compliments of one laboriously hiccuping window unit. But because the judge was hard of hearing, even that had to be turned off. When I spoke, I thought I was shouting. But I suppose I was whispering because the judge couldn't seem to hear my testimony. I was embarrassed to speak louder. I didn't want anyone to hear the crude brutalities and obscenities I had to repeat. It seemed that every time I got to a particularly difficult part of my story, the judge, even without air-conditioner noises, would say, "What's that again? Speak up. Louder. Be precise." It sounded as if my words were bounding off the walls in the damp silence of the courtroom as I repeated—seemingly shouted—the perpetrator's words "cunt," "bitch," "fuck," in front of people I didn't know. *I don't use those kinds of words. Will they know that?* My voice *must* have gotten more imperceptible as I spoke; the judge could not have been so cruel as to have me repeat such offensive language for sheer impact.

As I gave my testimony, many times I felt I was not believed. When I told the court that one man had been sequestered in our basement for hours that evening, the defense attorney tried to prove that I had willingly let the man in. The defense tried to convince the jury that he was someone I already knew. The defense attorney asked me about keys to my house and who had copies. He chipped away at my insecurities and vulnerabilities. At times I was made to doubt myself. The man had been waiting in the basement for quite a while; the police found used matches on the basement floor beneath one of the windows. It was only when the house seemed quiet that he'd broken through the door at the top of the stairs. And yes, he could have come in through those basement window bars. There was no other explanation. We had been in the house all day. Unless . . . unless he had somehow entered through the hatch doors in the basement.

The perpetrators knew many details about our lives. They knew our son rode a green bike. They knew which windows and outside doors were not alarmed. Ours was not a random hit. We had been "marked" for the burglary. I began to question myself as the days followed. Who had we allowed in who had been suspicious? Were we chosen because we were perceived as having too much? Had someone put a curse on us? Had we been too nice? Too believing? Was it because we were successful, owned a three-story stone colonial on a corner lot, had a gorgeous, intelligent child? Because we were a happy couple? Because my husband was a successful black man? Why not rape his wife? How disappointed the burglars must have been with so little to steal. As attorney Susan Estrich tells us in her *Yale Law Journal* article: "Rape has long been viewed not only as a crime against women, but also as a crime against the man who is entitled to exclusive possession of that woman."*

At points during the trial, I lost sight of why I had pressed charges. I couldn't separate the crime from the reality of what was happening *now,* in court. *Why am I doing this?* I felt again as if I were being forced against my will. But I also knew that as the main witness for the prosecution I was protecting other potential victims.

---

*Susan Estrich, "Rape," *Yale Law Journal,* vol. 95 (1986), p. 1141.

But the trial that was supposed to be in my favor violated me again and again, and I was given no time to prepare for a fight. I had been tempted many times to let it all go—to drop the charges. Was it worth all the agony? David never let me give in.

I still have difficulty separating the rape from my hysterectomy. I believe that the rape trauma contributed to the urgency of my surgery. My body was crying for itself. *Scoop out the putrid mess.* It seemed like further punishment—or maybe a purging. One day at court recess, weak from the heat and the grueling cross-examination designed to make me doubt and feel more guilt, I stepped off the stand and slumped into the arms of my friend. I turned to Bessie. "Why didn't they just kill me? It would have been so much easier." When I would let my friends and family offer me solace, they never let me forget why I was alive and why I came to court each day. They assured me of the necessity of my presence in their lives. Our parents took our traumas extremely hard; they were there for every step. My mother and father stayed in our home during the trial so that Matthew would have "other parents" with him. I remember my mother and Matt laughing together as they played—good belly laughs. And I remember my mother's tender concern for me.

David's father, a man seemingly with strength enough for everyone, reacted intensely. My mother-in-law said she had never seen him respond to anything with such emotion. I wonder what memories my rape conjured up in his mind? He'd spoken to me once of his grandmother who had been raped—the facts escape me. *Weeks after the rape, he treated me to a fancy lunch and took me shopping. I still have the robe I chose.* It was not until spring 1982 that we knew he was quite ill. Perhaps he had been ill longer; there was just so much happening at once and so many people to be concerned about. David's mother never let a day go by without a call; she kept abreast of the court happenings. She helped nurse me during my illness and hospitalization. After the rapes she immediately offered to rearrange her own home—and her life—so that the three of us would have a place to live. And all the while she cared for David's father, who died of cancer in December 1983, seven months after the sentencing. At least he got to hear the legal finish.

My own father did not talk with me about the rapes, except the few times I brought up the subject in shrouded and guarded ways. But whenever he hugged me and said, "I love you," I could feel in his arms his *own* pain and the desire to take away mine. He didn't know how to comfort me and I didn't know how to explain to him what I needed. *How does anyone know what to say or to ask or to do? And yet we need them to know.*

The time from the actual crime to the sentencing was four months short of two years. In reality it's been a lifetime. It has taken so many years to discard the secrets and shatter the silences. *Guilty: all six felony counts, all eight misdemeanors. Total sentencing: 30 to 60 years.* I know the parole date.

LOOKING FOR HOME

The best hiding place was love.
                    —*Toni Morrison,* The Bluest Eye

After nine months confined to the blue house—the place we once called home—our parole finally began. David had found us a way out. We took a leave of absence to North Carolina for one year. Gradually I learned to breathe again in the clean, cedar-drenched air of the Southeast. I could see the sky. In the trees surrounding our house there were birds of all varieties, and below, the quiet sounds of rabbits, chipmunks, and squirrels scurrying through the woods. It was comforting to know that there would be no drastic change in the seasons in our place of flight. And Matthew could play alone outdoors. Our time spent in this country setting would become precursor to the country myth that would inform our lives once we returned to Philadelphia.

In North Carolina we found new friends and were welcomed into the academic community and our neighborhood. We received invitations to dinner and invited acquaintances to our home. It was wonderful to hear Matt and the voices of his new playmates echoing throughout our temporary home. I enjoyed the luxury of taking work breaks (I was working feverishly on my dissertation) and having tea and conversation with my new neighbor-friend, Carole, whose young son became like my own that year. She knew nothing of what I'd left back in Philadelphia. We could talk about normal day-to-day happenings. I took long walks and felt the sun on my face. It was a gift.

Matt seemed to blossom, and David was able to work and think without interruption. Somehow in this new setting, I felt a freedom from the constant threat of break-ins and violations. I felt I could be alone in the town and no one would stare threateningly into my face. *I was ashamed to say that I was comfortable without black men in my spaces.* I started seeing a therapist who told me I was suffering from PTSD (post-traumatic stress disorder). My sleeplessness, constant anxiety, flashbacks, weight loss, and inability to feel emotion in the wake of the rapes had been sure symptoms. Comforted by a diagnosis, I believed that my recovery would take only a few sessions of therapy. That I would be given a check list of do's and don'ts, and, *voila!* I would be cured. But in fact, I stayed with this therapist for the entire year until we left North Carolina. And when it was time to leave, I was frightened, unsure I could take the next step without her. (As soon as I was back in Philadelphia, I sought further professional help.) But as I consistently worked with Rose, I was able to concentrate and work steadily once again. I arose in the dark of each morning, wrapped myself in a blanket against the predawn chill, and studied until daybreak. In addition to collecting language samples from children for my dissertation research, I was determined to receive my Certificate of Clinical Competence in speech pathology. I passed the exam and received certification in the field. Control, discipline, and lockstep precision were for me the key to sanity. What I thought was equilibrium was to be short-lived.

But the aphorism that we take ourselves with us wherever we go made itself manifest that year. When winter arrived, I realized that only the surface of my life had been altered. Most evenings I was able to sleep; David had new and challenging colleagues; Matt had more freedom and a modicum of happiness. But—we were the same people. And David and I remained locked in an outdated dance begun in Philadelphia. We planned our weeks; we worked; we occupied the same bed; we didn't touch. Our marriage was as brittle as the weather. It is not surprising then that when the next blow came there was no buttress.

I had experienced bouts of sight loss, numbness, and weakness since my early thirties, but I had always been able to successfully explain away the transient episodes. Not this time. A total numbing gradually overtook the right side of my body and could not be ignored. It was as if I were dragging something connected to me, yet foreign. This time, I couldn't pretend; I had a problem. *Another violation. Another betrayal. No time to mourn* and things fall apart. Tests, a trip back to Philadelphia, more tests, waiting for results. I eventually learned I had multiple sclerosis. Once again our lives flew into disarray. David agreed to give therapy a try. And I went into remission. Over the years we learned that my condition was a mild form—ironically called "benign multiple sclerosis." I was lucky.

Matthew grew more wise and sagacious than either of us. While we were unconsciously and assiduously building a two-profession status to avoid thinking and connecting, Matt asked us to enroll him in religion classes at the University of North Carolina Newman Center in preparation for accepting Catholicism. It was not my idea, but because I was Catholic and his mother, I was expected to accompany him, since he was only eleven. That spring at Easter, Matt was baptized Catholic. Matt drew us closer as a family and helped us celebrate his new life with the church and Father Tim. I learned an extraordinary amount that year about believing, forgiving, accepting, and relinquishing my armor. The boy-child was maturing before us, growing into adolescence, but we had little time or energy to process it. We would later realize that we had allowed our trauma and its aftermath to make difficult the years that were already calculated to be impossible for any teenager and his family.

In spite of the "progress" in our lives as well as the myriad complications, I still didn't talk about the rape to anyone except my therapist and my new friend, Father Tim. His words and prayers brought me solace. It was the first time I'd ever been friends with a priest. Priests were usually relegated to the confessional. With others, I maintained my silence about the rapes and continued to believe that somehow I had been responsible. *It was a secret. But from whom?* The rapes and other "woundings" became intertwined in my mind, a part of the everydayness of my life, causing chronic physical pain, blocking all emotions except fear, anger, and guilt. The horror of the rapes needed to be excised in much the same way that the tumors and adhesions had been cut away during my surgery. As Pat Conroy says, "violence sends deep roots into the heart."

I didn't want to acknowledge that I could no longer live where I wanted. That I didn't trust my own community. *I still hurt.* When we bought the blue house, it was our dream house, made of old stone, surrounded by beautiful mature trees, a good neighborhood for children, in a multiracial area. But since the rapes, I realized and accepted that I would never again be able to live in a racially mixed or predominantly black neighborhood. The realization frightened and saddened me. I had been betrayed by my own people. I no longer had choices. *Black men had raped and humiliated me. How could they do that to one of their "own"?* And so a different kind of lie crystalized—a lie of omission. I had to keep the rape secret—I had a responsibility. But to whom? For what? Almost as if the crime had been perpetrated by someone I trusted. *That night one of the men had whispered, "You don't want your husband to know—do you? I had replied, "Oh no."* Perhaps the secrets began there, with my assuming responsibility for the horror he was perpetrating upon *me.*

I didn't want my nonblack friends, colleagues, and acquaintances to know that I didn't trust my own people, that I was afraid of black men I didn't know. *Or was it that I didn't want those people to know "what I had been doing"?* I felt responsible for upholding the image of the strong black man for our young son, *and* for the white world with whom I had contact. I didn't want my son's view of sex to be warped by this crime perpetrated upon his mother by men the color of him, his father, and his grandfathers. I didn't want to confirm the white belief that all black men rape. Better not to talk about it. And so, I'd kept silent about what had happened to me. I didn't speak about my anger and my pain. I assumed silent responsibility for the infamy of others. My soul began to feed on itself.

When we returned to live in our original home city and state, we changed houses three times until we felt safe. The houses we lived in were never within the city limits and were not in interracial areas. *We used to believe in both.* But now the emotional price was too high. Another lie to tell. *"We love living in the rural/country areas!"* Actually we felt fortunate to find any house in which I was comfortable being alone. *I can never be safe.* A house in which I didn't have to constantly roam about in search of an enemy to destroy. At one time we thought we would have to move permanently to another state. I always felt detached and disingenuous when I lied to our friends as they mused about why we lived in the country. *I began to* believe *that I loved living in the rural/country areas.* For a long while during the after-trial years, I really had no close friends to whom I could tell the truth. I had ostracized myself with my silence and secrets. I thought I had everyone fooled. *Eccentric behavior.* They just knew to keep their distances. I continued to work and to make the most of daylight.

With the help of immediate and extended family, I pretended my world was stable. Only those people who knew me, and saw me regularly, recognized the vacant eyes. I lost more weight I didn't need to lose. When I look back at pictures of those years, I could have been an ad for the perfume Obsession or, conversely, a young starving woman with a prompted camera smile. *I* was *starving*. I was not surviving. But I kept plodding along with my graduate work, always watching but oblivious to most of life happening around me. I smoked. A drag on a cigarette blocked tears; then Valium took away the edge of fear. And my old, postrape coping mechanisms lingered. I remember that, after my late-evening graduate school classes, in order to prove to myself I had moxie—instead of asking for a walking partner—I would hold my breath and run from the time I left the doorway of a building until I reached my car. If the distance was too far for one breath, I would allow myself to stop, check my surroundings, and start again. With this talismanic behavior, I assured my status as victim.

Each day as soon as I awakened, I began thinking of how I would get through the night, much like an addict always wondering where to find the next fix. I remember very little about "fun" during those graduate school years. And I constantly wondered if all the energy, stress, and strain were worth it. During the daylight hours I made jokes with university friends and studied with a few faithful but unknowing colleagues. They afforded me moments of escape and forgetfulness.

After returning from our year away in North Carolina, we rented our first house just outside Philadelphia. Our plans to have the old, stone blue house sold by the time we reentered the city had not worked. We saw the farmhouse on a late-summer afternoon. Light was streaming through front windows that overlooked a field full of corn. Even before we agreed to rent it, David decided that the small second-floor room that looked out onto the field would be perfect for my study. "So peaceful. You can get a lot of work done here," he'd said. Again, David had given me the choicest spot. The farmhouse was away from the city, and it was safe. David would eventually take a small room on the third floor for his study, a room that in the winter would prove to be almost uninhabitable. It was next to Matt's; Matt had the upstairs heater.

We moved in and delighted in "making do" by putting up frilly add-ons, necessary curtains, and shades at the windows; clearing a yard space in back for Matt to ride his bike; and washing down the kitchen in order to make it "ours" for the short time we would stay. It was exhilarating to open the windows wide, smell the country, see corn fields all around. Matt was beside himself with the pleasure and freedom of open spaces. Winter, though, came with a vengeance. The furnace was inadequate and there were holes to the outside in some of the walls. We hadn't seen them on that gorgeous summer's day when we so desperately needed an "away house" to live in. We kept both woodstoves burning during the coldest part of the winter—one of the coldest on record up to that time—and still it was bitter. In spite of discomforts, we made a great "country Christmas" with all our parents visiting. *That year, David replaced my diamond ring. But it wasn't the same.* Between all the festivities of Christmas, David made regular trips to the cellar to rid the house of field rats that had been poisoned just before our arrival and were now dead and dying. He never complained of this death duty and, until much later, never told me exactly what he was doing on his trips to the cellar. And I had never asked. Basements were not my thing.

Self-pity can be a debilitating condition. As I looked around us in our frail, basic, unadorned farmhouse, I began to feel totally responsible for the makeshift quality of our lives. It was my fault that Matt was living away from other families and old friends and had to attend a new school with only his classmates as friends. Our lives no longer seemed to have purpose or specific goals. We were no longer a middle-class, academic family with plans for a future. Matt made one good friend that year; they frequently swapped overnights. But there was no exchange between the families. Our skin color was a new, sometimes curious, addition to the area in which we were now living. Yet we felt safe. This proved to be just another of the ironies of our existence. I continued to submerge myself in work, writing my dissertation. Two of my goals—running five miles in the park and finishing my Ph.D.—were like magical amulets: one kept me alive in its attainment, and the other would create possibilities for a future. If I held on to those charms, I believed I could manage.

David was excruciatingly unhappy during that decrepit year. I had become insular and private without even knowing. I had become aloof and uncaring about anything except the surface necessities of life—and how to get through the night. I smiled, but with no passion. I would flinch ever so slightly at David's unexpected touch. We were still roommates sharing the same bed. Fear still had me in its grasp. While being out at night was horrifying, being at home was completely intolerable. In the evening between Matt's bedtime and our own, David and I were tense and alienated, always seeking neutral issues for small talk. We never talked about *us*. To do so brought on accusations and fury. I thought seriously about leaving for good. I didn't know what else to do. Everyone was unhappy and I felt it was my fault. I didn't know how to ask for more help because I didn't even know I needed it. And I didn't know that David was dragging *his* feet through life, also wondering how and if we were going to pull all this together. Matthew began to have migraines. We never connected the headaches with the stress we were all feeling. We were careful to talk only at night and to hide the fact that as a married couple we were not doing very well. I wonder what people on the outside saw when they looked in on our family. We were so careful to protect our own parents and to present a certain face to the public, that we were neglecting ourselves. Our son was on the brink of adolescence and we hardly noticed.

During the time we lived in the farmhouse, a teaching position at a local prep school became available, and I was asked to apply. Before my dissertation was complete, I had been given a treasured position in their English department. The same school that would protect and nurture our son through the trying times of his adolescence would become for me, unbeknownst to my colleagues, the place to prompt laughter and self-confidence, a safe place to call home. Once I'd accepted the position, I worried about how I would get to school each day. It was the same area where the perpetrator and his family members lived. I managed. But then there were the faculty meetings that I soon learned were held in the evening. This meant I had to return after dark. While trying not to be fired for my absences, I quickly learned how to make excuses about missing meetings—"Sorry, a family matter has come up." "Sorry, I must be coming down with the flu." "Sorry, I have an important doctor's appointment." Sometimes David took me to the meetings and wait-ed in the car, away from the curious eyes of my colleagues. I hated myself for my dependency. I hated lying. I hated the pretense of my life. But I never told anyone at the school about my daily ordeal in and out of the classroom or about the toll it was taking on our mar-riage, our family, and my sense of self.

We grew to like the country. After a year, we left the farmhouse and actually went even farther into the country. We bought a home where each afternoon in late summer we could hear the geese going south. Once I realized why it saddened me to hear their wailing cry—autumn was approaching—I anticipated it and knew that a shift in light would soon occur. I used these signs as a reminder that my "trauma anniversary," as it is called in psychology circles, was near. And I learned to integrate these seemingly insignificant hap-penings of nature into my life. It was a good life in our newly purchased home, and it was now three years post-trauma. Our new community welcomed us with homemade dinners, and desserts that lasted for weeks. The day we moved in, teenagers—mostly girls—seemed to fill our front yard to meet the "new boy on the block." We'd found a real home. Although we kept our silences, it was while living in this country space that I gained the courage to try again to live in the city—or at least nearby.

After five years in the country house, we finally found a house of our choosing—"our choice house"—and made it home, months before our son graduated high school. It was much nearer school and friends. Through the years of waiting and wanting, Matt never lost his tenacity, his focus, or his love of family, *and* he managed to have a good time with life. He went to college and then graduate school. With his perseverance and determination, and knowing he always had our love and support, he discovered extraordinary and creative ways in which to excavate his past, and begin anew. David and I worked in counseling individually and together, and learned to trust again. I learned to sleep. He learned to stop blaming himself and caring only for the welfare of me and Matthew. I no longer traveled with pills in hand, and he no longer needed a drink to sleep. I gave serious thought to breaking my silence.

Therapy, in the end, saved me. I needed professional help in the crisis stages of my rape trauma, when I returned to our home city after a year away, when I moved into each of our new houses. And I have needed counseling periodically along the way. I suppose I will need what I call maintenance checks for the rest of my life. But now I understand their value; these reality checks allow me to continue to be productive. They allow me to never doubt my sanity. They allow me to live fully. I know now that I never lost touch with reality. Healing is a continuous process. Sometimes a struggle. Rape affects all parts of one's life and being, and one has to work continually to become whole and intact. Pieces of myself are slowly coming together. I am different, but I accept that. I still have flashbacks, but I know strategies for handling them. Most of the time I have control over my life. Sometimes I still need someone to listen while I retell my story from beginning to end—a therapist, or a "rape buddy" (a survivor like me). Each time I tell my story, it becomes easier to live with the truth. The event has less hold on my life. The wound to the soul is healing.

FULL CIRCLE*

I remember an incredible woman named Jody Pinto who twenty-three years ago pulled together a grassroots movement which had a profound impact on the city of Philadelphia. Those early women knew it was not enough to bind up the wounds of those who were sexually assaulted and send them out again. So together we challenged the rape culture. . . . The last time I saw Jody Pinto was the year of WOAR's twentieth anniversary. She said that despite our problems we should always "keep one hand in the fire."

  —Sara Bergstresser, recipient of "Victim Advocate's Award,"
  1996, Philadelphia WOAR

In 1995 I decided to search for Mark Lipowicz, the assistant district attorney who prosecuted my case. I had not fathomed what I would do or say, when and if I found him. Locating Mark was, for me, a way to bring personal closure to what had happened fourteen years ago. My friend and court advocate, Sara, helped me find Mark. One spring Friday, she accompanied me to Mark Lipowicz's office at Liberty Place. I was extremely nervous. Questions that seemed organized and appropriate the day before the visit now seemed naive and simplistic.

*The previous four chapters were written in 1994; "Full Circle," approximately two years after that.

Mark Lipowicz had left the district attorney's office shortly after the finish of my trial. He is now a partner with a Philadelphia firm, a civil litigation attorney dealing primarily with corporate cases. Had some quirk in my trial driven Mark Lipowicz from the DA's office and Philadelphia's Rape Prosecution Unit? Perhaps Mark had not believed me "beyond a shadow of a doubt" and had, because of me, become disillusioned with rape cases. How self-absorbed we become when consumed with our own terrors and traumas!

Mark Lipowicz's generous invitation to visit his law offices, and his willingness to relive some of his old criminal trial days in this new life and setting, unearthed for me missing pieces about the crime and the trial. I was uninitiated in the ways of the court, so at the time of the trial I could only surmise why things were being done or why some people were absent as witnesses. I had asked few questions then. I was a creature who followed orders and otherwise remained silent. Life happened in my head, not in reality. But leaving a person like me to speculate is certainly dangerous business. During those many years, I had carried a nagging feeling somewhere inside that I had made an error. Maybe it *was* another man who committed those horrific crimes. After all, the defense attorney *told* me I had the wrong man, didn't he? The gullibility that made me the brunt of many jokes as I grew up and led me to believe unequivocally in the goodness of every single human walking this earth was the same gullibility that kept me believing that the attorney for the defense was trying to help *me*. I was too broken, hurt, and vulnerable at the time to understand that every defense attorney must say those words and imply those notions when the prosecution of his client—the "alleged" rapist—depends upon positive identification by the victim/survivor. I was enormously relieved and validated by what I learned over the course of two meetings with Attorney Lipowicz. The stories I had conjured and carried for fourteen years were now being dispelled. I had spent years needlessly torturing myself with unnecessary doubt.

Mark Lipowicz remembered everything. He even remembered the defendant's name. I was amazed that he could so readily recover such ancient details from a case to which he had been attached merely in the line of duty:

It was a case surrounding a family, a child—a rape and burglary. A *family* was terrorized and there was conspiracy. A family had been traumatized. Your case is one I will remember for the rest of my life. The details of your rape were particularly horrendous. And you and [David] had such feeling and love for each other. I won't forget that. All had to pass through him before you could be approached. You were not to be violated again. There was a steep sentence because of all that. The judge saw it as a horrendous case—and because he [the defendant] was a second-rape offender.

There had been special security in the courtroom during the trial; people were frisked as they entered. "This was done because of the nature of the case and because the second man was still loose," Mark explained.

When the lineup identification was arranged prior to trial, Mark Lipowicz was seated behind me. I vividly recall that detail because in a room filled with people, I still felt alone. I was given specific instructions, and then the room was darkened. I kept checking over my shoulder to make sure Mark was still there. I distinctly remember the startled look on his face when I abruptly turned, reaching for him in the dark, after recognizing the perpetrator in front of me—on stage in full light. I desperately sought safety. For the moment, reality evaporated. I thought the man could see me. Was he pointing me out too? *Gonna get you.* "I saw your entire body shiver and begin to shake," Mark recalled. "That was proof enough for me that you had seen the rapist. That was a positive ID."

Mark had been surprised by my positive identification. He had *expected* David to identify the suspect since they had faced each other several times during that evening of the crime. Before the line-up, David had already identified the man from a series of mug shots. That's how he had been initially located. I, on the other hand, had repeatedly insisted I had not seen the rapist's face—that I had not looked. Now sitting in these beautifully appointed offices in 1995—protected high above the city—I realized how afraid I had been to say I could identify the man who raped and violated me. I had to believe the litany I had given to the two men that evening, *"I can't see you. I have my eyes closed. I can't see you."* I had to believe it in order to stay alive. It was all absurd and surreal. At the time of trial preparation I had thought: if I identify him, I condemn him. I would have to point and say, "That one." I did not want that kind of power—to condemn a black man, any man. It was sobering to think that with my words and the raising of a finger, I could send a man to prison, or—if he were exonerated—be afraid forever that he would hunt me down. I had no clear sense of the gravity of the crimes committed against me until many years later.

Attorney Lipowicz had solicited the expertise of the FBI for the trial since his case (the prosecution) rested on eyewitness identification and identification from photographs. The primary photograph, taken from an ATM camera, was grainy and needed analysis; the other photograph had been taken of the suspect after his apprehension. The FBI specialist in photo identification was to discern if the two photographs were of the same person. Mark commented,

> The then assistant director of the FBI's photo lab agreed to be a witness for the prosecution since he believed after analysis that the photographs were of the same man. He [the FBI assistant director] fit the bill—you could practically see the American flag waving behind him as he spoke.

Mark smiled. "The FBI was not usually brought in on local cases in those days."

On my second visit to Liberty Place, in 1996 (and this time without Sara), Mark Lipowicz arranged a conference call between the arresting officer, Joe Britt, and myself. Mark and Joe had remained friends over the years. Joe Britt's voice on the telephone brought back faces and emotions I'd buried for fourteen years. We spoke as if only months had intervened. In 1981, Joe Britt had located the defendant, then the alleged rapist, in another section of the city, standing in the back of a courtroom at another preliminary hearing. "He seemed to match the photograph that had been circulated throughout the city. Perhaps he was there to testify for a buddy," Joe offered. Joe Britt questioned him then, and later brought him in as a suspect—Joe, the gentle "man with a badge," who sat with me on the benches outside the courtroom waiting his turn to testify. We were both stuck there, victims of fate I thought. Now years later I was learning that our lively, seemingly spontaneous conversations and Joe's beyond-the-call-of-duty games of tic-tac-toe had been his idea of distracting and keeping me safe. I have never forgotten his kindness.

Mark Lipowicz and I both remembered that in the middle of trial preparation, Mark's expertise had been requested on another case in another court. Without my being notified, he was removed as "our lawyer." I then received an enthusiastic call from another Philadelphia ADA, introducing himself as the new attorney on the case, explaining that Attorney Lipowicz had been reassigned but not to worry, he had been thoroughly briefed on my case. After several phone conversations, I knew I could not trust the new man. I could never repeat all the horrid details and relive the traumas as I had done with Mark. Couldn't they, whoever "they" were, understand that this was not just a garden-variety robbery or a case of assault and battery? This was a case of *felony rape*. They really expected me to shred my emotions one more time for yet another man, another stranger? Attorney Lipowicz had gained my trust and proved his loyalty. We both had worked hard to achieve that. If Lipowicz could

not remain with my case, I would drop all charges. My final pro-
nouncement. My husband and others were incredulous.

District Attorney, Edward Rendell (now mayor of Philadelphia),
was quickly consulted, and the next call I received informed me that
Attorney Mark Lipowicz had been returned to the case. I still don't
know the reason for the turnabout, but I was content that preparation for trial would continue uninterrupted. I assumed the mayor
had spoken. Recalling this incident fired other memories.

In 1981, the Rape Prosecution Unit of the DA's office was on the
sixth floor of their old building on Chestnut Street. Each morning,
David and I arrived early as if for a workday. The Rape Unit was the
only office on the sixth floor. Whenever I pushed the sixth-floor
button on the elevator, I believed everyone knew where I was headed and why. But once I stepped off the elevator into the Rape Unit,
everyone played my game. All the ADAs and other workers allowed
me to be invisible. I was merely there on business. No one in the
unit ever disclosed his or her involvement with the case or acknowledged my ubiquitous presence. And yet they knew everything.
Because, as Attorney Lipowicz explained this day, "Many times I
needed to brainstorm. We all did that for one another. We were a
very close team and we respected each other." Each day *I* arrived,
however, eyes avoided eyes. And I was content.

With Mark's assistance, I remembered that the jury deliberated
only three hours. And I remembered rigidly sitting in court,
between David on my left and detective Gil Mathis from the Sex
Crimes Unit on my right, as we waited for the verdict. When the
jury foreperson read the first "guilty" charge, my eyes welled with
tears. *Why was I scared and dry-mouthed at this final hour?* And as I
heard the other charges—fourteen in all—I began to sob, the ten-
sion of years rolling off, dissolving. My teeth chattered; my body
shook uncontrollably. David put his arm securely around me. My
head fell to his shoulder and with his silent permission, I sobbed

more deeply. I had wanted to sit with my head held confidently high and look directly into the jurors' faces. But as the charges were read, I merely stared at the back of the defendant as he faced the jury. I should have felt gratitude. I felt unmitigated fear. *Guilty, guilty, guilty* . . . The foreperson continued to read the list of charges and for every "guilty," I inwardly mourned. I felt an extraordinary responsibility. I was sending a black man to prison. *What if he was really sorry? Perhaps someone could help him.* Gil Mathis, crossing his arm over to me, rhythmically patted my shoulder and said softly, "It's okay. It's all over now. It's okay. . . ." But really it was not okay—the aftermath of the trauma and my recovery were yet to begin.

Once the trial concluded and the verdict was in, the prosecution team met in the lounge of the old Bellevue Stratford Hotel to toast a "great success." I don't remember feeling festive. In a stupor, I followed the relieved and jovial group, consisting of Mark Lipowicz, attorney for the prosecution and "my lawyer," Joe Britt, Gil Mathis, other detectives on the case, and the entire Rape Prosecution Unit in the district attorney's office. The ADAs chatted excitedly about various details of the case. One woman told me that Mark had consulted her on some point of law, and she had been pleased that her suggestion had worked. And all the time, I thought no one knew about me and my case except *my* attorney. For two years, the team had all been extremely discreet. They all knew. Mark Lipowicz was now telling me, fourteen years later, that the defendant had been a repeat sex offender; that he had failed the lie detector test; that he frequented the areas in which he had used the various ATMs. According to Joe Britt, the arresting officer, "It was a tight case." All the pieces had fit together.

I always believed I had been treated differently as a rape survivor because we were middle-class and worked in a university environment. After several interviews in which I questioned people involved with the courts, I learned that if there *had* been a class differential in my case that granted privileged treatment, the case never would have been admitted. "In those days [1981], we [in the DA's office] were concerned to prosecute the rapist and to protect as best we could the woman involved. Sure, some cases were harder than others to prove, but we always believed the women. We had been trained to be sensitive." I certainly hope it was more than a code-book recitation.

Finding answers within the legal domain has been necessary to my recovery. Most of the gaps have now been filled in. But there is always a price to be paid for information gleaned. There are always more questions. The prosecuted and imprisoned perpetrator, the first one to break into my home, now has a reconstituted identity. He is still alive. I had obliterated him in my fantasy. But the fact of the crime is still "on the books." There was a part of me, I think, that hoped there would be no record of what had happened. In some ways it would have made life easier. But it is there. It *did* happen. I still have to contend with the fallout. Finding records of the case stored on computer and people who would talk about it has made the incident more real than the reality I had previously excavated. For years I had been collecting and repiecing the moments and years around the crime. One memory always triggered another. But with these new pieces, I had conjured up objective evidence beyond my own recollections. The crime was viable without my memory to breathe life into it.

When I left Liberty Place after talking with Mark Lipowicz, in that edifice of glass, metal, and marble on that Friday in 1996, the evening rush hour had begun. After making my way through a bustling lobby, past a maze of elevators and an elegant baby grand at the entrance, back through revolving doors to the outside— sound returned. Until I burst upon the cacophony of Market Street, I had not realized I was hearing nothing. I had seen rushing bodies, animated faces, but all had been engulfed in silence. It had been a brightly warm, afternoon lunch hour when I entered the building, and now the sun was settling in. My eyes worked to readjust to the light. My body was tight. I ached from the strain of sitting, tensely listening, and holding back emotion. At last, I could breathe long and deeply.

I am generally familiar with the downtown thoroughfares of Philadelphia, but that day I became disoriented, unsure of streets, directions, landmarks. *Strange.* I could not decide which street would take me back to my car near the university. I was distracted by the noise and crowds of people as if someone had just awakened me. I walked until I regained my equilibrium, feigning self-confidence as if someone were watching. Camera images intruded on the day. The shutter clicked repeatedly.

I recognized Juniper Street—the alley street David and I had walked years ago to get quickly from Mark Lipowicz's office to City Hall. *Click.* I looked to my right and there was the little hole-in-the-wall deli where we had eaten many a hasty sandwich during the court and trial days. The sun had felt warm and gentle on my face and arms after the harsh chill of the courtroom as we sat on the deli steps and ate in silence. *Click.* There was the parking garage we had parked in every morning during the days of the trial—just in time for the early morning rates. *Click.* The downtown area around city hall had been an integral part of our world in those days, seemingly so long ago—yet a blink. And there it all was, as if nothing had ever happened in our small, ordinary lives. How could I have forgotten so much? I was dizzy with old memories. Feelings reemerged and sadness swelled. Tears flowed as I maneuvered through traffic. When I finally reached my car after walking thirteen city blocks, I was emotionally spent. I felt overwhelmed and astonished by how much I continued to learn. I felt simply glad to be alive.

. . . .
(For all we know
the wind's inside us, pacing
our lungs. For all we know
it's spring and the ground
moistens as raped maids break
to blossom. What's invisible
sings, and we bear witness.)
. . . .

—Rita Dove,
from "The Hill Has Something to Say"

Part II

SILENT SURVIVORS

The Other Women's Stories

You are the survivors of a crime that does not exist.

—CONVERSATION WITH A MALE ALLY

I entered therapy for the first time immediately after my rape. Somehow I did not believe I could go through such a trauma and come out unharmed. I was assigned a counselor by a Philadelphia organization. It was not a satisfactory arrangement, so I kept trying until I found the right match. But it was not just a therapist I needed and was searching for; I was looking for another black woman— another rape survivor—who could understand the intricacies of my life and trauma, to whom I wouldn't have to explain my dilemma of being black and a woman. I needed a mirror. The ones available were all distorted. I now know that I was not as alone as I thought. There were, in fact, other black women looking for themselves in mirrors—equally without success. All of us were looking in the glass silently.

For black women, where rape is concerned, race has preceded issues of gender. We are taught that we are first black, then women. Our families have taught us this, and society in its harsh racial lessons reinforces it. Black women have survived by keeping quiet, not solely out of shame, but out of a need to preserve the race and its image. In our attempts to preserve racial pride, we black women have often sacrificed our own souls.

The unearthing of "silent survivors" and their narratives has taken time. But since I waited so many years to cease being silent myself, I had to continue to be patient until others were ready to speak with and through my efforts. They could not be forced again. Never again. I regret I could not present the stories of *all* the women with whom I've had conversations over the past four years, but their spirits are here. The narratives that appear in these pages, with the mask of new names, are spoken from the heart. They are not composites. Conversations varied in length from many hours to several days. In every instance the sessions were audio-recorded and later transcribed. As I conversed with the women, I made detailed notations about their affect (expressions) as they spoke. Later I merged the notes with my transcriptions. The narratives that appear in these pages were excavated from longer, more complex encounters and conversations. I tried to capture the essence of each woman, her uniqueness of person and situation. The women vary in age from eighteen to sixty-six; they are students, writers, homemakers, community workers, an actress. They have in common their survival of rape and their courage to speak the truth. They represent the myriad voices that wait to be heard. In their chorus perhaps you will catch a hint of the pain but also the wonderment of their survivals and a glimpse of the diversity that constitutes our lives, our worlds, our traumas—our silences—as black women.

This time when we speak, we move together—as a community of loving accord—into that same space occupied by Zora Neale Hurston's women in *Their Eyes Were Watching God*. Janie, the protagonist, gives love and trust to her friend, Phoebe, in the following words: "You can tell [the public] what you want to tell them, [Janie], 'cause my tongue is in my friend's mouth."* The women of our newfound community have let me into their lives. I speak for them, and I speak for all of us muted by circumstance. They have trusted me with their words. They have let me be their friend. And I am profoundly befriended. They have broken silences; they have borne witness.

*Zora Neale Hurston, *Their Eyes Were Watching God* (1937; reprint: Perennial Library, New York, 1990), p. 6.

RUTH

*I feel that we [black women] should write because after all there
are a lot of us out here that are hurting and don't know where to
turn and we keep it bottled up.*

—*Another survivor, age thirty*

Ruth is a writer. I talked with her by phone several times before we
met. Her light, airy voice seemed to run through all the registers of
the scale. I had pictured her a younger woman—tall, lithe, delicate—and was surprised to greet a woman of medium height, forty-
ish, robust. Her quick, warm, ebony smile belied the horrors and
tragedies held within. Her laughter was contagious; she was all that
her voice had promised. Ruth and I were comfortable with each
other almost as soon as we began to exchange stories. As the hours
passed and the sky began to darken beyond my office window, we
planned a second meeting.

Ruth has never married and has no children. She is open about
sharing her experiences as a survivor of child physical abuse and

adult rape. And she makes clear her distrust of men. So why does Ruth need someone to write her story when she is successful at her craft? And, for that matter, why wasn't she writing the kind of book I was, including the stories of other women survivors? She quickly responded, "I do only little pieces. And I don't think I could deal with other people's stuff."

In addition to her battles with post-traumatic stress—fear, anxiety, and self-mutilation—Ruth has had several surgeries unrelated to the rape that have kept her in bed for most of the past five years. She's had numerous encounters with doctors, psychologists, and "ill-prepared mental health care providers." She reports that "more than once, due to incompetent therapy, I actually ended up hospitalized or suicidal or one heartbeat away from overdosing."

Ruth has eloquently written about being raped as a "naive virgin of twenty" and about the ongoing aftermath of her trauma. In spite of her personal writings, she is a self-consciously private person who works conscientiously to hold in check her violence toward herself.

RUTH'S TELLING

My rape all gets complicated by the child abuse. When I left home at eighteen, I left home for good. If I had stayed, I would have been killed. The physical abuse was becoming very bad. It started when I was about nine. I just shut down emotionally. I remember thinking when I was seven that I would be at home only until I was eighteen, and then I'd go to college. I was going to be a doctor; I decided that when I was nine.

I can remember when I was seven trying to kill myself with a butcher knife in the kitchen. I remember mutilating my fingers. I still have some of the scars. I always felt physically threatened as a kid. I act like an incest survivor, but I don't recollect any incest. I know there was something wrong with me in terms of how I felt about my sexuality before the rape occurred and maybe that will come up now in my therapy. There was always something wrong. As a kid I remember always feeling like I had to protect my body and not really understanding why.

And now I bite my fingers; I've taken off the top layer of skin. It's healed over now. But whenever the anxiety starts, I start biting them again. I've been in therapy for twenty years. It's like a whole chunk of my life went down into the trash.

At the time of the rape I was a research fellow at college. I was twenty, and *I* had won a fellowship to medical school! I was so happy about that. After a few semesters, I dropped out. I had to retire on disability. I just couldn't take the pressure. Now I'm a writer.

I was raped on a date in Los Angeles. I was twenty years old; that was twenty years ago. I had never had a boyfriend; I was a virgin when it happened, and hopelessly naive. He said, "Well I thought we'd go out to dinner at my place." I should never have gone. I was in his car, and I didn't know the city well. Going to this guy's apartment and realizing that I was in trouble was disturbing. I really didn't understand what I should have done. I couldn't get out. He had a deadbolt lock, with a key from the inside. He had taken the key out and unplugged the phone. When we drove into the apartment garage, the bars came down. He said, "You should feel secure." I was disoriented. There was no way I could have gotten out of his apartment let alone this building. I was raped for eighteen or nineteen hours. I thought I was going to die.

He told me while he was raping me about the therapy group he was in. He told me he had a criminal record, and he'd done this dozens of times before. He was older, thirty-two. Hated his mother and the Catholic church. Hated virgins. I was a virgin. I just remember thinking about what I could hit him with. Every time I moved, he moved—all night. It was horrible.

I met him at a bus stop. At a bus stop! Can you imagine? He walked up to me and was very sweet and kind and started chatting with me and, you know, "Call me sometime; maybe we can go out." I'd *never* had any attention paid to me before. I didn't even start dating until I was twenty. And then to just meet someone at a bus stop and then go out to dinner and go to his place! There were some problems I must have been having, and this guy knew who to pick. He knew he could pick me. He knew I'd go off with him, stupidly.

The next day, after the rapes, he just dropped me off at the family where I was staying, and I just told myself, "Oh well, nothing happened." And before going into their house, I went to a park and sat on a bench and I just hypnotized myself and forgot the whole thing. Just shut down. I was all smiles. Didn't think about it at all until about nine years later. In my mind I castrated him. I have fantasized him being on a jail ward and in restraints and I would castrate him. And then he would go to prison forever until he died.

When the post-trauma of the rape hit, I was partway through medical school. I ended up dropping out. I wanted to be a surgeon. It's too late for me now. I really feel that way. I'm so gone in terms of my concentration, and the damage that was done was so huge. I know I can't get back what I lost.

In 1972, if I had reported a "date rape," I would have been laughed out of the police department. You know how some people laugh. We talk a lot about date rape, but people don't really understand the emotional fallout on that person and her community. They don't understand how institutions, like churches, set up families so that these problems are hidden—secret—and remain so. God! We're not even safe in our own homes—nobody wants to see that! And the only thing *I'll* say to most people is that I was date-raped and abused as a kid. Plus I say it in such a way that it doesn't really open the door for any discussion. Because I just want to say it and give some insight. Sometimes I say it to distance people. Because people don't want to hear it. You can talk about being mugged and boast about being held up at knife point on Market Street Bridge or something, but you can't talk about being raped. And I know if I do, I can't count on that person ever being a friend again. I can see it happen. And even if I wanted to try to bring them closer, it wouldn't help. They'd always treat me different. People have one or two reactions when they see you being needy. They either take you under their wing and exploit you or they get scared and run away. They abandon you.

One of my frustrations is knowing we black women *accept* being raped. And middle-class black women don't talk about rape. We sort of support society in viewing us as not being important as rape victims. Or we pretend it doesn't really happen. "She's just saying it." Or, "You could have gotten out if you wanted to." Maybe it's a defense; we don't have control over our own sexuality historically—ever—with rape during slavery and all that. We have an attitude that whatever your man does to you or does to someone else, you still have to stand by your poor lowly black man. And the desperation we have of hanging onto our men when it's obvious that we should go on with our own lives!

I think the better educated and more middle-class we become, our attitudes will change as black women because we will realize that we have a right to a nonviolent life and we have a right to say to a black man that what you're doing isn't right instead of the African American church telling our rapists, "We'll forgive you," and being so outrageously indignant when the rapist goes to prison. We are black, so we really have to mind our p's and q's a lot better. We have to take care of ourselves.

We all have free will, but when it comes to black men, all of

a sudden everybody blames *us*—black women—for what goes
wrong in our race. All of a sudden black men are not responsible for themselves. *We* have to be responsible for them. Then
we're blamed when they go to white women; we're blamed
when they kill each other. We're not valued as people to the
same degree that other people are valued. Even less so than
black men. A professor at the university said in class, in my
presence, that "you can't get raped unless you go slinking
through the ghetto." As if I'm not even a human being. I was
sitting there! We're very disposable people, black women. I—as
a black woman—have feelings. I get angry; I feel delight; I cry
myself to sleep. We have the whole range of emotions that anybody else does.

It's strange, but I get less support from other women than I
do from men. If anything, I find women to be flippant about
my rape. Usually white women, who don't see themselves as
"rapeable," are critical, judgmental, flippant about it. Black
women *blame* me—like they do other black women who say
they have been raped. But there are some supportive women,
like two of my friends, and also you. Just the few telephone
conversations we've had—they've been very healing.

The church was a part of my growing up. I've never really
belonged to a predominantly black church. But I was taken a
few times to a Baptist church because my mother, I think, was
Baptist—I think that's how we ended up there. At first I was
Methodist. Now I'm a Buddhist. I changed my name. That had
a lot to do with the child abuse and the rape. I changed my first
and last names three years ago. People didn't understand. I
think they thought: "Oh this is like the flavor of the month for
Ruth, being a Buddhist and changing her name." But it's very
deeply rooted. I think people see that now. My names had to be
something from the Old Testament. It had to be something
that would give me a sense of family.

The rape, when I was twenty, was the first penetration I'd

ever had—the first time for intercourse. I don't date now. I just decided I wasn't going to date. I don't have sex. I don't have the equipment to deal with it, to keep myself safe. So every man is a rapist and a batterer until proven otherwise. I have anger around not being taught what every young girl should be taught about how to protect herself. Then maybe I wouldn't feel that way. Just commonsense things. Like speaking up if something happens that you don't appreciate. Or if you can't do that—just don't go to his apartment on the first date. Get to know him better. But going off with that guy on that first date—I should have been able to pick up little signals. Looking back, I could have avoided that. But at the time I did the best with what I had. During the rape I always knew that God was there and that he didn't want this for me—it wasn't like He was punishing me.

I get really angry with my mother because she didn't tell me anything about sex or about my body or growing up. She never told me! Not even about menstruation—nothing! She told me nothing about those things. My girlfriends didn't want to tell me because I was this good little kid and, you know, they wouldn't include me in their boy talk. I learned it all on my own. My mother will say now, "So and so was raped." And I'll say, "Well I was too, Mother." Then I get this dead silence. She still hasn't even said, "I'm sorry," or "That's too bad." She hasn't said a word about me being raped. We haven't been together for years. She's still in very strong denial about my rape, which I now pretty much accept. I can't deal with her pain, and I'm not obligated to. I have to just go on and let go.

I think the more it's socially acceptable for women like us, as black women, to talk about black women who have been raped, it will get better. It's still not the thing to do for black women. A lot of people feel they're my friends, but my trust has been broken so many times that I have to trust people on different levels—and only up to a certain point. But I think the more of us who talk about it, the more support we'll have for ourselves and also to give to other women who are black and have been assaulted. It has to come from inside—from our community. We can't depend on support out there to help us to be well. We have to tap our inner voice and try to find our own strength inside ourselves. And I believe we can form a community— somehow.

SHARING WITH RUTH

You told your secret, Ruth; your writing has freed you. How brave you are! I wasn't able to talk about my rape for such a long time.

But finally, late one evening in 1994, thirteen years after my rape, I found a woman "like me"—one of the ones I had been looking for back in 1981. It's strange how these things happen. I met Jocelyn by phone, and everything I had sensed about other black women rape survivors hiding in the shadows of my world became a reality. We talked much too long at long-distance rates, but we found that our paths had almost crossed so many times, and had just missed.

I learned that her rape—the circumstances were quite different— had also occurred in 1981. Jocelyn had been raped, badly beaten, and left for dead. Her situation was much more dire than mine. I am glad she was alive to speak with me that night in April. It was wonderful to learn, that like me, she was a writer and an academic and that she had produced an extraordinary piece of writing with rape as the theme. It was reassuring—no, it was uplifting—that Jocelyn and I had experienced similar reactions as part of the rape aftermath. Over the phone that evening, we shared stories of our nightmares, paranoia, distrust, work obsessions, fear of losing a handle on reality—all of that trauma "stuff." She even had begun *her* rape project about the same time I decided to begin my interviewing. Neither of us knew the other existed. What a solace we could have been for each other!

Jocelyn told me that soon after the rape, she found a life partner—someone who became her healing support just as David had
been for me. He was someone who understood the weird ways in
which we now had to live as rape survivors—someone who understood that we would never be the same, even as we pined continuously for that day of "like before." We are always hopeful that one
day our carefully constructed walls of protection and silence will
crumble because of some unexplained, gracious forgiving that we
have earned. But we are certain, she and I, that we have a purpose
until that day arrives.

I hung up the telephone and felt as if a lifeline had been severed.
I knew we had to plan a meeting to make sure the other existed.
And then the doubts began: Had I told or promised too much?
What had I said to this stranger that was not to have been shared?
Having learned over the years not to trust, I knew I had to be cau-
tious until I met her. How else could I know if all I had sensed on
the telephone was real?

We have learned through trauma, Ruth, not to listen to our
hearts. Through your writing, encourage other women to share their
pain. Tell them not to be afraid, as I was. Tell them it's all right to
trust again.

GRACE

People always tell me that you forget the bad things, you forget pain. . . . But no, you remember the pain.

—*Another survivor, age forty*

It was at the conclusion of a class session, when I explained to my students my book project, that Grace passed me a note: "I think I am one of those women. I'd like to talk to you," it said.

She had been a fine student but extremely quiet and self-effacing. I learned her academic strengths, not because I heard her voice in class discussion, but through her clear, engaging writing style. In fact, until Grace came for an interview and we talked, I don't think I knew the sound of her voice.

She was dressed impeccably, as if for a special occasion. Her dark brown hair relaxed at her shoulders, and the unevenness of her milk chocolate skin was dramatically highlighted by the muted shades of a tan-and-beige pantsuit. As she haltingly told her story, her eighteen-year-old, five-foot frame seemed to disappear into the tweed of my oversized office chair. She had the look of an ingenue: tentative in this unfamiliar place, speaking forbidden words.

Grace is eighteen, a college student. She was raped at fifteen, during her sophomore year of high school. "It seems a lot farther away than that. It seems like ten years at least," she said. She describes her family as loving and supportive. She never sought therapy, although she finds it extremely difficult to speak the word "rape."

Grace sat nervously, with her arms folded and hands clenched. From time to time, tears welled in her eyes. Occasionally, she would let out an enormous sigh. But only once did she give in to the sobs that seemed always near the surface. Grace said this was her first time disclosing to a stranger. She seemed vulnerable, but her story spoke of her courage.

GRACE'S TELLING

I tend to block it out. Like my memory isn't as sharp as it would be with some things. You know? Like I know when it happened—it was on April 2, but I couldn't tell you the year. Cause I don't really talk about it much. I don't talk about it that much with *anyone*. I don't feel comfortable talking about it now.

My best friend lives in a city nearby. I had been seeing this guy off and on who lives near my best friend, and I went over to his house. My friend said, "I'll take you over to Petey's house, and I'll go see my boyfriend or whatever." I said, "Okay, fine." We were like: "Yeah, why don't we do that." When I got to his house, I guess both of our minds were in different places; he was expecting one thing and I was totally expecting something else. He was two years older. He was seventeen.

A lot of people say certain guys expect certain things, right? I mean when they're messin' around with a girl. They think if you're fooling around . . . well, certain guys expect it to go to the next step. I didn't know this; I had gone to his house only once before. Like the summer before. Nothing happened that time. We just fooled around, and that was it. So I expected the same thing to happen again. This time it was different. I told him to stop—maybe he didn't hear me.

I didn't hit him or anything. I was so scared I didn't know what to do. And plus I started crying a little bit and he shouted, *"Shut up!"* Right? And I thought, Oh gosh, he's gonna break my leg, or he's gonna break my arm. 'Cause he was a lot bigger than me. So I said, "Okay." But I didn't fight, I didn't scratch, and I didn't scream to the top of my lungs and stuff like that. At first I didn't even know it was rape.

After it happened, I couldn't get angry. Whenever I got angry I got physically sick. And I was really not looking well, and my best friend's boyfriend, when he heard what happened, was like, "Grace, that can be considered date rape." And I'm like, "No, no, no, no, no, no, no, no, no it's *not*." I just didn't want to hear it. And I just couldn't take enough showers and baths. It was like I was trying to wash it all away. . . . I still take two showers a day. *(She smiles.)*

I've never spoken to the guy who did it since then. When I got back home I didn't tell my mother. And, um, I told my best friend's mother, and I asked her not to say anything to mine. She said, "You know, I respect your decision not to tell your mom." But then I told my mother everything anyway—I mean—*almost* everything. And living with that was kinda hard 'cause, you know, I'm so used to telling my mom *everything*. I was hurting so much inside. I really wanted to tell her.

Then on the bus on the way back to school, I wrote the whole incident down on a piece of paper. Like everything that happened from the moment when I woke up that day. But that piece of paper got washed in the washing machine and all of it got run together. I've never rewritten it. But I did write it. I wrote everything down and it was in purple ink. I remember—on a yellow sheet of paper. I showed it to one of my friends who rode the bus with me back up to school. She started crying. And she was like, "Oh, gosh. You know this is horrible!" And I was like, "*Yes*. I know this is terrible. But I don't know what to do about it."

When I got back to school, I saw a counselor for two days, 'cause I was like, "I can't deal with this." I spoke with her and I was really upset. And I was saying to myself, "I have to tell my mom. I *have* to tell my mother." 'Cause I couldn't go on without my mom knowing. I called my mom and told her. My mom said: "Speak to your father. I can't handle this." So I spoke to him. I told him what happened. He got real upset. And that was that.

My mom then got on the phone and said she was going to call Petey and talk to him. And I'm like, "Pleeeese don't do that." I'm like, "Mommy, please don't do this." She called him anyway. Then she called me back and said, "He said he didn't do anything." And she spoke to his mom. And *his* mom was like, "Well your daughter is a little tramp for coming over to see my son anyway." My mom told her something like, "If my daughter says so, I'll bring you to court and it'll be a hassle for you and your son to get lawyers and such." She asked me if I wanted to do that, and I said no. Because I was in school and that meant I would have to take time off and go back home. I had already been sick and missed two weeks, so I couldn't afford to miss any more school.

My mom made my guidance counselor take me to Planned Parenthood. She made them check for venereal diseases and all that stuff. I didn't want to go to a doctor. I kinda worried about

being pregnant. They examined me and said everything was
okay. But I would have preferred not to think about any of it.
You know? 'Cause . . . I mean, if my stepfather didn't believe
me, right? . . . I didn't think a judge would believe me. And
since the situation was kinda tricky—I *did* go over to his house,
and since we *did* mess around, I didn't . . . I just couldn't handle someone telling me:, "Well, you know, maybe you should've
said no *louder*. And it is your fault 'cause you didn't." So I
thought, well, the judge might not believe me, and I don't
wanta go through all that 'cause that would just be devastating.
I think a lot of people would say, "No, this is not rape." Or
they would say it was my fault for not speaking up louder or
for not kicking him or punching him in the face. A lot of people don't realize that when you're in that situation sometimes
you're so scared you don't know what to do. You panic and you
don't want the person to hurt you so you don't do anything.
Physically hurt, I mean—like slapping you or breaking your
arm. And also, I was just scared. I don't know why at the time.
I was just so scared that this guy was gonna *do something to me!*
The more I try not to think about it, the more I think about
it—and it's something I think about every day. *Every* day.

For a year, my mom wouldn't let me go to the city where he
lived. And when I *did*, I was always looking around—expecting
him to pop out of bushes somewhere and shoot me. My mom
had told him over the phone, "If what my daughter says is true,
then you'll be punished in some way." And she told the same
thing to his mother. Two months later there were riots in his
city, and a kid got shot by a cop. Petey witnessed the shooting.
He had been arrested for rioting. My mom was like, "You see
that—you see?" So I guess what she said was true. A part of me
felt, Good, I'm glad that happened. But then, I'm just the type
of person who doesn't wish any harm on anybody. You can step
on my foot and treat me like crap, but if your parent dies, I'll

feel bad for you. You know? And I was really sad for him that his friend died in the way he did, and I wasn't happy that he went to jail for rioting. But this Petey was obviously not a good person. After the riots, my best friend told me that he had said to her, "Your friend thinks I raped her. What do you think about that?" I never got all the details of the conversation, but I know he said to her, "I don't think I did anything wrong." After he had been in jail for rioting, he was in jail again for attempted robbery. At that time, I said, "Well, good for him. That was stupid." But I didn't feel like he was being punished for what he had done to me.

After I graduated high school and went to college, I met a girl from Petey's hometown. I asked if she knew him and she did. She told me that he was getting married and that he and his wife-to-be "had a daughter; about a year and half." *(Grace's rape had been two years before.)* I called home and said, "Mom guess what? I ran into somebody that knows Petey, and I found out that he has a daughter and guess what her name is? . . . It's Grace!" I was so upset; I still am. So after I met this girl . . . she didn't know what had happened between the two of us . . . the whole rest of the day I felt like I was walking in a time warp or something. *(She cries.)* I felt like I was in a twilight zone. That's the last I heard of him.

I always get really tense whenever the topic of rape comes up in a group. Then there always has to be one person in the group to take things to a higher level, like: "I wonder if any one of *us* has been raped?" I get quiet. Some people just don't think that there's a need for their voices to be heard or that people want to hear it. I guess sometimes people are just uncomfortable about speaking about certain things, and they just don't say anything at all rather than put themselves in an awkward position. A girl in my college did a survey. She had three situations and she wanted to know if people felt that it was rape or not. I thought most of them were rape. The guys, especially, didn't see it as being rape in any form. I think a lot of people are a little confused or they don't know; they think the boundaries are really thin. I think a lot of guys on my campus, if my situation was put on a piece of paper and they were asked, "Do you think this was rape or not?"—a *lot of them* would say no. Or they would say, "It was her fault."

My mother tried to talk me into going to group therapy, but I always saw therapy as being this anonymous body of people— strangers I can't talk to. So I never went, and I never called. I don't know how I deal with most of the things that have happened to me, to tell you the truth. *(She laughs.)* I have a chronic disease and my mom was a battered woman, so I grew up with that. I lived with my grandmother until I was five, and then lived with my mother. I find some comfort in talking with my best friend and a few other people about "it" and about my life, but these are only people I know who won't ask me more questions that I don't want to answer. Or people that won't judge the situation in any way or won't view me in a different light. I really hate to tell somebody what happened and then they're like, "Oh, poor thing. That's so horrible. You poor child." I hate pity.

I don't think I clearly understood what "it" [rape] was until after the incident happened. I had this thing about kissing a guy, right? I said the first guy I'm gonna kiss has to be so special to me, right? So my mom was like, I have nothing to worry about with this girl 'cause she has all these crazy views. She's not gonna do anything with any guy too soon. So there was never a need to warn me. Everyone always *knew* Grace could take care of herself. "She takes care of her younger sisters." So a lot of people felt, "We don't need to talk to Grace about it cause she knows already." But I *didn't* know. *(She cries openly.)* I didn't know.

Petey was the first guy I had kissed. That happened one summer when I was fourteen. So it's like I went from crawling to
running almost, you know. In such a short space of time. I
didn't even know him that well, to tell you the truth. He was
just some guy who was nice to me whenever I went to visit my
best friend. He was some guy at her school who thought I was
cute. And I was, like, this guy is really gorgeous—blow me
down, knock me over, beautiful. My best friend told me, "Well,
he's a player." And I was, "So what? He's really cute and he
thinks I'm cute too. So I'm gonna see this guy despite what you
say." My mom said to me after the incident happened, "Grace,
you need to pay more attention to what people tell you about
other people, especially guys. If they say negative things about a
person, then you need to take it more seriously or take it into
consideration when you deal with these people." That was
about as much advice as she gave me, 'cause the topic makes
her really uncomfortable.

About my rape, first my mother said, "You clean it, polish it;
you watch it shine. You set it up on a pedestal for everyone to
see." *(She cries.)* And then she said, "I felt like somebody took
my diamond and put a scratch in it." *(She cries hard.)*
"Something so special—just hurt it so. I felt like someone took
my diamond that I had placed on this high pedestal and just
slapped it to the floor, knocked it over. They didn't care. It
hurts me so much to think that someone would do that to you
because I know that you're a good child. I know you do everything I say. It really hurts me." That's what my mother said to
me. It hurts *me* to hear her say something like that. I still feel
like it's my fault for going over to this guy's house. She told me
not to. You know, I went against everything that she ever taught
me. I never like to do anything to make my mother upset.

I don't know if I can ever think of myself as a [rape] survivor.
Maybe one day. *(She laughs.)* I have never said it; I guess

because it was "date rape." It's like something will happen—the walls will crumble—if I say the word. Even though I've heard many people confirm it and say that what happened to me was date rape, there's still a part of me who's not sure if it was. I always wish that there could be at least one day that goes by when I don't think about it.

SHARING WITH GRACE

Your talk of taking lots of showers and desperately trying to get clean, Grace, reminded me of a moment with my aunt in whose home we stayed for a time after the rape and burglary.

What a loving and intimate thing she did for me. The day after the rape she orchestrated a douche for me, using her personal douche bag. And it *was* an orchestration! It was done the old-fashioned way, the kind I remember from my childhood. No "Summer's Eve" to be sure. You know—the contraption that is the cousin to the enema bag. What horrid associations! I remember lying on the floor of her bathroom gazing up at cold white tile, feeling water flow into me. During that time, like you, I seemed to stay in or around water every chance I could get. I just kept washing everything, over and over. Would I ever really be clean again?

It was so hard getting his smell out of me. . . . But I do remember the soft loving feel of her hands and the sun slipping through the bathroom curtains.

MATILDA

I had a choice of either being raped or being murdered.
—Another survivor, age thirty-two

Matilda's message on my answering machine was not long or complex. Her full-bodied voice left only the necessities: her name, the person who referred her, the times she could meet. "Call me back; let me know when I should come. Thank you," she said as she rang off. That's how I was introduced to Matilda. I thought, What a powerhouse. Who is this young woman?

When Matilda swept into my office on the day of our meeting—precisely on time—I could see the youthfulness just under the self-assured, no-nonsense surface of her twenty-year-old bearing. A third-year student at a local college, she was colorfully dressed in loose-fitting clothes—long skirt and shawls of African textiles. Scarves tied into a *gelee* (African head wrap) hid her hair but accentuated her pretty, angular face.

She made it clear that she knew why she had come and what she had to say. As Matilda found a chair and adjusted her wraps, her story and all its details spilled out without any getting-to-know-you preliminaries. She attempted nonchalance.

MATILDA'S TELLING

I was raped when I was ten years old. And here I am ten years later. Just fine. My story is a little out of the ordinary in the sense that I have not kept this a secret. I told right away, and I called the police. So it actually went through the court system. I got a conviction and all that stuff. I don't keep it a secret—but I don't broadcast it either.

I feel different from most survivors who talk about rape because I was a child when it happened. The incident was so clear-cut for me. It was a stranger who forced his way into my home. There were no gray areas at all. I was home by myself. I opened the door . . . and I shouldn't have and all that, but I did. So I'm not gonna kill myself over that—or I could have. But my mom is different. My mom feels guilty about it still and thinks it is her fault because she had to leave me at home alone.

My aunt lived two floors up so I would go upstairs with her when she came home. But this particular day, I didn't go. I came home and when the person knocked on the door, I opened it. I didn't think about it. Actually the first time he knocked on my door he didn't really do anything; he just asked if I knew where so and so lived. I said, "No, I don't," and told him to go downstairs to the super, and I didn't think anything strange about what had happened. I was just like, Oh someone's looking for someone. I mean, it was a big apartment building. When he came back, I thought he must not have been able to find the super's apartment. I opened the door again. But he was totally different this time. You know? He wasn't asking about the person. He was asking if I was home by myself. That's when I was . . . I mean it happened so fast. I didn't want to answer his question, and I guess he could tell since I didn't answer. Then he was like, "Can I have some water?" And I yelled, "*No!* you *can't*." The next thing you know, he just hit me. He just came in. There was never a gray area.

And then, he left. But he just kept saying not to tell, not to tell. Not to tell. I thought about *not telling* because it was just stuck in my head. But what happened was, when I went to clean myself up, there was blood all over and all this "stuff" dripping down my leg. I realized I couldn't *not* tell. So I called my aunt upstairs. I didn't say anything to her except—I yelled sort of "I was raped!" I didn't say "hello"; I didn't say anything. I just said, "I was raped. I don't know what to do!"

Actually I thought for a split second about not telling cause that's all he kept saying throughout the whole ordeal—"not to tell"—but he wasn't overly violent or anything. The only time he ever hit me was when he tried to come into the apartment. I mean, the whole act is violent in and of itself, but I mean, I wasn't—you know—beat up or anything like that. He just would keep threatening that if I screamed or if I didn't do this or that then he would hit me. So I wasn't trying to scream or anything. I just wanted the thing to be over with. I just didn't want to have anything else to do with it.

So my aunt came downstairs, and the next thing I knew there were two dozen people in my house. The police were there, and the ambulance came and got me. I had to go to the hospital. My mom and everyone was just rushing around. I guess, my life was never the same after that. It was like the cutting point of my childhood from nonchildhood. I can't say from "adulthood" 'cause I wasn't an adult yet. This happened March 20. It was like the end.

I still don't know to this day how I knew I was raped. Where did I hear this? Who told me this? I don't know! I'm not fabricating. I know that's what I said to my aunt: "I was raped." That's *all* I said to her. I don't know how in the world I knew that, but I knew that's what was happening to me. I know because I remember before he actually physically violated me—he had told me to take off my clothes and do all this stuff. And I was like, you know I'm only a child. I said that to him. I said, "I'm only ten years old. Please. Please. I'm just a child. Please don't do this to me."

He didn't say anything. He didn't answer my questions in any way. You know, he was like, "whatever." I knew somehow that . . . I knew what he was gonna do . . . and I really . . . *(She laughs nervously.)* I *knew* that it wasn't right. This was not supposed to be happening to me. But I don't know *how* I knew that word "rape." I guess it was my mom. She was very open with me about sex education and all that: "If you have any questions, just ask me," she would say.

I was hurt. Real bad. I had to have stitches. That was my injury. I was torn. My vagina was torn, and I had to receive stitches. But other than that, nothing was wrong with me physically. Everyone was saying that I was brave. When my mom got there, she *broke down!* And I was saying, "Mom, I'm okay. Really I'm fine. Look at me, I'm fine. Nothing's wrong with me. Everything's fine." She was like, "*No*, everything's *not* fine." She tried for my sake not to be upset, but she could not help herself. She was there with me through the whole thing. This is my mom. She went into the emergency room with me. She would not leave my side for the whole rest of the time. Wherever I was going, she was going. And no one was speaking to me unless they spoke to her first.

I remember when my mother came to the hospital, she was more devastated than me. This was strange to me. I've always had a sort of take-it-in-stride character, even as a child. That's how I was. You know, stuff would happen and I'd be, Oh, well, it happened. It's over; just deal with it. So when *that happened to me*, first of all I didn't even really feel anything at that moment. I was just *there*, not feeling anything. I had to stay in the hospital for two or three days. I didn't know why. But my mom knew why. You see, basically, they were investigating *her* to see if she was fit to take me home. I didn't know that's what was going on then. I know that must have hurt her badly.

I had a ball in the hospital! I was in the Pediatrics Department. Surprisingly, there were four other girls there who were raped—in *my* room—in the same room with me on this ward. And we were all ages ten to fourteen, so we had this little posse. It was this big, huge, city hospital. We were all there at the same time. All the circumstances were different, but they were there, just like me. It was real strange. I mean, maybe they [the hospital administrators] did it on purpose and put us there so we would be together—I don't know. We didn't talk about the rape at all. We asked each other, "What are you here for?" And we would just say, "Hey, I was raped." When you're a kid, you don't care about these things. We just formed this little clique, and we called our friends on the phone. That's what we did for the few days. I didn't really think of myself as incapacitated. I was just there. Everyone came and acted like nothing was wrong—I guess because I was a child. They wanted me to feel like I was okay. I didn't really understand why, but I was a little celebrity for the time being; my [school] vice principal came to see me in the hospital.

So I went back to school like nothing had happened. As a child you don't have the tools to deal with something like that happening to you. Everyone would ask me how I was. I guess they didn't know what to ask me or what to do. I was like, "I'm fine!" You know, I'm back home now and stuff is back to normal. . . . But it really wasn't.

I had to go see a psychologist. I had to go as part of the police procedure; I don't remember for how long. Of course, my mom wanted me to have the best, so I went to see some private psychologist—a white woman. I didn't like being there. I remember wondering what she was doing. I was a smart child—like nothing went over me. I would play games with her, and she would try to hypnotize me. And I thought, I'm *not* going to be hypnotized. But I think I faked it. I remember my mom wasn't allowed to be there. Two weeks after I got out of the hospital, I had to go to the police station to look through snapshots. I *saw the guy*. I picked out his picture, and I said, "That's *him!*" The strangest thing to me was that he was already in jail at the time I picked out his picture. He had been arrested already for trying to steal a car. Then I had to pick him out of a lineup. That started the case. I remember meeting the lawyer, and then I was on the stand. Actually that was the only part of the case that I remember.

For a year, I was paranoid of *every man on the street*. I thought I was being followed. I would just watch people. No one knew that this was going on, but I was really, *really* paranoid. I hid from people thinking they were following me; then I would turn and go a different way. Or, if I saw someone following me, I would duck behind cars. All this stuff I had to do just to get home every day. I didn't talk to anyone about it. Someone was always following me . . . just *always* . . . and that was just so scary. I don't know when it stopped. For that year after the rape when I was in the sixth grade, I sort of dropped off the face of the earth. That year was a blur for me. I don't really know how many of the details of the rape I've blocked out. I was in a new junior high school, and I had to take tests, but I do not remember my life there at all. Except for the fact that I had some friends, and I was there every day. I gained a lot of weight. I was always unhappy looking. And this was the same time I was going through the trial. I don't remember my life there at all.

I remember the man who raped me. But I know that one of the results of what happened to me is that I have a very bad memory to this day. Certain things I remember . . . certain things I don't forget . . . like I didn't forget his name. In general, my memory is *very selective*—about everything. Even now, I'm very selective about what I see. A lot of times I don't remember men's bodies. I remember their faces. I'm an observer. I definitely think this has to do with the rape. As I get older, I realize that I can block out things like they never existed. Or detach myself from things as if I wasn't really there.

If I'm sitting and I'm talking about the rape—like now—I'm not feeling it. I'm just describing what happened. I was there certainly, and I remember it. But I do not remember *how* I felt at the moment that the rape was going on. And I haven't been able to pull that back yet. I would like to at some point. Actually I guess that's what I'm working toward, 'cause I go to therapy all the time. I have yet to remember the feelings. I guess I've subdued the pain of the rape. *It hurt! Wow! Did it hurt!* But, you see, I do not allow physical pain. There seemed to be such greater hurts I could have—like my arm could be cut off or something crazy like that. I have a big phobia about physical pain. I don't know when it began or ended, but I don't like to think about the pain.

I remember a lot of different things happened in my life after I was ten, after the rape. My mother's boyfriend was a very mean, abusive man. Not to me. More so to my mother. I find this a lot with black women; they will let things happen to themselves, but not to their children. It's like, "If you cross that line and you do something to the child, then it's like, *now it's not acceptable*. But if you do these things to me, we'll work around it." That's what my mother did. He would never beat my mother up to the point of bruises, but he would terrorize her. And he might hit her once, then walk away—or push her. But he *would* terrorize. Constant threats. I used to take up for my mother. My mom would be scared for her life. He would hit her and she would say, "Matilda, call the police!" Then her boyfriend would say, "Don't touch that phone. If you do, such and such will happen to you." I remember that vividly. If you feel that your mother's life is threatened, that's probably the scariest thing that can happen to you. That was such a traumatic thing to me as a child. But I would find a way to call. And I would scream, "Don't touch my mother." Maybe that's where my "courage" came from. My mom was my best role model even though she was in situations that I didn't think she should have been in. I hated him. But then . . . I loved him too because he was there. He wasn't always like that.

I'm in therapy now, and I'm working on how I relate to black men. How I *don't* relate well to black men must have something to do with my past state and my present relationships. The man who raped me was a black man. He actually had a family. I didn't know all this until I went to court. And there he was with his family. That was his alibi—that he was at home with his family. He had a child and a *wife*—I was so taken aback! That to me was astonishing. You know, I really didn't know how to take that. I mean I've *never* had a black man in my life who I've looked up to in a good way and respected—except for my grandfather, who died when I was a kid.

There was a whole length of time that I was seeing only white men. I look back on that, and now I can see why. All through high school I dated one guy. He was white. In fact, he moved me to college—him, me, and my mom. We thought we were going to be married and have kids. We were inseparable, to the point where we were very dependent on each other. There was nothing we wouldn't do for each other. Then we realized we needed to go our separate ways. We didn't break up in a bad way. I still consider him a friend. But I was an escapist—I had been living a segmented existence. There was my neighborhood—very harsh and rough—mostly blacks and a few Latinos and lots of crime. And then there was this little white school where everybody had money, and I had financial aid. I don't date white men anymore, *at all*. I came back to life in college, and I've starting dating black guys. I've changed so much now that I would never accept a white man in my life. As far as I am concerned, I was dead before. And I say I was dead because I was living lies. My whole life was a lie. I hadn't accepted any part of myself that was true. I've made a lot of changes. I guess I've been working my way back "home."

I think I got my coping strength from two different sources. People have energies and they have spirits—from the second they come out [of the womb]. I was always a very outgoing child. I was always courageous. I was a go-getter, and I didn't let anyone get in my way. My mom never really wanted me to be that way. She always would say, "Matilda, why can't you be dainty like all the other little girls?" I just was not like that. She used to dress me up in little dresses and I looked cute, but I was loud and just like a little tomboy. I didn't hang out with the boys. I was just a very blunt child. I sort of laid down the rules, even as a child. My mom was not very strict with me. She let me do my thing. My mom is not like me; she's exactly the opposite. She's very soft-spoken. She won't speak her mind.

Everything about me has become exaggerated over the years—which can be good and bad. I always want to be the *best*—not in relation to other people. I want to be the best *I* can. I don't know if I was like that before the rape or not. There was such a small part of my life *before* that happened to me that I don't even know. I wasn't developed. I mean, there almost was no "before." I say that because I think my memory has been damaged. One of the things I want to get to is to be able to rebuild it. I do not remember my childhood. I sort of separate my life: like "before rape" and "after rape."

Black women and sexual assault don't exist on campus. Like, it's not a reality. That's because people don't respect women, period. And black women get *no respect* by anyone—even ourselves. Black women don't have respect or love for themselves or even see themselves as legitimate beings who have every right to everything that everyone else does. Talking about rape is like taboo, and we all *know* it's taboo. I think I know people who have been raped, but I don't know anyone who has ever come out and *said*: "I was raped." They may say something like, "Well, yeah, something sort of like that happened to me too," but they won't go into it. Or they sort of allude to the fact that, "Well I can understand because . . ." It's always "something similar," but people won't just call it what it is. If I ever chose to deal with rape in a public way—and I may or may not in the future—I wouldn't just deal with rape. It's not just the rape thing. I would deal with sexuality too. I would deal with rape in the context of other things. I'm very woman-centered. Rape is a part of *my* sexuality because it has made up what's happened to me. Rape is an act of violence that can or cannot shape the way you see your own sexuality for the rest of your life. And for me it has. What happened to me, happened before I was a sexual being. I had no frame of reference except rape.

A *lot* of women don't feel they have the right to say no. And for black women it's a taboo "to tell"; the brothers are hurting so bad we don't want to hurt 'em anymore. God forbid we should put another worry on them! If it were date rape—a person I knew—I would have already said *no*, first of all. So there would *have* to be a violation cause I would have said no. There wouldn't be any gray areas in *my* mind. *(She smiles.)* I don't know if I would report it to the police. But he would have to suffer some consequences for violating me. However, . . . I don't know what they would be. I would make sure *everyone* in the black community on campus knew what happened. But now that I think about it, I wouldn't call the police cause I wouldn't want to ruin his life. Him going to prison and being another statistic to me is almost as great an evil as what happened. I love black people. Even when we're sick.

People have asked me—and I've thought about it—if I could go back and live my life over, would I erase the rape? And *no*, I would not. This is part of me, and I don't believe in erasing the past. It's sort of like—written. It's done, and I don't mess with it. I just deal with it and move on. I incorporate it and use it. Part of the reason that there are some good things about me now, I think, is because that happened to me.

I'm a Virgo. I'm a thinker, analyzer—that's what I do. I may not have answers, but I *think* about everything. I think all of this has made me—along with other things—a survivor. I survive, and I *will* survive. Like, *nothing* will get me. That's the way I approach things. I take even the most horrible things and I squeeze the goodness out of them because I believe that's why they're there. I'm a fighter. I'm strong. To me strength means resilience. Not, "It's gonna be my way or else." If you're unbending, that's weakness to me. I believe everything that happens to you, you're supposed to learn lessons from it. If you don't, then you're not allowing it to be what it should be. This belief has helped me deal with the pain. Not the physical pain—the emotional pain.

SHARING WITH MATILDA

I have tried so many times to sit and talk with my mother about my rape—about how I feel now and, yes, even the horrid details of seemingly long ago. Like you told me about your mother, Matilda, my mother is also *my* role model. We live different lives, but who she *is* I respect. As Lisa Jones says about her mother, we don't always agree about things, but "we don't stumble on it."* My mother is soft-spoken too, but she's a real fighter. We are extremely close and can talk about everything—except the rape. I wish she didn't take on my pain. I wonder if my mother worries that there might have been something she forgot to tell me. Perhaps that's why it's so difficult for us to talk with our mothers. We can't seem to separate ourselves out.

*Lisa Jones, *Bulletproof Diva* (Anchor, New York, 1995), p. 34.

EVIE

I think [religion] acts itself out in the healing, and I think it really acts itself out in the silence.

—*Another survivor, age fifty-nine*

Evie is a petite, pixielike, nineteen-year-old college student. She wears her long, highlighted brown hair pulled tightly into a small knot at the back of her head—as if to hide some of her beauty. During our talk she smiled infrequently. Her light complexion foregrounded large pale green eyes, which held me to her every word. But whenever she talked of herself, her eyes had difficulty making contact. Evie's small voice sometimes got lost between broadcast and reception. Often I had to lean in to make sure I heard the entire utterance.

Evie and I were having lunch in downtown Philadelphia. I had no idea our spring "getaway" would end with talk of trauma. We had only known each other about a year. We had worked together on a community project. We enjoyed discussing women's issues whenever our very busy schedules allowed. This was such a day, away from the bustle of work on a bright, breezy afternoon. Just after our sandwiches and before our final cup of tea, I told Evie about the book I was writing. I'd become mired in the details. When I looked up, I saw that she was not registering; she seemed in another space. Where had she gone? What happened? She quite suddenly had become "dark" and pensive. "Is there something wrong?" I asked. She began to shake and to cry softly.

I reached for her hand and held it tightly. It was almost as if we were on a bumpy roller-coaster ride and we were both holding on to stem the fear. And then I knew. "Are you a survivor, Evie?" No answer. She began to sob and shake her head, no. It was good that the hour was late and most of the people in our section of the restaurant had gone. "Evie," I repeated slowly, as if she wasn't hearing me, "Are you a survivor?"

She began to shake her head frantically.

"No, no, no, no, no," she chanted, her eyes closed.

"Then what?" I insisted, still holding on.

"I'm fine. It's nothing," she shot back—not looking at me but speaking through gasps and sobs.

I held on, "You *must* tell me, Evie." My frustration rose. "Are you a rape survivor like me? Please, please—you must help me. I need for you to tell me, Evie."

A very tiny voice came back, "Yes."

My heart sank. Not another one. And she's only nineteen. Once she had spoken "yes," Evie began to cry uncontrollably. I kept holding on to her, reassuring her that I was not going to leave.

"May I ask how old you were?" I felt that this memory had come from long ago.

"About three years old. I'm not sure. I know it was before I went to school. I don't remember exactly how old I was."

When I embraced Evie at the end of our afternoon, to thank her for sharing, I was not startled to feel an ever-so-slight quiver run through her shoulders. It was like the subsurface eddy of faraway, underground water—or an imminent earthquake. During our time together, I learned only a few of the secrets Evie had been keeping tucked away. I knew she would not share again for a long while.

EVIE'S TELLING

Maybe I was around four. I'm just not sure of the age. It was my cousin. I guess he was a teenager because he's in his thirties or forties now. I still know where he lives. I never told my mother. Oh, I want so much to be able to tell my mother, but I don't know how. She's worked so hard to bring us up. I think if I told her, it would kill her.

After my father and mother were divorced, my mother had to go back to work. She has always tried so hard to keep us strong and together—me and my sisters and my brother. I love my mother very much, but since I'm the youngest I didn't really get to know her very well. She had to go to work, and that's when it happened—while she was at work. She would never forgive herself . . . if she knew. My cousin was supposed to be watching me. He hurt me. Real bad. And I knew what he had done was wrong. But I just couldn't tell anybody. I haven't ever told *anybody* in my family. I guess I've been carrying a weight around with me all these years. But I haven't forgotten what happened. . . . Not any of it.

I have never been in therapy. I just can't stop to do that now. I know I need help. But I feel I might become something . . . like dysfunctional . . . for a while anyway if I began to talk about what happened. I just can't talk about it now. I *have* to finish school, and I want to travel. There's just no time to go into therapy. It would just take so much time.

But I do feel that there are some things I am not able to do because of the rape. I am so nervous about so many things. I'm afraid to do things. I just get so frustrated, and I cry—a lot. I am desperately afraid to put myself in some situations—not sexual—*life* situations, and I know it's because of what happened to me. It just makes me so angry . . . so angry.

(She begins to pound on the table and rock back and forth. She twists her fingers in a childlike fashion and cries openly.)

When I think that my whole life has been ruined by what happened to me when I was just a child, it makes me angry. I don't know anything else. These memories have been with me all my life. They have determined what and who I am. Sometimes I wonder what I would have been like—who I would be now—if that hadn't happened to me. But I don't know anything else.

That's all Evie would tell me.

SHARING WITH EVIE

When I was teaching high school English just after my BA degree, I loved watching my students learn to write and get "turned on" by the creativity of it all. In one of my classes, after assigning a writing exercise—to create a story of suspense that would keep a reader enthralled—I received one paper that gave me serious pause.

For this paper, I asked that names be put on the back of the last page; I wanted to enter fresh into the suspense of the stories and pretend I didn't know these "writers" personally. As I read the story in question, I began to feel strange. I knew that either this person was an undiscovered short story writer who would one day surely be published, or the student was in trouble and was indirectly asking for help. When I discovered the author of the paper, I despaired. I knew it had to be the latter, since I had expected the assignment would give her some difficulty as previous ones had. I asked the student how she decided on such a fantastic, imaginative piece and what process she had used to write it. Had someone helped her with the story? "No" was her answer. She had had previous opportunities to consult a ghost writer and had not done so, and she did not fit the profile of a cheater. I gave her every opportunity to tell me that the story was so vivid and graphic because it was true. She maintained it was a fiction.

As any teacher should, I took the paper to an administrator and explained the classroom assignment and why I thought it represented a *possible* case of sexual abuse and needed to be investigated further. I was summarily dismissed. I was told that this was an *excellent* young woman; she was always appropriate; she came from a "*very* good family." This could not be the case. I was mistaken. I had gone too far, I was told. I took the matter no further.

Now years later, I regret that I didn't take things further because I don't think I was wrong in my assessment. What I was lacking was not insight, but experience and strength to fight a battle alone. I doubted myself and my instincts. I will never forget that student, Evie. I know I let her down. I remember her smile. I remember the conference we had about her paper. Somebody there was in need. If only I had had the voices of this book to sustain me. But now I know what I didn't then—my gut was right. There are children suffering in silence, not knowing how to say the words that could bring them comfort. Just like "your child," Evie.

YVONNE

I literally told him, "You're hurting me." And I thought he would stop. But he just came on worse.

—*Another survivor, age thirty*

Two words adequately describe Yvonne: gorgeous and proud. Yvonne is tall, seemingly shapely (her figure hidden by her overly loose clothing), with smooth coffee-and-cream skin and just a touch of blush. She has a commanding yet not overpowering presence; her smile lights her face and the space surrounding. You would expect to see the likes of her in print and media ads. Complementing her extraordinary looks was Yvonne's flair for style.

Yvonne is twenty-three, an honor student in her second year at a local college, married, with one child. She took a leave of absence after her first year to become a mother and set up home with her husband, several years her senior.

During an extremely tumultuous childhood, Yvonne endured rape and repeated molestations in addition to negotiating other complex family situations. After being raped by a stranger as a preadolescent, Yvonne never received validation or support for telling the truth. Prior to the rape, she had been molested and violated by those close to home. But she never bothered to tell because she felt no one would believe her stories. Everyone loved the man who called himself her "uncle." Only Yvonne knew him for what he was.

Her determination and ability to focus enabled her to complete high school, finishing all courses with grades of A. No one in Yvonne's family had been to college; in fact, on her mother's side no one had finished high school. She was determined to succeed because her mother and grandmother had been on welfare, and "no women in [our Southern town] had anything or were anything."

She expressed herself eloquently, telling her stories of unrelenting lifetime horrors with the equanimity of someone who has been to the bottom of the pit and found a way up. She was determined not to give in to self-pity. Once she graduated high school, Yvonne said she never thought of not going to college: "I had no choice. I got my vision of going to college from Oprah Winfrey. She was the first black woman on TV I saw who was successful. I liked her story. I wanted to be like Oprah Winfrey."

YVONNE'S TELLING

I'm the oldest girl and the first grandchild. I have four sisters and a brother. I was always the smartest, brightest, so everyone always looked at me with high regard. When there was a pageant at school, my mother would *never* say, "I want you to be in this pageant; let's get in this pageant." I would beg her to pay the money for me to get admitted, and then I would do everything myself. My family never came to any of the things I did in school.

I don't necessarily *have* to talk about the rape, but sometimes I like to talk about it. I don't feel ashamed to talk about it to any particular person. . . . I can talk about it to anyone. Before . . . I couldn't. But I think as I got older and started to think about what had happened and after hearing in the media all the time, "It's not your fault; it's not your fault," I probably started to really believe that it wasn't my fault. Once I believed that, it was easier for me to talk about it. Now it's not hard at all. I was fifteen when I first wrote about what happened. I wrote a short story, a kind of fictional autobiography. I've been developing that ever since tenth grade. I'm still working on it.

When I heard that you were gonna do this book, I had already been thinking about doing something like this, . . . writing about black women that had been raped, because I felt the same way. And also because where I had lived in the South, any time a black woman said she had been raped, she was never believed. In my community, they always made her feel like she did something to deserve it—or she was lying. When I left my community in the South to go to the West Coast, where it seemed to be taken a bit more seriously, I think that's when my change started . . . and I wrote that story for my class. Everyone was writing happy stories, and then I came in with this very sad, depressing story. I got very graphic. My teacher, though, was very impressed that I wrote.

I was twelve when I was raped, but I also had been molested when I was eight. I was molested from eight years old to ten years old . . . by a man down the street from us. He called himself my "uncle." So my family trusted him a lot. When it started, I had just come back to the South with my mother because my parents had gotten divorced. We lived with my grandmother in a three-room house. It was only three rooms. Me, my sisters, my brother, my mother—she was pregnant—my grandmother, my grandfather, my aunt, and my real uncle. . . . We all lived in this house!

My grandfather was an alcoholic, and so was my mother. But she wasn't drinking as heavily because she was pregnant. She would get a Social Security check, and my grandfather would go shoot the whole thing and give money away because he would be drunk. My mother would do the same with the government check she was getting for us. We would have no money. After the first three days of the month, we'd have no food. A lot of times we didn't have hot water. And so they would go to Mr. Hatcher, my "uncle," and he would always give us money to buy food.

One Christmas my mother . . . she had just had my sister . . . was a week out of the hospital and she went off on a drinking binge. We hadn't seen her for days. She took the government check and spent the whole thing, and my grandfather had done the same thing with his Social Security check. It was Christmas time. We had no food; we had no toys. We didn't have anything. Mr. Hatcher bought my aunt a boom box; he bought me a used bicycle and a jogging suit; he just bought little things for all of us! He bought us food for Christmas. My family really trusted him.

My aunt—who was my age—would go over to his house and do sweeping for him and wash his dishes for two or three dollars. In the summer she had gone to stay with some relatives, so he would tell my grandmother, "Oh let Yvonne come over and do some sweeping for me." I was eight or nine years old. And so I would go over there and sweep for him, and he'd have me play checkers with him. I would do dishes for him and go and get soda from the corner store. Then one day he said, "Let me see your teeth," and I'd smile real big. I was real gullible.

(She says with disgust.) I was only eight years old. He says like, "Oh you have such pretty silver caps on these teeth. Open up." So I'm opening my mouth real big and wide. He's touching my silver caps. Then he says, "You know, you're such a pretty girl." And I'm all happy: "Why thank you!" You know. . . . Then he says, "I'm going to give you a kiss." So he gave me a kiss and that's when it all developed. From that moment. Every time I would come over to sweep or whatever, he would give me three dollars; and sometimes he would give me five dollars; and sometimes he would give me ten! You know, that was a whole lot of money for me.

We never had money to begin with, and then bein' nine years old—I was really happy. And I was like, "Oh, I love my uncle, Mr. Hatcher," and then he would kiss me and sit me on his knee. One day, he said, "Give me a kiss," and he was kissin' me a bit more than a friendly kiss. I looked over and saw one of my aunts was looking through the little glass on the front door. I didn't think anything was wrong. But then when I saw her, and she just got down and ran, I felt funny. She never mentioned it to me . . . not to this day. In retrospect, it kinda made me think that he was also molesting her. She never said anything. He was like rubbing me when he was kissing me, and she was in the window. She never said anything to my grandmother. He kissed me in my mouth. Before he would only kiss me on my cheek, or kiss me on my lips like—. *(Here she pecks the air with her lips.)* But now it was actually a deep kiss. He also had his hands around me—not on my behind, but near . . . very near. I wasn't comfortable with the way he was kissing me. This is what my aunt saw. At the time, I didn't think anything of it, but as I got older, I'm thinking, Why didn't she say anything? If I brought it up, it was as if it never happened. But obviously something was wrong. She didn't knock on the door.

She looked in, she got down, and she left. She was about thirteen or fourteen then. I was nine.

Then things started getting *really* bad. When we didn't have hot water, we wouldn't take a bath the whole week. Then on the weekends my aunt and I would go to Mr. Hatcher's house to take a bath in his tub. We would take a bath together. He told us to leave the door open. We shouldn't shut the door, he said; it would lock on us. So the door would stay open. It was an old-fashioned tub, and we would sit on the rim of the tub to wash up. We would get in the water just to rinse off. This is so funny because when you're older and you look back, you say, "Why was I so naive and why was I so stupid?" I thought everything was perfectly fine. He would always walk by and come in and ask us, Did we want anything?

So at that point things started to get worse. He started to touch me more, and he would tell me the typical thing that molesters tell kids: If I told my grandmother, I would be in trouble; and, "I'll stop giving you guys money and you won't be able to eat. Your grandmother is depending on us." I would usually go over there by myself and say, "Mr. Hatcher, you need me to sweep up for you or something?" And then it got to the point I didn't like to go over there, but he would *make* me come over. He'd say, "Well, I'll tell your grandmother. You know they really need me. And next Christmas you're not goin' to have any toys because I'm not goin' to buy you any." And then he would start to fondle me . . . and this is . . . I've never told anybody this part. *(She whispers.)*

He had these black things, and they were in the shape of penises. They were different sizes and he would, like fondle me with these black things, and um . . . I don't really know what a dildo is. But they were firmer maybe than a penis. They were like this big and then like this *(She demonstrates.)*, and then like this, and then they got a little bigger, and then they got like bigger in circumference. But they started off small. He would actually insert these things into my body. And he would . . . like . . . make me perform oral sex on him. And, um, it just had gotten so bad. I would cry all the time.

I started feeling very . . . *dirty!* And at that point, I *knew* something was terribly wrong, but I didn't know how to get myself out of it. Because he would, like . . . after doing this stuff, he would give me two dollars and say, "Now go buy yourself some chips and soda." So it was almost like he was paying me for sex. And it's not like I didn't know what a prostitute was, because I *did*. And that's how I felt. He never had intercourse with me himself. But he would rub up against me. He would undress himself. I was nine or ten. I was depressed a lot. I was really depressed. I went on a Diet Coke diet in fifth grade. I wouldn't eat any food, and I got very sick. I was even in the hospital for a couple of days. I prayed a lot.

Then I went to the West Coast to stay with my other father. Every summer I did this. I was very sad. I wrote myself a letter: "Dear Self." And I said all the things that Mr. Hatcher had done and about how I was feeling. I was, like, asking myself, Could I be pregnant? I hadn't even had my period yet, and I was writing this. I didn't know if I could be pregnant by the things that he was doing to me. My other father's girlfriend found the letter I wrote and read it to him. He sent me back South 'cause he thought I was just having sex with boys. He said, "You girls are just getting out of hand." He was coming down on me and he sent me back South. So I *never*, ever mentioned it again.

I think I wrote that letter hoping someone would find it. I think that was my intention 'cause I never wrote anything like that down. I would always keep it to myself. And I don't know what happened to the letter. Mr. Hatcher died right after that.

He was a really old man . . . like a grandfather, . . . about sixty,
. . . somewhere in there. A real distinguished man. I was about
ten and a half when Mr. Hatcher died. I was very happy!
Everyone expected me to be really sad. My grandmother was
like, "You know your 'uncle' just died, and I know you're hurting so bad." In my mind I was so happy. I wished I could tell
everybody what he had been doing. But no one would believe
me. Or they would think that I was . . . that *I* had initiated it!
Everyone in the neighborhood looked up to him. He gave *big*
donations in the church; I know cause he would always show
me. He *promised* me that when he died he was going to leave all
this money to me. He didn't leave *anything*. After he died, a lot
of kids were saying how lucky I was to have Mr. Hatcher to be
my uncle. And I think he was also molesting other girls in the
neighborhood because I noticed that other girls my age would
go over there. I can only assume that if he was doing it to me,
he was doing it to them too. They weren't just going over there
to get sodas or ice cream or whatever. So when he died, I was
very . . . *very happy*. I never talked about what had happened to
my grandmother. We never ever talked about it. To this day,
nobody knows what happened. The only person who knows is
my husband.

Now, when people mention Mr. Hatcher with such great
respect, it hurts me to listen. Because I *know* what he was
doing. I know how he was manipulating me, and I think it had
to do with the fact that he was giving my family a lot of money
to help us survive. I felt obligated to my family because my
family was so screwed up. I've always felt like the savior of my
family. And that's something I'm dealing with now because now
I know that about myself.

I've kept going, but I've avoided men. I didn't like to be
around men. And to this day I don't feel comfortable being
alone with men. I don't look men in the eye. And I don't feel

comfortable being in the room with other people's husbands or
boyfriends either. Almost as if they could find out something
about me that I don't want them to know. My husband is different; I feel comfortable with him. He said when he first met
me he *knew* I had been molested or raped because I didn't look
men in the eye. I was fifteen going on sixteen when I met Bill.
It was during high school that I told him about my molestation
and the rape . . . while I was still at boarding school. I told him
over the phone. I said, "There's something I want to tell you
about me that you might not be able to handle." He was twenty or twenty-one at the time. And he was like, "Whatever you
tell me, there's nothing too bad because I love you. You can tell
me anything." After I told him about being molested, he got
real quiet—very quiet. He was like, "Yvonne, I'm sooooo
sorry." He kept saying it. "I'm so sorry." I said, "It was not *your*
fault." And then I told him about when I got raped.

I was in the South when I got raped. Delores was my very
best friend in school. She was having problems with her mother, and she would run away to my house. We would tell my
grandmother that Delores's mother had to go out of town for a
week, and since I was her best friend, her mother wanted her to
stay with me. I kept telling my grandmother that her mother
said it was okay. I always tried to be "fast," but I was too concerned about school. But Delores was *very* much that way. She
would want to stay up real late, and I was like, "I have to go
to school 'cause I have a test." I always tried to act cool. I
really wasn't. Delores wanted to see this guy who was in *high*
school. . . . We were just in middle school. She wanted to go to
a club or something like that, and it was a long way from our
house. She said, "Will you walk over there with me?" We
walked everywhere in that town. It was daytime when we left.
We were dressed alike. We had bluejean skirts on, and colorful
headbands tied around our heads—and plastic shoes were "in."

On the way back, we stopped to see some of our friends. Then it started to get dark. And I was like, "My grandmother's going to kill me. I'm going to hear my grandmother's mouth." And my grandfather was *always* fussin'.

And then this guy drove up. He says, "Do you know where such and such is?" We gave him directions. But he was still driving slow. I whispered to Delores, "Maybe he doesn't understand. Maybe we can get a ride from this guy. You know I'm going to get in trouble if I don't get home soon." And he drove up again near us. He said, "Hey, could you guys come and tell me how to get to Monroe Street and Park one more time?" So we walked over nearer to the car, and he started talking to us: "Do you know you guys look like sisters? You both are really pretty." That's the last thing I remember him saying. He opened his door, and grabbed my arm to snatch me. Delores grabbed *his* arm . . . and I really love her for this because she didn't just run and leave me. Then she grabbed my other arm and *she would not let me go!*

He was pulling me hard . . . and this was a *man*. And she, a twelve-year-old girl, would not let go. She was screaming and saying, "You're not gonna take her; you're not gonna take her!" She was pulling and he was pulling, and I just remember being in the middle and being in a lot of pain. He actually dislocated my shoulder from this. He pulled me into the car, over the driver's seat, put something to my neck. . . . I don't know if it was a knife or not, . . . and made me put my head in his lap. Delores got left.

I tried to feel where we were driving so I could know where we were. But I wasn't going to try anything 'cause I didn't want to die. He had been drinking a lot, I could tell. He smelled like a distillery. Then he took me into this house. There was a mat on the floor. I was having my period. My family still didn't have money, so I didn't have any sanitary napkins, so I had paper

towels and tissue all wrapped up and I had had this thing on all
day. It was soaked. I was just lying there and looking around.
First of all, he took off all my clothes. When he took off my
shirt I was screaming because my arm was hurting every time
he moved it. I said, "I can't take off all my clothes. I'll have
blood everywhere." He said, "Don't worry about it." I was sitting there when he went into the bathroom and I was thinking,
Should I just run out like I am with no clothes on and try to
get away? Or if I try to get away and he catches me, Would he
kill me? I came up with the idea that I was going to make him
feel guilty about what he was doing.

So when he came back, I tried to make myself seem younger
than I was. I said I was only ten years old. And I said, "Do you
have anybody in your family that's ten years old?" He didn't
answer any of my questions. It didn't work. He said, "Just lie
down and close your eyes. It'll be okay." He started consoling
me 'cause I was crying. I was like, "*Please* don't do this. *Please*
don't do this. I'm only ten years old. Please don't." He just said,
"Lie down and be quiet." I laid down and got quiet. Then he
raped me.

And then afterwards . . . he just helped me put my clothes
back on 'cause my arm was sore. And then I told another lie. I
said, "My grandmother only sent us out to get sugar and she is
going to be missing me. I'm going to get in trouble. You're
making me get in trouble . . . bad trouble." He said the weirdest thing: "I'll write your grandmother a note." And then he
said he was going to drive me home. "I'm going to tell your
grandmother that we just went for a ride, and I'll write her a
note." But when we went out to the car, the tire was flat. Then
he said, "Let's go call a cab. I can't drive you." And so we were
walking, and I tried to look around to see where I am, 'cause
you basically know everything if you live in a small town. I see
a little steeple-type church, but I'm so in pain. . . . I'm really

confused, and I don't *see* where I am. Then I see McDonald's.
He takes me in and walks with me to the phone booth. He
called the cab and gave me three dollars. He said, "Here, catch
a cab." He left. He was maybe in his thirties.

I got in the cab. . . . I just started crying. I'm thinking
what I should have done. "I should have just called the police."
But then I'm like, "I'm going home. He didn't kill me, and
I'm happy." I got in the cab and said, "All I have is three dollars." . . . I didn't go home. I went to another friend's house
who lived on the next corner from me 'cause I was scared to go
home. It was late and I thought I would get in trouble for coming home so late. When I got to my friend's house, my grand-
parents were already there; they had started looking for me. I
started crying and told 'em, "He raped me. He grabbed me in
the car. Me and Delores were together. He grabbed me in the
car!" I couldn't stop crying.

Delores was already at the police station, and when I got
home I was supposed to go to the station. I told them just like
I told you: that I was trying to see everything and I was trying
to make him feel guilty. But he *still* raped me. The police drove
me back over the area. I couldn't remember the house. . . . I
couldn't remember the color of the house. . . . I remember it
was dirt in the backyard. We went to one, but it was the wrong
house. *(She gets very agitated.)* They kept asking me, "Which
house . . . which house?" The next morning the investigator
came back and again we went driving. I got scared because I
didn't want the rapist to see me. I remembered that I had said I
wouldn't call the police and get him in trouble. It's a small
town. I didn't want him to try and kill me again, . . . so I was
really scared. I didn't know anything. That was the last time the
police investigators came to see me.

That night, after the police station, they took me to the hospital to have me examined. I was bleeding. At the hospital they

said they didn't know if it was the first time I had ever had intercourse. I said, "Well, I just *told* you." . . . But I hadn't told anybody about Mr. Hatcher. Nobody knew what he did. . . . And so they did all their tests and they gave me the pill, . . . the one for after the second day, . . . and I had to have a thing for my arm because it was dislocated. I didn't go to school for six weeks after that. I was really happy that he didn't kill me. But I was just staying around the house and I couldn't even do my hair. I was just a mess and I just felt bad. I *knew* I hadn't done anything wrong because he *grabbed* me and abducted me in his car.

My grandmother and my [older] aunt didn't try to console me like, "It's not your fault." Instead they said, "See, this is what happens to little girls that run the street at night. Now you know to stay home because *he* is still *out* there." They made me *so* afraid. Even when I felt better, . . . like going to school, . . . I was afraid. I told them I was still hurting and couldn't go to school, but really I was afraid 'cause they had *got* me so afraid. And then my aunt started tellin' me about boys. About how they get you feeling kind of funny and then take advantage of you and get you pregnant. Then you drop out of school and you don't make anything out of your life. She started telling me about venereal diseases. So then I *did* start getting scared. Like, "Oh my God. What if he had some type of disease. I don't think they checked for this at the hospital." All *this* came out of the rape. They started tellin' me these things. They had me so scared.

I was so saddened. When I started going outside, I still had to think because people were asking me what happened. I told them I was sick. But they put the story in the paper about the rape. . . . Not my name, but they described my uniform. They said I had my cheerleading uniform on that I wore at middle school. I didn't have it on, but they said I did. And so anybody's parents that read that, *knew* it was me. And all the kids *knew* it was me. I was *so* upset and *so embarrassed* to go around people 'cause I didn't want people to know. I didn't want my little brother and my sisters to know. But my grandmother just talked about it all the time. I felt like I had a sign around my neck: *"I was raped."* Nobody asked me what *I* wanted. My brother, . . . any time he'd get mad at me, . . . would say, "*That's* why you were raped." He'd say stuff like that. He would tell his friends that I had been raped. So everybody knew. The boys in the neighborhood—like a bunch of hoodlums—would say, "I heard you were raped. How'd it feel?" They would laugh at me like it was a joke. So I stopped going outside. I *hated* to go to school. I didn't really get turned off going to school and doing the work. . . . I just didn't like going and being around the people.

I had a spell of being angry with God: "Why are you letting all this happen to me?" I even contemplated suicide several times. But I guess what I thought about the whole time growing up is that I'm *going* to do well. This seems kind of what people say you should do. It seems kind of corny, but this is what I did. I actually said, "I'm gonna do good, and I'm gonna make something out of myself very, very big. I'm gonna be in control of everything 'cause I won't have to worry about people controlling me. I'm gonna be able to control *them* because I'm gonna have so much power and so much money and so much fame that no one's gonna be able to hurt me." I think that kept me going. I became an overworker and overachiever because of that. And I kept telling myself that I wasn't going to be like my mother. My mother's a very good, loving person, but she was raped when she was young by a group of boys *(a long pause)* . . . and I don't think anyone believed her either. I'm spiritual, but not very religious.

My mother didn't know about any of what happened to me.

I wanted to tell her, but I just felt like she was having her own problems. And she was already feeling like she hadn't done what she should have been doing as a mother. She was already feeling guilty, so I felt that . . . I didn't want to give her one more extra thing to say like, "I should have been there to protect you." I've always felt that if I told a man about the things that happened to me, it would totally turn him off towards me. But it didn't with my husband. So that made me happy. But any time I feel like I want to talk about it, I've never gone into too much detail with Bill because I felt he couldn't handle it. It's hard for him. He gets so upset at *himself* for things that happened to *me*. I guess he feels like he should have been there to protect me . . . when there is no way he *could* have been there. He's always telling me how *sorry* he is. When I try to tell him certain things, I can't . . . because I don't want him to become disgusted with me. So in a sense, I'm *afraid* to tell him *too* much detail. A few years ago I told a male friend I had been raped. After I told him, the first thing he said was, "You *know* it's not your fault, right?" That was the first thing he said, and that was great. And I was like, "Yeah." *(She smiles.)*

I lost my virginity. I didn't take pride in my body after the rape. After it happened, I became a bit promiscuous; but not overly, . . . not a whole lot, . . . just so I wouldn't fall in love and get left like my mom. Everyone *thought* I was bad; so I thought, I should just *be* bad. After the rape it was like sex really didn't matter to me. It didn't seem like anything special because I figured if people could just take it, . . . if they just had to have it enough that they would take a little girl and put a knife to her neck and *take* it, . . . that it had nothin' to do with love. "See, that's what happens to girls who run around." Everybody was saying that. In retrospect, I think it affected how I felt about sex and how I felt about my body. Sex didn't mean anything. And no one said, "I'm sorry." No hugs.

Having my first sexual encounter be the way it was . . . made my body the center of everything. I always felt like I had to wear tight clothes because people wouldn't *like* me unless they saw my body. That changed when I met Bill. He would always tell me that my body didn't mean anything. He was like, "Your body is secondary. What I like about you is *not* that you have a 'fly' body." So that's when things started to change for me. That's when sex actually became a matter of love for me, . . . when *we* became sexually active. I was about sixteen or seventeen. Bill helped me re-see myself. I had put so much emphasis on my body . . . I thought that was the only way I could be seen. Because I was smart . . . that didn't keep me from getting raped. . . . It didn't keep me from getting molested. I did well in school, but that didn't keep me from getting raped. And in the beginning, my husband didn't *care* that I was smart. But when he found out, it mattered and he wanted to find out more about me. That made me wait. I'm really happy that I have him. At first I didn't feel comfortable sleeping with Bill, my husband, because I *loved* him, and I thought that was weird. 'Cause sometimes rape would flash in my mind. And if I'm having my period, I don't even like to *hear* sex . . . still to this day. So I know that there are some things still to be worked out. I've considered therapy, but I was thinking that I'm figuring all of this out . . . on my own. I *know* that the rape was not my fault. But at one point I did think that the molestation was somewhat my fault. Having Bill's family has been so helpful to me too.

I talked to my grandmother about a year or two ago about the rape. I mentioned it to her and told her that when I was growing up I never felt like I had anybody on my side. "When I got raped nobody made me feel like I was important. Nobody showed me love or compassion." With that, my grandmother was like—'cause she was always on the defensive because people

always put her down about how she raised us—"Well, I've done
the best I could with you guys. As far as that rape, the police
said it never happened—that you were never raped." That was
the *first* I knew of that and it started a whole lot of emotions.
She said the police said, "*That* didn't have anything to do with
rape." I was shocked. I just didn't want to talk about it anymore
. . . to anyone. *(There is a long pause.)* I guess that's why the
investigator never came by again to have me try to find the
house. It never went any farther than that. I guess that's why
my grandmother was telling me all those stories about boys.
She believed the police rather than me. That really hurt. I didn't
scratch the man. . . . I never had fingernails, . . . so I couldn't
scratch him, . . . and I wasn't going to try to fight a man that
had a weapon. I was just going to try to be his friend and
maybe he would forget about killing me. And they said that I
wasn't raped!

Sometimes I wish I could go back in time and change things.
The first thing is I would definitely tell someone about Mr.
Hatcher. Definitely. But with the rape I don't think there's anything I would do differently 'cause I would want to live. I think
I would have wanted people to embrace me more, . . . *hug* me.
And I would have wanted the police *(She laughs.)* to put more
effort into finding that person and punishing him for what he
did. I would have wanted the police to seem more . . . involved
. . . and seem as if they *cared* more. To me it really seemed like
they were just going through the routine. They didn't care
whether they got the guy or not. I think it was racial. I believe
if I *had* been white it would have been totally different. They
would have got more passionate about what had happened. I
believe that they would have put out a description of the guy
and actually made a little composite, and put on the news that
there's a rapist out there in our neighborhood. I don't think
class would have mattered 'cause in that little town, class and

race are pretty much the same—I mean, you're either rich or black. *(She laughs.)* I wish my grandmother had believed me.

When I was growing up, I was always told, "Be a nice girl so you can get a nice husband." Now what I say to my sisters is, "You be nice so you can be a good woman for *yourself*." I guess I made it this far because I've had lots of angels in my life.

SHARING WITH YVONNE

Yvonne, when I was on the stand testifying at my trial, I remember having the feeling that no one was believing me. I saw staring faces. My voice seemed to echo as if I were in a tunnel and the faces were not hearing what I spoke. I remember the stolid expression of the defense attorney and the overpowering sense of aloneness. The attorney made me feel as if all I said was a lie—but then, perhaps that was his job. How much more devastating it must have been for you at age twelve, and then later when you found, after so many years, that even your family had not believed you. Maybe fear of rejection was a partial explanation for my own silence. Perhaps I was afraid I would be doubted—that my story was too sensational to be believed.

When I think of my own growing-up community, I remember the bonding that occurred when one of our own was maligned. Like your Bill, I am sorry, too, that you were unable to enjoy the security of such protection. In your new life with a new family of your own making, you are creating a solid, loving, and stable community for *your* children. Perhaps if we work together toward that end, all our children will be free to scream, be heard, and, most of all, believed.

JACQUELINE

. . . by our silence I think we're saying it's okay.
—Another survivor, age twenty-five

Jacqueline is a pleasingly attractive woman of thirty-eight, the color of ivory with a voice of velvet. She enjoys the sound, the feel of words. When she arrived for our talk, she was dressed casually in tailored, dark khaki trousers with a soft pastel blouse; her barely shoulder-length hair was brushed away from her face. She laughed, and gestured when she talked—full, throaty laughs. I learned quickly, however, that her laughter did not signal merriment but nervousness—and sometimes irony. She was witty and charming, an actress. The quick observer might have assumed Jacqueline and I were meeting to talk about innocent, even pleasurable, pursuits—a recent cocktail party or where our children might go for summer camp.

Jacqueline was in her first year of college when the rape occurred. She became withdrawn and soon thereafter "failed out. I just stopped going to classes." The rape entirely altered Jacqueline's life. She did not complete her degree. Seven years later she returned to college to take courses. She is now a professional in the entertainment world.

Jacqueline told her story in a matter-of-fact way. We talked for quite some time before she allowed me to see the timid, insecure side of her personality. Although she was outwardly in control, her words—when she began to talk of trauma—revealed caution, fear, and silent vulnerability.

JACQUELINE'S TELLING

What I did after it happened was convince myself that I had just had sex. I didn't want to think that I was raped. It was just easier to say that I had sex with somebody. For about a week or two, . . . I'm not sure how long it was, . . . I acted as if nothing happened. Then suddenly I was waking up in the morning and throwing up. The first thing I thought was, Oh my God, I'm pregnant! And I knew what it was from. That's really when a lot of emotional problems started. I might have been able to deal with what had happened to me if I hadn't gotten pregnant 'cause I would have just *lied* to myself. As a matter of fact, I lied to myself for *so long* that after a while I actually forgot . . . kinda . . . what really happened. I never told my family. They just found out a couple of years ago.

I blamed myself for what happened to my sister—she was raped when she was in college—because I felt like if I had just told her about it. . . . You see, no one had ever talked to *me* about rape. I'd never heard of date rape. I *never heard that ter-*

minology. I thought that being raped was when someone snatched you off the street and took you in the woods and raped you. I thought that's what it was—*not* what happened to me. I mean, I had just met this guy. He came in and met my family a couple of times, seemed like a nice guy. He came and had dinner with us the night he raped me. He had even asked my mother, Could he take me to the Jersey shore? We went and I had a good time.

Later that night we were leaving the shore, and it was one of those deserted roads. . . . I think we were only at the shore for a couple of hours. He just drove up into some wooded area and turned into *a monster!* He was really, really violent. I actually thought he would *kill* me. I think that's where my survival just kicked in. I was in the middle of nowhere! I didn't know where I was. All I remember seeing up the street was one of those little convenience stores. But it really wasn't; it was a hick, rundown type of gas station with a little store attached to it. It was closed. I had thought of running at first—getting out of the car and running. But then I said, This guy is acting crazy. If I run and he catches me, I'm already in the woods. And the gas station is closed, and there were no cars coming up the street. So I thought, I better not run.

He went wild. He grabbed me by the hair 'cause at first I was fighting him. He pulled out hair! That's when he started getting really, really rough. I combed my hair later and a big mass of hair came out. I basically just lay there and let him do what he wanted to do. I just *hoped* that he didn't want to harm me any more. And then—basically—he just dropped me off at home.

When I got home, I convinced myself that what happened didn't happen. You know? I created a *whole different scenario*, until I found out I was pregnant. Then all of a sudden I became schizophrenic. I mean, I was just like *crazy*. I was trying to *kill myself*; I was trying to throw myself down the steps. I was punching myself in the stomach. I wasn't eating. I was *losing it*. I was losing it. Then I became real secluded. I had an abortion. I swindled someone so I could get an abortion. I didn't tell my sister that part. That's another story.

I just didn't deal with the physical pain. I don't even remember if my body hurt. I took a very long shower; I stayed in there a long time. Threw the clothes away that I had on. I had already put it in my head that what happened didn't happen. I'm probably still like that. The hardest thing was not having someone to tell . . . to talk to. Know what I'm saying? I just became very closed off. I wasn't prepared to tell anybody anyway, but it was to help *me* deal with it. So I just created a totally different scenario. It made it easier for me. And then I didn't have to think about what really happened. Have you ever seen those science fiction movies? Like where they close a room off and all of a sudden steel plates come over the windows, like *chk, chk, chk, chk*? Well, that's what I did. *Chk, chk, chk, chk, chk*— all around me. That's what happened to me. I just started dealing with it in my own little way. Still to this day—fourteen years later—I have a hard time saying the word: "*rape.*" . . . I have a *very* hard time saying that. I avoid saying it.

It was my first year of college when it happened. I was coming home on vacation. I took the train home, and that's where I met the guy who raped me—at the train station. I ended up failing out of college 'cause I was just sick all the time. I didn't go to classes. I got into a singing group and started singing, and that kind of took me away from my thoughts. And then I just stopped.

For years—and still to this day—I get angry with my mother. I sort of blame her, . . . but I know it's not her fault. I get angry with her for not scrutinizing this guy. He came to the house a couple of times; it wasn't like my mom met him just one time. He hung out with the family, and finally he asked my mom if he could take me out. And I felt *comfortable* with him. I just wished that she hadn't let me go out with him. You know? But how would she know? How would *I* know? I had to create so many stories about it. But I remember his first *and last* name. After the rape I started learning how to pull things in and store them—until my head filled up, and then I would blow up at people. My anger is real bad— phenomenal.

I really didn't have anyone to talk to; that was the hardest part. My sisters were *real young*—four and eight years younger. I was real angry, all the time. I just turned into another person. I didn't really have a lot of friends because my mom was very, very strict with me. I was the oldest girl, and I wasn't allowed to hang out. So as a result of not being able to go to parties or things like that, I didn't have many friends. I had maybe one or two, but I didn't tell them. I just kind of shut down. I was *real suicidal—real, real suicidal.*

I tell people this to this day—and I tell my sisters all the time—the only thing that stopped me was I always was told as a child that if you committed suicide you would go to hell. And I *believed* it. So I believe that had I not had some kind of faith at that time, I would be a statistic. I mean, I literally had pill bottles sittin' on my dresser, ready to take them. Then I would always think, I don't want to live the rest of my life in hell. That would always stop me.

I used to get so mad that I would hold my breath. Then I would push until I had blood shots around my eyes and my mouth. I was crazy. I was going crazy; I really was. I think I was having a nervous breakdown. My mom took me to a psychiatrist. Then . . . I got mad at the psychiatrist and walked out on him. Because I felt like no one had been there before to help me through the ordeal of the rape. I had no one to talk to and I had dealt with it all those years—by myself. So I felt I could still deal with it; I was still alive and kicking. I felt, I don't need nobody coming here and telling me what to do and what not to do. I just really had the attitude that *I can do anything*. I'm not saying that I don't need people, but I guess I'm not going to beg. I will do it myself. I won't ask for help. But my sisters and I have become very, very close over the years.

After the rape, I became *extremely* overprotective of my sisters—like a mother goose. *(She laughs.)* It was weird because when they were younger, I had nothing to do with them. You see, I was like the bad seed in the house. I was always in trouble, and everyone thought something was wrong with me. I became like a scapegoat for my mother, who was having a hard time with my stepfather. And then the rape happened. I just took care of everything, and I started living with it. I never told anybody, not even people at the abortion clinic. I just told them I had sex and got pregnant. I never told *anybody*—until that day in the bathroom when I told my sisters.

I told *just* my sisters. I started to realize that something happened to me and I was lying to *them*, and the lie was worse than what actually happened. Because I *wasn't* sexually active. You know what I'm saying? I didn't just *get* pregnant. For *years* it was just easier for me to let them think that I was pregnant from having sex. But as I got older and started dealing with it, I wanted them to know the truth. I felt I was making myself look worse by saying that I had sex, got pregnant, and got rid of it. That story was worse to me. But at the time of the rape it was a lot easier to just let it go. Plus they started dating. I wanted them to know. No one told *me anything*. Telling my sisters has made our relationship much stronger.

My mom knew about the abortion, but I had fabricated a story to tell her about how I got pregnant. It wasn't the truth.

This is embarrassing! . . . You see, instead of just saying what happened, I created a *story* for the abortion. Can you believe it? You see, before the rape happened, I had this boyfriend. He didn't come home with me for that vacation. Before I left college for my vacation and before the rape, he had wanted to have sex. I was always afraid to. I was a virgin. I had heard stories about having sex. So one day I convinced myself, I'm going to do it. I really like this guy and I'm going to do it. Right? *(She laughs.)* We got in bed; we didn't have any condoms. We get ready to do it, and he tries to, but it wouldn't go in! *(She laughs again with embarrassment.)* We never had sex. It wouldn't go in. So I said *stop!* And that was the end of my newly found sexual experience. Then a week later when I went home for vacation, the rape happened to me. Here's where my *lie* comes in.

I was kind of naive. But I *had* heard stories where even just that little bit we [my boyfriend and I] did, could make me pregnant. I convinced everyone that I had gotten pregnant from that. I thought they would believe me because someone had told *me* that it was possible. I took the story I had been told and put it with what really happened. I took pieces of truth and made it into a story—into my story. I made the truth into a lie. I convinced my boyfriend back at school that I was pregnant by him—from that little bit that we did. I convinced him that that's what had happened. I had no other way of getting the money. I *had* to get the money from him for the abortion. I broke up with him after that. I just shut him out because I knew it was a big lie. I had a hard time facing him. He came to see me just to make me take a pregnancy test 'cause he didn't believe me at first. I mean, anybody in their right mind wouldn't believe me 'cause it really was so impossible. I mean he literally *touched* me—that's all. Of course, the pregnancy test came up positive. My boyfriend gave me the money; I got the abortion.

I feel bad about it now. Talk about going out of my mind! I was going out of mind because I felt like if I can't convince him that this is true about the pregnancy, I am going to end up doing something to myself. I am *not* having this baby . . . from a rape! I feel *real* bad about that now. I think about it a lot. If I could have only just said something. I mean, I affected *his* life. You know what I'm saying—this innocent guy who was my boyfriend! I went through *aaallllllll* that crap, just to hide the truth. But I would have *got that money*—somehow—any way I could. I didn't want to discuss the money or the abortion with my mother. She knew I was pregnant because she overheard me on the telephone. *I* was not going to tell her what really happened; I would not have been able to talk to her about it. She used to always say, "Don't bring no babies in this house unless you're ready to take care of them."

I think if I had gotten pregnant from having sex, I really think I might, . . . I think I would have *kept it*. And the weirdest thing about it is, even though I knew I was pregnant, I didn't even see it as a child. It just never was. I never felt any guilt over it. *Never*. I saw it like a sickness that I had to get rid of. It was like taking lots of showers or having antibodies. Maybe that's why I never understood this big abortion thing: "Don't kill your baby." To certain people—I'm sorry—it is *not a baby!* It is a disease. That is just how I saw it. On Phil Donahue, this woman who was raped kept her child. Can you imagine? I give her credit. I could *not* have done it. I would have abused it.

I never told my mother about the rape. She knows, but *I* never told her. The only people I have ever talked to about this are my two sisters—and my brother. He took it upon *himself* to tell everybody. And that made me mad. But they never said anything to me. I knew my brother had told my mother because she started treating me differently. Actually my mother's response was that she had a different respect for me. But she denies it. We never sat down and talked, but things got a *lot* better. I didn't think anyone would believe me anyway. That is one of my biggest regrets—not *saying* something. That's my regret in the whole ordeal. Because he probably went out and did it again. Matter of fact, I *know he did*. Maybe the second time, he ended up in jail.

Sometimes now when I think I'm getting ready to talk about it, then I can't. Like, my husband and I had gone to counseling—marriage counseling—and there came a part where I had to slip out pieces of the rape. That's when I just stopped going to counseling. When it comes time to talk about "it," I have to mentally prepare myself. Even spending a night at someone's house . . . I can't when it's impromptu. It has to be a preparation. Everything has to "be prepared" for me 'cause I don't know what's going to happen from one moment to the next. Maybe that's a result of the rape. Maybe, I don't know. I have to control things. I've even become a little anal-retentive. After the rape I became real spastic about things—like color coordination. Like when I fold my towels in my closet, I have to put the colors together. In my cabinet where the cups are I have my pink cups lined together and my yellow cups together and . . . And I think that control has spilled over into my relationships with men too. I like to be in control. I like wimps. Because I *am* afraid of men trying to control me. I am. That's a number one fear of mine. If I feel like that's happening, I'll get out. And until I was raped, I would date black guys. Now I have no trust; I'm scared to death of black men. I've been married to a white man for three years.

Before the rape I was *totally* different. I was just so much nicer. I guess, in a way, naive. I would let my heart go to someone. I was dating a guy in high school before this happened, and I really liked him. I let my feelings go with him. I have *never* done that since. I think I've fallen in love after that as a matter of convenience and not as really being in love. I don't think I'm capable of loving anyone at this point. Not the *right* way. I get attached and I love people, but I think it's not an "in love" thing. I don't think I know how to do it. Before I wasn't tense about loving. I was more giving. Much more trusting. I don't know how to give anymore. I don't like sex. I don't like to be touched. I felt like I was a whore if I enjoyed sex. I just *felt* that way. I caught myself falling in love with my husband. . . . I think I loved him. Also I think I used him . . . 'cause he was really, really good to me. And I didn't want to lose that. I think that's why I married him. And now I see where that was wrong. He still is good to me. We just separated, and . . . I'm happy. That sounds bad, but I'm *happy* now.

At first I wasn't going to come here. I was like, "I don't *want* to talk." But when my sister told me why you were doing it, I was like, "Wow!—and it is specific to black women." I was like, "Yeah! Start contributing." So this is my first contribution to the cause. *(She laughs.)* When something like rape happens to a white woman, I see it totally different. I think we're just stronger people. I'm not talking physically; I'm talking mentally, spiritually. It's a result, I think, of the struggles and things that our ancestors had to deal with—different issues that were passed down to us. I think the black *family* itself is just so different from the white family. When a black woman is raped, it kind of weakens her as the female part in that family. I'm not saying that white women are weak. But I guess I am saying that when you compare a *sister* to a white woman, the sister is stronger any way you cut the cake. I think you learn it from watching your mother. Not being taught, just watching. I know *my* mom, when she would do something and injure herself, she'd say, "Damn." Then she'd wrap something around it and go back to what she was doing. She'd say, "Blood coming through there, but got to keep going."

Black women are quick to get up. They may not be ready to stand on two feet, but they do it. You know? They say, "Okay. I need to put this back together. Let me get up." Say she had this beautiful porcelain vase and say that represents her life and it gets cracked by something like . . . like a rape. Boom—it splatters everywhere. A black woman would do something like—she would take something like rope and put those pieces together. Wrap it up real quick and wrap that rope around, round, round and the vase would be put back together. It may not be as pretty as the white woman's vase—taking all that time to put crazy glue on every spot and put it all together real nice and pretty. It may not be pretty, but it works just the same. That's the way we go about putting our lives together. May end up having some kind of little drawback or maybe we have to deal with things like anger and controlling our temper, but we do it. It may not be beautiful, but it gets fixed fast. And it works.

SHARING WITH JACQUELINE

It was important to me, Jacqueline, what the men in my life thought of me—and how they acted toward me after the rape. I looked for ever-so-slight changes in their behavior when I was present. From men I didn't know extremely well, I still looked for gentleness, acceptance, affirmation, and appropriate physical contact. I needed to know if I was attractive. Or had this thing transformed me into an asexual being? Could others "see" the ugliness I felt?

Like everything else, making love became a pretense. David was understanding and sensitive. But how many times can one preplan and stage a bedroom scene with proper lighting (there *had* to be lights), no shadows, and proper attire before beginning to have an intimate evening. And *if* any unaccounted-for noise occurred, and *if* there was an inadvertent "wrong" move, and *if* words spoken were not in the "script"—everything was ended. Many an abruptly finished evening.

I was always afraid to close my eyes. Afraid I'd see *his* face when David and I made love. Afraid I'd feel what I felt that horrendous night. It was extraordinarily difficult learning to separate something forced and evil from a private, mutually loving moment. David and I talked endlessly. We cried. We learned together to reclaim the space of our bedroom. I wish for you, Jacqueline, such a reclamation.

ADRIENNE

My husband just rolled over one night and said, "Look, I'm not the rapist. We're gonna do this just so you know it's okay. And I will be patient." And it was okay. And that was the end of it.

—Another survivor, age fifty-nine

Adrienne is a forty-year-old nurse who, in her spare time, counsels abused black women; most of her clients are "walk-ins." As Adrienne encouraged young women to interview with me, she one day realized, "I need to call that number for myself. I need to talk about my own life."

After several abortive efforts, Adrienne and I finally met at my office late one afternoon. We had talked several times by phone, so when we met, we were each familiar with the details of the other's present life. She was extremely pleasant, a café-au-lait, slender woman whose self-possession immediately put us both at ease. Adrienne had successfully reared a family of sons and took joy in talking about their lives. She was slow, however, to speak of her own traumas.

We engaged in peripheral conversation about her hospital case-load and my volunteer work at Women Organized Against Rape (WOAR); we shared stories about mothering. I realized early on that I was not the only one interviewing; Adrienne was deciding whether to stay and what to tell. It took us a while to find a place of comfort. Finally we began to talk.

Adrienne has been raped twice: once by her father's great uncle when she was seven, and again by her mother's boyfriend when she was twelve. She now spends most of her time at work convincing women who have been physically and sexually abused that they are worth much more than they believe, that the rape or abuse is not their fault. Adrienne proclaims the worth of these women but does not always acknowledge her own.

ADRIENNE'S TELLING

I remember just like it was yesterday. My grandmother had gone shopping, and she had put some pies in the oven. I was seven. Uncle Larry was watching the ball game, and I remember him calling me over to him. In fact, he wasn't watching the ball game; he was listening to it on the radio. And so I went over, and it was nothing new for me to sit on his lap. The next thing I knew he started putting his hands up my clothes. *This* was something new. And the next thing I know he ended up raping me. I was so young. I mean, I didn't understand what was go-ing on. I remember him saying that I should *never tell* and that he would buy me things. All I knew was he hurt me. Real bad.

Then my grandmother came home. I was so hysterical he couldn't calm me down. He told her he had spanked me, and after that, my grandmother told me to go over and sit on the back step. But I couldn't get up. Now, my grandmother is the kind of person who expects you to do what she says *right then.* When she saw I couldn't get up, she went over to me and said, "What happened?" I told her that he had hurt me, told what he did to me. My grandmother took the lamp and hit Uncle Larry—she caught him right in the back of his head—as he went to run out the door. He was just lying there. I'll never forget that.

Then Grandmom picked me up and took me to the bathroom. I remember she turned the water on and was washing me up. She was crying, and she was talking to me as she was crying. I was crying too. But I couldn't understand what *she* was crying for.

I never told my mother what happened. My mother was away visiting my father; he was sick in the hospital. We had come to live with my grandmother because of all the expenses we had. My father was hospitalized for about two years before he passed away. My Grandmom had met Uncle Larry at a family reunion. She had been recently widowed and had a big house, so Uncle Larry moved in. We were all living there in the same house. He was a heavy drinker, Uncle Larry. But he wasn't abusive. He was really nice . . . and, you know, it's hard to look back and say that. But all in all he *was* a really nice man. But when he was drunk, he was a completely different person.

And then I remember the fight. My Uncle Wayne came over the next night 'cause my grandmother called him and told him what had happened. After that fight, my Uncle Larry left for a long time. I didn't know where he went. The rape was something I never talked to anybody about except my grandmother. Different times I would get really upset. But I could always talk to my grandmother 'cause, you know, it was like she understood.

What Uncle Larry did to me, I'll never forget it because it
was the worst thing in my life. It seemed like I would never
stop hurting. There were times, too, when I had problems with
going to the bathroom, urinating. But instead of Grandmom
taking me to a doctor, she took me to see some lady in the
neighborhood who helped people who were sick. She gave me
some powders, and they helped. Grandmom never said, "Don't
tell anybody." But it was like something unspoken, you know?
Uncle Larry was the *only* one who told me not to tell. And it
wasn't until I was in my twenties that I found out that my
other uncle, Wayne, went to jail for assaulting Uncle Larry for
what he had done to me. I really felt bad when I found that
out. We were all talking one day and it happened to come up
that Uncle Wayne had spent time in jail. I asked him what for.
He said, "Oh, for the fight I had with your Uncle Larry years
ago." It seems Uncle Larry had been hurt pretty bad.

About four or five years after we left Grandmom's house,
Uncle Larry came back to live with my grandmother. We had
moved out by that time, but we were not living too far away. It
was really hard at first to see him again. He moved back in, but
wasn't allowed to hug us or touch us. And if he gave us anything, he had to give it to us in the presence of my grandmother. He tried to really be nice, you know. But it was hard. He
would buy us kids all kinds of treats. My other sisters loved
him. He was always giving us money and stuff. I would take
my money and give it to one of my sisters or I would give it to
my brothers. He never hurt anybody else. After what happened
to me, he wasn't allowed to be left alone with any of us.

My father died the same year I was raped. I guess that's why
I remember it so clearly. They allowed us to go see him in the
hospital. I remember asking him when he was coming home.
My father was thirty years old when he died. He was a career
serviceman. He had contracted tuberculosis, and they had

brought him back to the States. He was in a hospital when he
died.

After my father died, my mother took up with another man.
We never liked him. *Never!* And that was the second time I was
abused. And to this day, I hate him. I was twelve. That's the
hardest to deal with because I was older and I knew more. Also,
this time, I did go to my mother and tell her . . . and my
grandmother too. When I told my mother, it was like she didn't
want to believe me. And I don't think she did at first, . . . when
I told her that he raped me, . . . that he would sneak out of her
bed late at night and get into my bed. It was like she thought I
was lying. I really *hate* that man! And I can't get it out of my
head! My mother found out for herself a couple days later.

After I told my mother, she wouldn't let me go to school the
next day. Then she wouldn't let me go to see my grandmother.
She made me stay in my room. Nothing was said to him. I was
hurting and I was upset and I just wanted to leave. Then the
very next night, he tried again. My mother came into the room.
She caught him for herself. She had him arrested. I still see him
every now and then, and I still *hate* that man.

I keep telling myself that hate is too strong an emotion, but
I know I will always hate him. At first I couldn't understand
why the hate was so deep. I really hated *myself* because I felt
that it must be me—you know—that caused this thing. *Two
times!* I used to tell my grandmother that it must be something
I did. And she would always say, "No. It's not you. It's nothing
you did." She never said why, though.

When my mother had her boyfriend arrested, a man cop
asked me all these questions and I felt really, really dirty. He
asked me, Do I "switch" around the house? Some of the things
he said to me just stick with me—even after all this time. And I
never got any counseling for any of it—never. I couldn't tell
anybody about those things! . . . I just talked to my grandmoth-

er. She played a big part in getting me through a lot of things. Now I know that if early on I had got some counseling, a lot of decisions I've made in my life I would have never made. I never felt that I was good enough. I thought other women and other girls were better than I was.

All the time I was a teenager, I never trusted boys. I always felt that they were out for one thing. And if a boy asked me out and I really didn't like him, I would get nasty and abusive— *really* nasty. And so that ended a lot of relationships. I was afraid. And so then I started choosing boys who my mother would say about, "Why in the world? What did you see in *him?*" They seemed to be safer than the others. During my teenage years, I would find myself in class daydreaming. I couldn't concentrate. I almost flunked out of school. Like maybe one little thing would happen and that would bring a flashback—and then I was lost for a while. Now I'm able to deal with the flashbacks. Right now, just thinking about what happened, I can see everything. I see it in my mind, just like it was *today.*

I passed up getting married several times. The first time I was supposed to marry this young man just before he went to Vietnam. He was really nice. His family was nice; everybody treated me great. And then all of a sudden one day, I knew that I just wasn't good enough for him. So I broke it off. Then when he came back from Vietnam, I ended up getting pregnant by him. He asked me to marry him again. And almost up until the time of the marriage, I said okay. Then I broke it off again. His mother had a talk with me and wanted to know why I wouldn't marry her son. I told her I didn't love him. That was a lie, but that's what I told her. I just didn't feel I was good enough for him.

But he's the father of my first two sons. He couldn't understand why I wouldn't ever marry him. He still can't understand.

Even when he was getting ready to marry the woman he's married to now, he kept calling me. He would come over and say, "I'm giving you one last chance. Marry me." He was serious. . . . I just wasn't good enough. We're still good friends.

Later I met Nigel. He was a nice person—a *safe* person. The reason I considered him safe was he was married, and he didn't ask for anything. He made no demands on me. We've been together now for twenty years. Now he's divorced and he keeps asking me the same thing, "When are we going to get married?" I tell him not to worry about it. I had his son. He knows I'm not gonna go anywhere.

Nigel talks to me and tells me different things about himself. Like he was sexually abused by a man when he was a child—someone in his family. He had to live through that. He told me a lot of things that most men, I guess, wouldn't come out and tell another person. But I've never shared *my* sexual abuse with him. I've never shared really with anybody except you—and my grandmother—and one of my clients. She's very young; she needed me to tell her because she's going through the same thing I did. She became suicidal. Her life was like a replay of my own life. I had to tell her. It's easy for me to talk to her and see what she's going through. But I really couldn't look at myself.

There was a time when I used to stuff myself with food. If somebody said, "Oh, you look nice in that dress" ('cause I was small for a long time), I couldn't accept that. I used to just eat for the sake of it—things not good for me. And if a *man* gave me a compliment I *really* couldn't take it. Then when I did get heavy and people said, "Oh, you look nice heavy," I would say to myself "Hmmmmm." *(She laughs loudly.)* There was a time that the clothes I chose, my mother called "ugly." But you see, I felt I could wear 'em and didn't have to worry about anybody looking at me. I didn't want to be looked at. And I didn't want anybody to compliment me. I say to other women all the time, "*No,* it was not your fault. You had no control over what happened." I used to ask myself, "Why can't you tell yourself that?" It was like I was saying to them things that my grandmother used to say to me: "It was not your fault."

One day, I went to a bridal shower and he was there—the man who raped me when I was twelve. We spoke. Someone asked, "You know him?" I said, "Yeah. I can't stand that man." That's all I had to say. Then one lady said *never* be alone with him; and if you have any daughters, never, never leave them alone with him. Once that woman started talking, then *another* person started talking and then another. It was like they all knew him, knew what he had done. One of the ladies said that all the girls he had raped were under twelve years old. Then one said, "It's a wonder nobody hadn't castrated him yet." I was really shocked! I realized the man had been doing this for a long time and getting away with it! Getting *away* with it!

When I told my mother what I had heard those ladies saying, she said, "I don't know if you remember, but I did press charges." Then I remembered being questioned by the police. My mother said that the police made it seem like it was *not* his fault. He did not serve any time, not even two years. My mother was so hurt. "You know, I never knew about the other rapes," she told me. "That shows you how people are because I met that man in a church. I thought everything was okay."

I think times are changing now. Back then when I was raped, so many things were kept a lot more quiet. Sexual abuse was something you mentioned in whispers. Women didn't talk openly about it—especially not black women. It was a "shame." I felt like *everybody knew.* I felt dirty. I felt like I wasn't okay anymore. My mother would always take us together to buy new things—me and my sisters. My mother would say, "Well, pick out what you want." My sisters would get something new. I

didn't want *anything,* even if it was plain or ugly. It didn't matter. I didn't want anything at all. You start to lose your self-
worth.

I've always taught my sons to respect women and respect
them in such a way that if a girl says no, she means no—
regardless if she says no and is smiling. If she says no and has
her arms up for you to come on, it *still* means no. I can only
say what I did for *my* boys. I never want them to get into that
type of situation. I've always told them that boys, by nature, are
stronger than women. The only thing a woman has to fight
with is her mouth—by telling him no. Her body is sacred. I
used to try to explain the difference between love and sex to my
boys. I guess I harped on it so much until now my teenager
says, if I'm on a roll, "Mom! I *know* the difference!" The
only way things are gonna change is if we educate the young
ones.

I think sexual abuse and dating and all that is different for
white women. White women are usually put up on a pedestal.
With the black woman it only takes one smudge, and you carry
that smudge with you for the rest of your life. Most white
women feel that black women should be used to being raped.
When I was going to high school, I went to a racially mixed
school. When we got to studying the Civil War, most of the
white girls I went to school with felt that black women enjoyed
sleeping with the masters. To me that was something that was
passed on to them by their families. I figure that's how the
white man justified raping black women back then; it was okay
because "they enjoyed it."

When we discussed slavery in school, sometimes I would
lash out and say, "How would you feel if a man *made* you go to
bed with him and then beat you in the morning? What would
you do? Would you try to fight him off by saying no knowing
you were going to get a worse whipping and maybe even hung?

Or would you submit and surrender?" I made my classmates
stop and think. They had never thought of it in those terms.
But I look at it now and I feel that that's how a lot of white
people feel about black women—that they are used to being
raped. So for us black women, it's really no big thing. I still
think a lot of white people feel that black women shouldn't be
upset about rape. But it hurts us just as deeply as it hurts white
women. We just find other ways to cope. We turn to other
black women for help, and hope somebody will listen.

Black women tend to keep quiet about rape and abuse. I
guess we feel we *have* to keep quiet about it. It's just something
within us that says, "It's not to be talked about." If you talk
about it, a man will think it was your fault, or he'll think less of
you. I think that's why I never told the men in my life, because
I've always been afraid they would not look at me in the same
way. We all live in the same neighborhood. If something happens to you, *everybody* knows.

Professional black women need to help black women. I don't
like the idea of some white lady tellin' me, "Well, you should
have handled it *this* way. And you should have dealt with it that
way." I *know* how *I* feel. I don't feel that white counselors
understand us as black women. I don't know what they think
our life is like because when you listen to them, most of them
feel all our homes have a single parent. Or if it's not a single-
parent home, then our mothers or fathers—one or the other—
is an alcoholic. I think they believe that there is no love in our
homes, that there's no communication. They always act like
they know just what is right for *you* and that you *don't* know—
that you have no concept of how to do it right without their
help. You know, I believe that I can help them straighten out
their lives. *(She laughs lightly.)*

Time has a way of healing. Now I can look back at those
memories and really see what happened. Like, I never consid-

ered talking to a preacher even though growing up I went to church twice a week. At first, after I was raped, I thought I had committed a sin against God. I really did—for a long while I thought that. I felt *I* had done it! Once I was reading along during Bible study—I was in my twenties—and I happened by accident to read in the Bible that a woman would not be punished because of a man's taking her. It's in the Old Testament; I'm not sure where. After I read that, it was like a burden was lifted! I realized, I'm all right. It *wasn't* my fault. Before that time I always thought I had sinned. I didn't know that the sin was against *me*. Now I can step out of myself and see that little person who was raped. I still feel her, but I know that I've outgrown her. That's the way I feel most of the time now. No matter how often my grandmother told me that the past didn't matter, to me it was there and it was stamped on my forehead. It was always there. But now I look at myself in a different light. Now what I see in the mirror—I can deal with.

SHARING WITH ADRIENNE

Some things, Adrienne, you never forget. Disclosing is a trauma in itself.

Fourteen years later, I can still see the exact arrangement of furniture in their tiny, newlywed living room in the house they were renting. Rinna was on the edge of the sofa. Gary sat elsewhere. They were both tensely poised to hear why we had come—whatever could it have meant, our urgent, mysterious phone call: "We're coming over. We have something to tell you." I knew David needed a friend in his everyday world of running, someone he could turn to in an instant and without explanation. And we needed to break out of our self-imposed confinement. I didn't know what *I* needed.

David and I decided to tell Rinna and Gary because they had

been such loyal Philadelphia friends. It would be only a matter of time before they both realized David's and my behavior had become bizarre. So with reluctance and ambivalence, we set out on our first trip to disclosure. "Maybe they don't need to know. Maybe we'll be sorry we told them." We rode in silence. I was scared to reveal what I had made a secret.

We told—I told. I don't remember the words exactly, only the fear turning my stomach, reeling in my head. I felt ashamed as I sat alone on a hassock in the middle of the room. Everything slowed. I could see Rinna, and David's gaze was frozen on me as he listened to my recounting of the bizarre happennings of a rape. But where was Gary? I couldn't find him through my tears. Then I sensed a presence and felt a firm arm ease around my shoulders; a hand began patting me calm. *"Sh-sh-sh."* It was Gary's lullaby; he looked at me softly. He didn't seem to mind touching me, looking in my face. I still remember my amazement. He said, "It's okay now," as he patted my back. And I believed him. I let him console me, and I cried even harder at the awareness of this extraordinary, unsummoned gentleness.

This was *my* first "public" telling, Adrienne.

TANYA

If you let the man go unpunished, then in a sense what you're doing is punishing yourself again.

—*Another survivor, age forty*

When I began this project, I had decided only to interview women in Philadelphia and surrounding areas; I would then be able, if needed, to refer the women to support services. I did not want the women I interviewed to feel marginalized or abandoned in any way. Then I met Tanya by phone through a mutual friend who knew my work. Tanya was a rape survivor and wanted to talk with me. I followed with a note; a correspondence began.

Late one night after telling her story by telephone, Tanya said, "Please use it for your book." She felt safe after our conversation, believed in my work as necessary to others, and trusted my confidentiality. Her trust changed my notion of community yet again. We *could* reach out across miles and connect. As I began to shape her story, Tanya and I had not yet met face to face.

When we finally met, she and I had already become telephone buddies. I had expected Tanya to look much older than her thirty-one years. There had been something about the weight of her voice and her labored phone sighs that led me to picture her that way. She is, in fact, bubbly and seemingly fun-loving. When we met, she was dressed in a tailored suit with bright accents of color that gave depth to her brown complexion and short, dark brown hair.

Tanya moved confidently, smiling through the crowds at the cocktail party we were attending. I watched her interact with others the day we met, and no one would have suspected she had suffered. When we were alone, she was cautious but not embarrassed about the intimacies she had shared. She was direct and precise as she again recounted her story, this time in person. She wanted to get the details right. She wanted readers to have the correct sequencing and all the pieces of her story.

Tanya is a sociologist in a small, New England college. She was raped by a well-respected, senior researcher at her college; someone she thought was a friend. Her plans for academic promotion have been drastically affected by her rape. She has not talked with her mother and family: "They wouldn't understand."

Tanya's rape narrative is especially important because of its complexity. The situation surrounding her rape was complicated by "bipolar disorder," which during her college years she was diagnosed as having. Bipolar disorder is a condition commonly known as "manic depression." One side of the disorder may present itself more emphatically than the other. That is, a person can seem more manic than depressive during any one episode, or vice versa. Symptoms manifest themselves in erratic behavior and unpredictable mood swings. An episode can vary from days to months in duration. Medication and psychotherapy are usually prescribed to alleviate the behavioral symptoms.*

*For more information about bipolar illness (manic depression), see Kay Redfield Jamison, *An Unquiet Mind* (Alfred A. Knopf, New York, 1995).

Tanya reported that earlier during the day of the rape she had felt symptoms of her illness. She became desperate for help because her medication schedule had been altered due to the unexpected change in her travel plans. She had been back in the United States approximately twenty-four hours when the rape occurred. She had been looking for a friend to give her assistance. Tanya explained that the manic side of her disorder had always been more pronounced than the depressive side.

During the many times we talked by phone, Tanya recounted her ordeal with a calm, decisive, careful voice, only becoming outwardly disturbed as she told of the rape, her loss of control, and her treatment by the police. Everything was clear, and each time she spoke with me, the details never shifted.

TANYA'S TELLING

I was sexually assaulted. It was my first full day back from a leave of absence that I'd spent engaged in intensive research. I spent most of my leave time at a research university in the United States, but the final two weeks of field work I did in another country. I had just gotten back the night before, about midnight. I was exhausted. My travel arrangements had been made at the last minute, so getting back had been extremely traumatic. I found out when I got to the airport that I would *not* be a passenger on the evening flight back to the U.S. as I had been told. And the next flight to the U.S. was not until the following week! When I heard that, I felt myself get sick. I had to wait one more week to get back home! I panicked. I was alone in that country, and I had little money left. I was not prepared for that turn of events. My greatest fear was that by the end of the week I would have a hotel bill I couldn't pay and that I would not be permitted to leave the country.

Worse still was what these new events meant for my physical health. I have bipolar disorder. I'm a manic-depressive. I was diagnosed in college. My episodes have usually been brief and rare—spaced about every four or five years apart and averaging about five days in length. Under those conditions, I was always able to ignore and forget about my illness and dismiss it as just one of those things that happened. My last episode prior to accepting the job at the college had been very embarrassing, however. So I started being prepared for the possibility of illness. I got under medical care and went on medication during times of extreme stress. I was on medication the whole time while I was away. But when I heard about the flight delay, I realized that the bulk of my medicine was deep in my luggage and I didn't know when I could get to it. That scared me.

I'm also hypoglycemic.* It was hard for me to eat the food in the country where I was researching those last two weeks; I had diarrhea the entire time that I was there. It got to the point that I was neither physically nor mentally able to deal with the challenges of being alone in a foreign country. I became ill and then had to spend another week under very stressful and dubious circumstances. I spent four days traveling with no sleep, only to return to the States to find out that I was fast running out of medication for my bipolar condition. The change in diet and round-the-clock traveling caused my body chemistry to just go out of whack. I returned to the U.S. one week later than planned, in the early stages of a manic episode.

I managed to get back to my home. I called my doctor as soon as I got there, only to find that he had moved his practice out of the state. Since I didn't see him very often, I hadn't been aware of his plans to move. There was only an answering machine saying that he would get back to me as soon as he got

*Hypoglycemia is an abnormally low level of sugar in the blood.

his messages. I couldn't wait for him to pick up his messages and call me back. I was desperate. I tried everything—other numbers and names; there was no one to see me, to help me. I needed medicine. And then there were racial complexities: I was black, working with one white therapist in town *and* with a black woman therapist in another neighboring city. And now I was trying to get help from a new, white psychiatrist. The number of psychiatrists in this small town can be counted on a few fingers. I could not see the use of explaining to strange doctors that I was in crisis. I felt cornered and trapped. I needed help from someone right away. I was afraid—and panicked.

This was the state of mind I was in at the end of my first full day back—the day that I was sexually assaulted. I lost track of time, my eyes burned, and I had a terrible headache. I went on a shopping spree and stocked up on all kinds of fruits and drinks and then bought about ten pairs of sunglasses. About 11 P.M. that night I felt seriously ill. I had not had anything to eat except a bit of pizza. I thought I might go into a hypoglycemic coma and not be found for *days*. I had nothing to eat in the house—I'd just gotten back, and it was the weekend. I didn't know what to do. I had to *call* someone. If I could just eat something, I thought I could settle my blood sugar. I called for a pizza takeout, but the restaurant had just closed. I tried to contact other people, but no one was around. It was summer; most of the college people were gone. Then I thought of James, one of my colleagues. I knew he was hardly an angel, but I had done a lot of favors for him in the past. I rationalized that he owed me this one favor. I was willing to risk asking him for help in order to stay private about my bipolar problem. It's hard coming to grips with having bipolar disorder. It's so private. People don't always understand. And now it's difficult choosing which brings the worst shame: being known publicly as a person with bipolar disorder, or having been raped.

I thought about it a long time before I called him. I was fairly sure James knew I had some problems because he had seen me in the psychologist's office one day when he was doing his errands in town. After he had seen me there, he made some cracks in my presence about "crazy people." When I called, I didn't tell him that I was a bipolar manic-depressive in crisis, but he *knew* I needed some kind of help. I told him that much. I didn't want just anyone to know I had this disorder. I had spent many years keeping my illness private, and I had started a new life at the college. When I asked him to help me and he said, "Come on over," I thought it was safe. I just wanted him to get me to a doctor. I didn't *look* sick, but I *was* sick, and I knew I couldn't help myself. If he had gotten me to a doctor— if he had just helped me—he would have had a friend for life.

After I got to his place, I'm sure he knew something was wrong. When I'm in a manic phase, people say it's like I'm "flyin' high." I had not slept in four days, and I didn't know the extent to which I was ill. He gave me something to eat; it was waiting when I got there—a hamburger patty with some cheese. After I ate, we talked and I gave him one of the souvenirs I'd brought back from abroad. I was there one or two hours before I got ready to go home. All I wanted to do after eating was sleep. That's when he said, "You can't go home." I didn't ask questions. I didn't know how to resist. "Okay," I said. I feel so vulnerable when my body chemistry is out of whack. I can't think straight. That's how you feel in a manic phase. I figured he recognized that I was sick and in no shape to be alone—that he was saying this to me as a friend. I had wanted to use James as a mirror—to say to me, "You're *not* okay. You *do* need to get help." I thought the message was coming back to me through James's "eyes" that I did not need to be alone and he was going to help me. Anyway, I was too scared to stay alone that night. Then I said, just because I knew the way he was,

"But I will *not* take off my clothes to sleep, and I will *not* have sex with you." I just said that right up front. "Alright," he said.

I followed him up the stairs. And I said again, "I'm not taking off my clothes and I'm not going to have sex with you." I must have said that at least three times. I don't recall he said anything that time. There were no signs to indicate he was going to rape me. He showed me to the bed. It's difficult to describe the physical changes that happen when my body chemistry is out of whack. My head felt like someone was taking a metal flashlight and smacking me on my brains directly with it. My body alternated from feeling like it was a loose collection of fluids held together by a thin membrane of my skin, to a dry overly stretched piece of cheap vinyl about to implode from combustion. I removed my sandals and lay on top of the bed with my clothes still on. All I wanted was quiet and to be left alone.

Then I realized that James had removed his clothes down to his briefs and had climbed into the bed beside me. By this time, James had begun fondling my body—his head was on top of my chest. Despite my protests, intercourse seemed inevitable. I knew I wasn't going to be able to stop him. So, I said, "Go get a condom; I don't want to get no AIDS." That was my state of mind in my condition. Judgment is definitely altered with bipolar disorder. I just felt if you're going to rape me, don't give me AIDS. It's like getting mugged: "Here, take my wallet; just don't cut me." I didn't want to get "cut." Know what I mean? I felt him leave the bed, but I couldn't move, and there seemed to be no time between events. He had an erection to get in, but he had difficulty staying inside of me. He started over and over again. I remember the opening acts, but I don't remember the denouement. At some point I blacked out. I'd had blackouts before, but not like this one. My next memory is of James driving me home in my car at daybreak—about 6:00 A.M. I often wonder whether he drugged me.

Once I got there, I wandered around my house in a daze for a few hours. When I came to—that's when I discovered the bruises on my body. There were dark purple marks on my shoulders where he had held me down. And there were five fingertip marks into the flesh of my thighs where I guess he had borne down on me. I carried these marks around for at least three weeks. I don't remember fighting. I know I did though. All my fingernails were broken the next morning. And I was not in the same clothes. He had dressed me in a pair of his jogging pants. I would *never* have done that on my own.

When I came to my senses after I got home, I remembered what had happened. I panicked and thought, Oh God! I'm not going to have his baby! I took wash rags and repeatedly showered and washed my vagina. I scrubbed. I showered again and again. Then I called a friend from my department; she and another white woman came over. She called the local police and a male officer came to my home while I was still dressing. The two women took me to the police station to make my statement against James. There was not time to eat anything. I carried a bottle of water with me and dissolved a couple of my last few lithium tablets inside to sip on during the interview. I was determined to block a manic episode if possible. I had several months of a refill on my medication, but it was in my luggage, which was still at the airport. I knew I also needed to see a doctor to have my dosage reassessed. I had been under a lot of stress. And also the hypoglycemia had complicated things.

It was around 3:00 in the afternoon. I was finishing up my statement for the third or so time to another white male officer who was the captain of the local police station—I learned that part later. I don't remember all that I said during that interview, but it was taped. He did ask me a lot of embarrassing personal questions about my past medical history in front of my women colleagues—all white. I burst into tears as I painfully described all my last manic episodes.

At one point he must have asked if James was wearing a condom, and when I answered that I wasn't sure but that I had asked him to wear one, he must have come to the happy conclusion that this was consensual sex. I did not remember that part of the interview, but later I read a copy of the transcription. It read: "So you agreed to have sex then." My answer was a garbled grunt of some sort. It was *not* a "yes." In my state of mind at the time of this third or fourth interview at the station, I could not explain to this elderly white male official that by that point, intercourse with James was inevitable—that I had no fight in me, that I felt I was being held captive in his apartment, that I was dependent on James's mercy. He was already on top of me, no longer wearing his underpants, with his head all over my breasts, my clothes pulled up and down. My head felt like two freight trains were colliding repeatedly inside it. Apparently that bit of information about the condom was all this official wanted to know. He did not order a rape kit.

Back to the mugger—if a mugger is holding you up and you hand over your wallet to keep from being further harmed, you do not say to your friends, "I just made a charitable donation to a stranger who needed some money." Instead you say, "I was mugged." That's how I feel about James's raping me. But it also probably explains why I keep referring to that event as a "sexual assault"—because of my own sense of guilt about it all, even though I know I was the victim. The woman who took me to the station returned the next day to file a complaint against the captain for not ordering a rape kit.

And that woman officer was the one who took me home after the interviews. Neither of us felt that I was safe. James had my house keys and could easily have made copies of them; they were on the chain with my car keys. I'd left everything at James's. I still had not eaten that day and was without sleep now going on five days. She decided to take me to a local hospital to have a rape kit done. Polaroid snapshots were made of my bruised body, pubic hair plucked from my groin, and the medical examiner noted the five fingertip marks indelibly pressed into my thighs. Then the local police were called to the hospital. When I was released from the hospital, the doctor took pains to give me a violent-crime medical form to fill out. She was convinced of my being a sexual assault victim and had written on my medical form that "[she] appeared calm except when talking about the assault at which time she became very animated." It was now after 10:00 P.M. I still had not eaten.

The same woman officer took me home from the hospital; she had night blindness, but I decided to take my chances with her. I had no other way home. Then, when I got to my home, I proceeded to cuss her out pitifully for driving me in her car knowing that she could not see at night. I didn't know my behavior was erratic. About that time, the police from the hospital drove up behind us—a woman and two men. She pulled the woman officer aside to talk; I was still trying to find a way to get in my house since the front screen was locked and I have so many keys. The woman officer who had taken me to the hospital and brought me home drove off. And then the male officers came after me. I resisted. They wrestled me to the ground as they handcuffed me from behind. "I didn't do anything wrong," I sobbed and screamed. Apparently the noise woke up one of my neighbors who knew I had been away and had been looking after my place. I didn't see him, but he told me later that he had asked the detective what was going on, and she had said, "not to be alarmed." This was just the "normal response of a woman who'd been raped." The truth is, I was out of control because of my bipolar illness.

Instead of going to the station, the police took me to the state hospital as a precaution. I found out later that the woman officer who had driven me home from the hospital told them I'd "lost it." I sobbed and screamed in the back seat of the police car all the way to the state hospital. No one said anything to me. They put me on a twenty-four-hour emergency hold, plus a seventy-two-hour hospital hold. I was given drugs by injection and still no food. I was in the state hospital *four days!*

I had been manic when the rape happened and manic when I gave my report to the police. When I'm manic, I can't settle down and my thoughts start racing and I have this great desire to sleep, and I don't make much sense. People say I act like I'm on drugs. I don't get severe depression, just low-grade depression. No extremes. I mostly experience the manic phase. I had been in a manic phase when the police arrived that next morning at my front door. They treated me like *I* was the criminal. The police didn't believe me about the rape. That hurt a great deal. I guess they thought it was a case of rough sex or "acquaintance abuse" or something like that. You see, James is a reputable citizen of the college community, and the town and the school are very close.

By the end of the four-day period, I was released from the state hospital. My manic symptoms had disappeared. I had begun eating food again, though my normal sleeping pattern had not returned. One of my white colleagues at the college brought me clothes and personal items. I had no close personal friends, at the time, to help out.

In the past, I had always been able to "catch" an episode when the symptoms began and to deal with it. This was my first episode at the college, and because it was coupled with hypoglycemia and the rape, it got out of hand. After I got out of the state hospital, I didn't want to tell *anyone*, especially black people. I knew it would spread over the campus *and* all over town. One black woman called and left a message on my machine. She said she called just to check on me and to see about my trip. But I knew she really wanted to know more about the rape allegations. She had already heard. I didn't call back.

In this state where I live, rape charges are *only* possible if you can, one, prove that sexual intercourse occurred, and two, prove that intercourse occurred without consent. I had already showered, so there was no evidence of semen. And James had told them that we had had consensual sex. It was his word against mine. *I* knew I had been raped. But I had never told anyone. And no one knew I had bipolar disorder. I really tried to keep that part of my life private since I had not had any manic episodes since my arrival in town. My medication had been working just fine. So since I couldn't prove that I had bipolar disorder without dragging out my entire medical history, and I was not known as a manic-depressive with a mental problem, I couldn't prove that the sex had been nonconsensual. I was raped. I remember him penetrating me.

There *are* medical reports from that night indicating that I was raped and that I had all those bruises. The police had pictures of them, but I was advised by my lawyer to go for a lesser charge—of battery. I refused. My lawyer told me that since James had said he was innocent of rape charges, I would have to give over all my medical files and have my private medical life exposed before a jury if I insisted on charges of rape. The lawyer said he "felt" for me, but that he did not advise prosecuting because it would be too difficult a case to try in this state. He said that if they were to bring this case to justice, they didn't think it would be in my best interest. That it would be better to put it all behind me.

When my attorney called to say that James was not going to be charged, I couldn't believe it. Everyone had assured me that I had a very strong case. My goddamned illness had been outed when I tried to do the right thing by reporting the rape, only to have things end with James getting off scott-free—except for his legal fees. I flirted with the possibility of suicide because it was too hard to believe that life could be so unfair. I had suffered the humiliation, and I had not gotten criminal charges filed against James for it.

I really have gotten very little support through all of this. Several white women from the college were the ones to go with me to the police station, the doctor, and to the hospital. They stood by me. If it hadn't been for them, I would have had nobody. And I think they believed me.

Whatever sense of community I had at the college has been ripped apart. I think, even though most of the black people here believe me, they don't want to see "another brother" in police custody. One note left on my door by a black woman colleague told me to let the charges go otherwise it might hurt my career. She suggested I settle out of court so it wouldn't make minorities look divided. Another message from an anonymous colleague named the white people I could trust. *No one* came forward. Throughout it all, though, the black woman therapist I had been seeing gave me unconditional support. She called me long distance every night for a month to see how I was doing, and sometimes she counseled me for over an hour.

Black people have no power here. I think they're afraid if they say anything, they won't get to stay at the college. Only thing you can do is try to keep people safe because I don't see anyone doing anything to try to stop the incidents of harassment and sexual assault. James is free. No one is cutting back his power or his salary. In fact, the college said that the rape incident didn't happen on campus so the only thing the college could charge him with is "moral turpitude." The irony is that I was here at the college before James arrived. But he has rank and I don't. Black people could be such great help to each other, but because of our silences we can't be. With no sense of community, we end up killing ourselves.

My first year back to teaching after the rape and after my leave were extremely hard. I am a very good teacher. Prior to the incident, I had received teaching awards and recognition for my service to the college community. Upon my return I had no way of knowing what students knew about the case—which stories they had heard and what they believed. No one asked *me* about it. So it was very hard going back into the classroom.

Certain illnesses just don't skip over us because we're African American. I hope someone will read my story and say, "That's me. I see myself." And for those people in the community— any community—who are covering up things and keeping the silence: know that your "self" is at stake, your integrity. And any black women who are engaged in "unholy alliances" where silences are kept, there is a need to stop doing that. There are too many silences in our community.

I spend a lot of time now at home. Since the incident, I shy away from activities or events on and off campus that would bring me into contact with James. His actions have made it extremely difficult for successful promotion at the college. I stay because I hope I make it; I've put in a lot of time here. I keep to myself. I've turned my home into an oasis. I also try to travel when I can. It gets me away, and that's good. I have periods of high productivity, and then some very low times.

My spiritual centering helps me to cope, to survive. I'm as confused as anyone else as to why these things happened. I do know there is a God—some consciousness out there that is above and beyond it all. And in time, I will come to understand why this happened. Knowing that keeps me to the core. Also, in time I think writing will be a way of healing for me. I sort of feel at peace because I've done all I can do about an egregious situation. Now I'm moving on. I have survived because I am a survivor. I still believe in myself.

SHARING WITH TANYA

Why can't men, in general, be more sensitive, Tanya? Why can't they understand that our bodies are always at risk? Why do we have to instruct them?

It happened at a celebratory, business dinner at a very public place. I hadn't really wanted to go because I had worked all day on my writing and was weary. But I thought, it's an evening to relax with David, and so we went. As I am always careful to do, I checked the name cards of my table partners so that I could seem amiable when they arrived, especially since I was tired. Two men would flank me.

The first was an elderly gentleman who engaged me in chatter about matters of the workplace. The second man arrived with a jolly manner and blond smiles, and he introduced himself as Noah. When I introduced myself, he confidently replied, "Oh, I know who you are! I've been waiting to meet you." And then he left with no further explanation, to shake hands and greet colleagues. *How do you know* me—*and why?* Eventually, the jolly, blond smiler came back to the table and to the conversation he had so dramatically begun. "I live in your old neighborhood," he announced. "I want to know the *real* story about why your family left the neighborhood." I froze inside. *We're not going there, are we?* More banter as I tried to steer clear of the topic. "Tell me the story," he said flippantly, staring directly into my eyes. Conversations continued around us. I felt cornered. *Could he tell, I wondered?* "So what *did* happen that night? Tell me." I replied coldly. "Why don't *you* tell it? This is your story, not mine," I said. And he did. In doing so, he repeatedly used the phrase, "personally accosted" when referring to my rape. *Whatever could that mean?* He said, "I heard you were personally accosted. *Were* you?"

After weeks passed, and after David told him of his insensitive behavior, Noah called to apologize. He didn't understand what he'd done wrong. I could only think of his wife and children. I accepted his apology. But I wanted to say to him: "Take good care of your wife and daughters, Noah. They need your vigilance because there are men like you who 'mean no harm,' but wreak havoc nonetheless. And as your sons mature, teach them, if you can, to watch, listen, and feel—with sensitivity. Teach your sons to console—for the woman in the seat next to someone like you might be their mother, sister—or lover."

HARRIETT

*A lot of times what we don't realize is, we got to take care of our-
selves before we can take care of other people.*

—*Another survivor, age twenty-three*

Harriett is a retired real estate agent and the oldest rape survivor
interviewed for this book. She is now engaged in her own computer business, and works from an at-home office. Divorced, Harriett
lives alone. She has two sons; one lives with his family in a nearby
city. Her rape occurred two years ago, during the burglary of her
home. She still lives in the house where the violations took place.
That is where we conducted our interview.

Harriett could pass for forty-five, easily. Her unblemished, rich,
coffee-bean complexion made me want to rush to the nearest mirror to check my makeup. She is beautiful in her sixty-six years. On
the day we met, her lipstick was perfect, her nail color a precise
match. Her white, peppered hair was in the latest short style, appro-

priate for her age and professional bearing. I was captivated. Sitting and listening to her talk, I had difficulty not searching her face, her body for a flaw. Secretly, I knew nature would betray me long before the age of sixty-six.

Harriett told her rape story in a straightforward, restrained manner, as dignified as her appearance. Only during our second meeting, after we had shared personal reminiscences and established a trust, did she share her growing-up years and the more intimate details of her life. It became clear as I played back our interview that Harriett was trying *not* to talk about so many family traumas in her life. There was a sadness in her telling, but she held in check her outward emotions. "I was always the one who had to be tough," she said. These added details helped explain Harriett's ability to survive and cope with her rape trauma. After several meetings, Harriett allowed herself to cry.

HARRIETT'S TELLING

I wasn't ashamed. It wasn't so much that it was easy for me to tell others as it was an escape . . . for me to get rid of some of the details right away. I told the mailman. I told my neighbors. I told everybody. The people who had been in my house had not been caught, so I figured the more people who knew about it the better. They just might see three boys hanging around together doing nothing. So I felt if I could tell people, they would be looking out. I found that that helped me . . . *(She whispers.)* during that time. I wasn't that much together . . . except I felt I had to do some of the work myself because I didn't feel the police had done an adequate job. After I pushed my alarm system, they didn't show up. *(She chuckles.)*

You see, I had been out and had just come in the house. It was July, and it was hot. What I usually do is leave my security door open with the screen in. When I came in the house that day, I had to go to the ladies room *real* bad. So everything in my hands I dropped right in the middle of the floor and ran up the steps. Prior to that I had seen these three people walking down the street; it was a natural thing for me to look over my shoulder. I sort of stood on one leg and then on the other as I sort of watched them pass the house. After they passed, I ran in and flew upstairs to the bathroom. My security door unfortunately is not one of the newer ones where it closes and automatically locks. You have to lock it with a key. And I didn't take that extra couple of seconds to lock it.

It was on my mind, rushing that way, that the first thing I had to do after, was run downstairs and lock that door. But when I went to do that—I was on my way back downstairs—I happened to notice a shadow on the wall. I have a picture window with a tree there, and sometimes that tree would blow and sway. I thought maybe that was a shadow from the tree. But it wasn't. It was a young man standing in the middle of my living room.

I never screamed. I never did anything. It was a shock to me. But then I said to myself, "Okay. It's me and it's him." And I said to him, "What are you doing in here?" He answered, "Oh, I'm looking for an address." When he told me the address, I said, "Well you don't have the right number." I was thinking to myself, "This is not right. He would not have had to come into my house to ask me for an address."

Then he proceeded to ask me, Was my husband at home? I said that he was upstairs. "What do you want with him?" But of course, since I didn't call anybody, he knew I was faking. I never moved from that spot on the stairs. I didn't try to run. I didn't do anything because I figured even if I had, I still would have had to come down the steps and all he had to do was cross the room and he would have caught me. So I was rational in my thinking. He looked fairly young, and I figured I could out-smart him. He looked like he might have been in his late, late teens or early twenties.

As he walked toward the door, I said to myself, "Oh my God. I'll never do *that* again." You know? I was so relieved. And as he was walking out the door, the first thing I did was grab my keys and lock the door. "He's out! He's out." What I did not know was that there were *three of them*. When I turned around there stood two others. It never crossed my mind that he had been one of the three fellows I saw coming down the street earlier. These two had been hiding in my dining room while I was talking to the other guy. One young man had a knife pointed at me. He told me to give him my money and my jewelry. I said, "I don't have anything." Then they proceed-ed to ask me for the key to let the other guy back in. I said I didn't know where I'd left it. But it was lying on the table so they just picked it up and, naturally, let him back in again.

I thought about trying to run, but then I figured if I did, I would probably run right into the arms of the other one. I only saw one weapon, but I kept saying to myself, "I can't believe this is happening to me. I don't believe this." I was naturally nervous. I did not scream. I just kept saying, "Don't hurt me. Just *don't* hurt me." And, "I don't have anything." They kept saying, "You *look* like you have something around here." They told me to take off my rings and my jewelry. I had on one very good necklace that I don't usually wear every day. I had gotten it in Europe. I had been wearing it for a couple of days and hadn't taken it off.

Two of them went upstairs, and one stayed down here with me—watching me. They never even shut the door; they just left the door open. I sort of kept walking toward the door, and the fellow that was here first just kept watching me. Finally I got too close to the door, and he said, "I think you better go back the other way." He didn't have a weapon. But I told the guy with the knife—I had said to him—"Look, you have to put that knife away. I can't stand this. I cannot *think* with you pointing that knife at me like that." And he did. At this point I thought to myself they might have another kind of weapon—or they even might beat me. I didn't want to take a chance. I know I cannot handle three people. No way, I thought. And I said to myself, If I make a lot of noise and draw attention, they're going to close the door. Then that's goin' to be less chance for me to try to get away. So I just sort of went along with it. I called myself basically *surviving*. I thought, I'm not going to put myself in a situation where these guys have to really *kill* me. If I can prevent it at all by being as calm as possible I will. I felt my calmness. I was complying to their wishes, but in the meantime, I was still trying to outsmart them 'cause I didn't feel that they were so sophisticated.

They were all about the same age. And I could see how neatly they were moving things. They weren't dumping things all around—no burglar's going to take time to do this or that. So then I figured these guys are kinda new at this. They seemed to come from better homes; they weren't just bumming out there. I did note their sneakers and things like that. These guys were like, "I'm new at this." They were nervous, too, because I said to the one watching me, "You're just making me nervous." He said back, "Yeah, well, you're makin' me nervous too."

So I asked him for a drink of water. When he said yes, I started walking toward the kitchen through the dining room. In my dining room there is an alarm panel. As I walked close to the wall, I pushed the two alarm buttons—and I was shaking. It is a silent alarm; it *did* go through [to the police station], I found out later. When I got to the kitchen and got the plastic bottle out, I was so nervous I couldn't get the cap off. He took it off *for* me. That's why I thought these boys—or these young men—had been properly trained by someone, 'cause that was not an ordinary thing to do given the circumstances. That was one of the things I told the police—about the water bottle. But they weren't able to get fingerprints from it. Later when they tested the fingerprints, they were mine.

When I came back into the dining room, I faced the door waiting for the police to come. The guys had not locked the door, so I thought, when the police get here, I'll make a dash for it, right into their arms. You know? And I waited and I waited and I waited. No police. "I don't believe this. I don't believe this." No police. Finally the other two guys came down from upstairs and had my VCR and other things. Then the youngest guy in the group said, "Hand me that belt." He was going to tie my hands behind me. It was a leather belt . . . real soft. . . . *(Her voice becomes more quiet.)* He couldn't get it to stay tied. I wasn't struggling.

While he was trying to tie me up, the other two walked out with all my stuff. Then I said, "You need to go. You got what you want. There's no reason for you to stay." I thought to myself, Oh God. What's now? And then, it came to me: he's up to something else here. I said, "What are you doing? Why don't you go? Why don't you go?" I just kept saying that. He was the one who had the knife. He shoved me into the kitchen.

He said, "Lie down!" "No, no, no, no, no," I yelled. "You don't want to do this. You don't want to do this." I *knew*. Then I just looked him in the eye and said, "Would you—how would you feel if someone would do this to your mother or your sister?" He got very nervous. There was no weapon in sight. Later on I thought back that maybe I should have fought more. Maybe I should have done that. But then, by that time, I was kind of gettin' drained. And I figured there are knives in my kitchen, and I'm looking at them. If I refuse to comply, is he going to then take another weapon out or grab one of mine? Then I figured, I'm alive. So I did whatever he wanted me to do as far as I could. I got down on the floor.

I kept saying, "*No.* You don't want to do this." *(Her speech gets faster.)* "Don't do this, don't do this, don't do this." As he tried, I sort of lay on my side a little. He kept telling me, "Spread your legs, spread your legs." I said, "I can't do that because I have one bad leg." Which I don't, but I said it anyway. I figured at least he will not get to do what he wants to do fully because I'm gonna keep staying on my side. Whenever he pushed my leg, I made a lot of noise. This unnerved him. It wasn't full penetration because I would *not* cooperate. The other thing that came to my mind was that if I cooperated *somewhat,* the rest of them wouldn't come back and find out what was going on. Maybe they *knew.* But if they had come back and tried the same thing, I don't believe I would have really been as sane as I am today—had it been three people. I know that someone would have held me—or something. You see?

They did not come back. When he finished what he was doing, he grabbed things up . . . his pants. He was trying to get them up and trying to run out the door at the same time. I thought, If I just had something I could hit him with. But here again it was *fear* of them coming back that stopped me. That was the one fear I had. I felt that I would possibly get hurt more, because at this point there was no physical punching or slapping. They didn't harm me in that way at all. I was afraid, but I tried to stay calm. I think the others knew what was going on. I think it was a decision made by that one guy. He didn't get enough out of the house. I never could understand why this guy would take time to assault me when earlier he was so busy trying to get the others to hurry up and come downstairs. I did say to him as I was standing near this door right here—I looked him right in the eyes and said, "I don't understand. Why would you *do* something like this? You look like a nice young guy." He just was so nervous as I was talking to him. He never answered me.

They left. The police still had not come. Then I called 911. The police had been notified twice. The first person I told was my neighbor; the alarm company has his number, and he was coming over to see if I was okay. This all took place within about half an hour. Actually it seemed like *hours. (She laughs.)* Oprah was coming on. . . . I remember . . . 'cause when I came back down to lock the door, I could hear the music. The police got there within the next half hour—*after* the detectives. Oprah was still on. Everybody got here about the same time. I don't go around trying to blame the whole police department, but if they *had come* . . . they could have prevented the rape. *They could have caught him* had they come. That's the way I've always felt. And it makes me angry today.

When the detectives and police finally get here, they're running in and out of the house. You know, everybody's in a big hurry. Every time I would start to tell the story to one group, then here comes someone else. They wanted to hear it again and again. I didn't go to police headquarters; they took me immediately to the hospital. The policeman that took me was very nice. But here again—I was in a *police* car. I just felt so bad about that. I was sitting there in that car by myself, and everybody was lookin' in at me. I was breaking down more and more in the police car because it was degrading to be just sitting there every time he stopped the car. That was a time when a person needed tinted windows—especially if you're by yourself. My hair was ruffled, and I looked like I'd been crying. People could think *anything*. By the time I got to the hospital, I really broke down. But mostly by myself . . . and with some of the people who came by to see me—people who knew me. Not with the nurses and the doctors. *(There is a long pause.)* Oh glory! . . . just one second. *(Silence; she becomes emotional.)*

You know, another thing that bothers me even 'til today—out of all the things that happened—was the fact that most of us think of our home as safety. When it happens in the street, at least you can say to yourself, "I'll get back home, and I'll be safe." But when it happens in your *home* . . . well, . . . it's different. I find even today sometimes I'll come in—even with the alarm system on—and look behind doors, look behind shower curtains. Everything. *(She sniffles.)* I have put a little chain on my cellar door, *knowing* that if they went down there they couldn't relock the door. But I *still* look. And I guess it's because I'm always afraid that maybe if someone *did* get in, that somebody else is hiding somewhere like it was before. It's terrible. If odd things happen right in your home, it takes a while to feel secure. I always go to the door at night and recheck to see whether or not I can do anything more.

It was after 5:00 when I got to the hospital. And I did not get out of that place until 11:00 at night. I had to wait soooooo *long*. I was in the room most of the time by myself. I thought, "Maybe if I scream, somebody will come." There was a caseworker there from WOAR. She was the first one who talked with me. She explained everything that was going to be happening. I knew what to expect. But I was still by myself. I thought to myself, How long do they think I can *stand* this? I felt like, *If I don't get a bath soon I will die!* My friends came later and stayed with me until my son got there. My son took me home and stayed with me four days. He brought a weapon with him, and he said, "Now Mom, this is all you have to do with this." And he showed me. I think he knew I was not afraid to use it. And I'm not. Most women will scream out at the drop of a hat. Not me. I am not really a hysterical person. I'm not afraid to have a gun in the house. And if I ever point a gun at

you and say I'm going to shoot, *I . . . intend . . . to . . . shoot.*
'Cause you can get shot by your own gun. You have to be serious about what you're doing.

The next day after the events, there were a lot of visits from
people I know. Someone wrote a letter to the commissioner of
police to ask *why*—if this was supposed to be an emergency,
panic type of thing—*why* it was not answered quickly. His reply
was there were so many calls that they had to be done in order
of priority. They didn't have the cars; they don't have this and
that. And I've got to listen to all of that! When I pushed the
alarm button, they couldn't know if my throat was being cut—
or what! And when I called the 911, I told them it was a robbery
and rape. They have a record down there when the first call
came in from the panic button. Now, on other occasions my
panic button upstairs has been pushed by mistake when people
thought it was a lighter—and there have been police *just like
that! (She laughs.)* Now I do not understand the difference here.
After the rape, I made *sure* I told people in the neighborhood. I
knew if I told one or two neighbors, they would spread the
word. They might see something next time. Because these
young men walked up the street with my stuff under their
arms—in broad open daylight. I am constantly looking out my
window now. I watch. If I see something that's not right—I can
call the police.

After things died down, I went to a couple of counseling sessions at WOAR. I signed up 'cause that was one of the things
they told me to do at the hospital. I had a couple of individual
interviews, and then I chose to join a group. It helped somewhat. I met a woman there who was a hooker and had been
raped, and she thought about killing the guy. And I thought to
myself, a lot of people would say, "Well she asked for that—the
kind of lifestyle she leads and all." But I could see she was still
hurting. So one day, I called her and we talked. She was ever so

grateful—you know—that somebody understood and put it in
its right perspective. Some of the stories I heard were a little bit
depressing. But then, sometimes when you hear worse stories, it
gives you a feeling that, "Well, maybe I was blessed." So I
stopped going. I feel so thankful that I've gotten to my age and
this had never happened to me earlier.

I had a male friend at the time of the rape. I never really had
that feeling some women get where they can't be touched again
and all that type of thing. I never really felt that way with him.
We had been friends for a long time. So I had to think of it
as—he would never do something like that to me. If I said no
to him, he would just honor that. There's *never* been a question.
So I did not treat him like there *would* be, to make him feel
worse. Because he had things to go through himself in order to
cope. But a couple of times he did say things that really struck
deep and hurt—like he more or less accused me of allowing
them to come in: "How could you be so stupid not to lock the
door?" The more I tried to explain, the more aggravated I got.
He just could not understand. So I just let it go. But I told him
I would never in life forgive him for bringing that up. You
know, men can't tolerate the fact of someone else touching you
to begin with—and in a case like this it's even worse! They have
this crazy thing in their minds, "Well, what did you do to stop
it? Why didn't you stop it?" . . .

And then the following year, when the day the rape happened came around again, I was real upset. I wanted that day to
get over quick! My friend didn't understand that either. He said,
"I don't know why you would still feel shaky. You need to put
that behind you. It's *not* the same day." And I said, "You've *got*
to be kidding!" And I can't say what else I said to him. *(She
laughs.)* So I may not even mention it this year when the day
comes around. If I get over it, I just won't say anything. We're
still friends. . . .

I don't believe men have the same kind of thinking about rape. I think they're pretty well set in their ways—not the same amount of flexibility there. I think they let their little invisible protective shields down just a little bit, and say they're being helpful. And we're *not* supposed to cry. We're supposed to snap right back as if a rape never happened. They think—no, they *expect* the woman to be that way. . . . They just don't know, do they? They just can't think in terms of how women really think.

I have some ideas that might help other women who have been raped. Like, now, I talk about the rape. I *tell* people. Women should try, if they possibly can, to muster up enough strength to get some of their stories out 'cause it does help other people. Do you think being quiet about rape goes back to the fact of how women, black women, were used in slavery and probably never complained? . . . But then, now that I think about it, they couldn't complain. Who would they complain *to*? I think in the end it's not just about rape; it's about how we survive the rape. It's about how black women were *taught* to survive. I would say to other women, if rape happens to them, try to think as rationally as you possibly can. I know fear overtakes part of you, but I'd say, no matter what, *stay alive.* Do whatever it takes for you to stay alive. But your decision has to be quick *(a loud clap)* and positive. It's just like CPR. You can't wait. *Stay alive.*

SHARING WITH HARRIETT

We can't expect everyone to rush to embrace us when we tell them our secrets. Once I told a trusted black male friend that I had been raped. I just knew he would stroke my wounds and make me feel important and needed. I wanted him to touch my hand, give me a hug, or just say how sorry he was. He said nothing, and he didn't touch me. That encounter only reinforced my sense of being a pariah. It was not what I had expected or wanted. But he had done nothing wrong. I think later I decided he just didn't know how to be compassionate, didn't know how to comfort. Perhaps his family never showed him. Perhaps he was inwardly grieving my loss.

We can never know what is lurking in another person's storehouse of trauma. That's why we have to be willing to test the waters until we find what we need—without feeling that somehow we have stepped over an invisible boundary. We must be patient with our male friends, Harriett, and help them to negotiate with us, our very precarious pathway to recovery. We need them to help us heal.

JENNIFER

My pastor even said, "Some things you bring on yourselves." But I don't believe that.

—Another survivor, age twenty

Jennifer was waiting when I arrived at our designated meeting place. She greeted me with a generous, open smile. She was tidily dressed in a simple skirt, jacket, and blouse of muted greens and browns; she looked very much the corporate paralegal that she is. She seemed shy, somewhat nervous. And her softly cropped hair and small frame made her seem younger than twenty-five. Once settled, Jennifer watched me intensely as I spoke, trying, I surmised, to decide if she would tell me everything—or anything. She spoke carefully, monitoring every detail, answering only the questions I posed. Jennifer had been a volunteer counselor for the hotline at WOAR; she heard of my "call for interviews" through that organization. Our conversation moved slowly. It was as if she had come for a job interview.

As we talked, she relaxed. She reveled in the details of her recently acquired job. Jennifer explained that she was a recent college
graduate and had returned to the city to be near family. She was living with her significant other. As afternoon became evening, we
laughed, shared our lives, and engaged in serious conversation, talking of the traumas that had brought us together in that space.

Jennifer was raped when she was thirteen. On her way to a neighborhood store one winter afternoon, a nineteen-year-old stranger
abducted and raped her within blocks of her home. After the rape,
Jennifer was told, simply, "Go home." As soon as she arrived home,
even with the rapist's threat of "I'll kill your family if you tell" ring-
ing in her ears, Jennifer told her mother and older sister. The
youngest of seven children, Jennifer found refuge and solace in her
family.

JENNIFER'S TELLING

Rape is very much a secret thing. In African American culture
it's to be handled within the family, and that's as far as it should
go. That's the way my family wanted to handle it. The family
decides *what* should happen and *how* it should happen. And
that's that. We don't need to bring in outside people to help us.
We can handle it. In my particular case, when I came home
and told my mother, *immediately* certain family members were
notified, and it wasn't really taken further than that. But the
family *had* to know; the family knew what was goin' on. They
then took it into their hands and decided—my little caucus of
support—how it should be handled. It really wasn't ever a big
issue—seeking outside help. I mean, like, I went to WOAR on
my own—just for myself personally. My family asked me if I
wanted to go, and I said yes. But they weren't really pushing it.

In a lot of other cultures the parents would say, "Let's take the child to counseling immediately, . . . make sure they're okay." But within my group of friends and people I've known, it's always been like this: families deal with it, and that's how it is taken care of.

I was thirteen when I was raped; it was a couple of days before my birthday. I'm now twenty-five. It was a Sunday afternoon. It's bizarre. . . . I remember certain stuff, and other things I don't. I had gone to church with my mother and my family, and we had just come home. I had to go to the supermarket. It was December and it was about three o'clock, so it was relatively light out when I left. On my way back, . . . I was maybe a block from my house, . . . like I could see my house from where I was standing, . . . there were people everywhere. . . . This guy approached me from behind and said, "I have a gun. Come with me." There seemed to be people everywhere. I didn't see the gun 'cause it was sorta behind me. I looked down at my block, and there were kids playing and there were a few people walking around. I don't remember if there were any adults out. . . . I think if there *were*, they would have said, "Hi," to me. "Where are you going?" 'Cause my neighborhood is very much a community. Everyone knows everyone else's business. I don't remember anybody speaking to me like that.

And so he and I began to walk. He said, "Hold my hand." I guess so as not to arouse attention, since this is where I lived. If someone saw me and I was holding this guy's hand, it would be okay. So we walked the block that was parallel to where I live. He was making casual conversation, which was really bizarre. For some reason I believed he had a gun. The whole time I'm thinking, Oh, my God, don't let him hurt me. I just want to go home. I never really thought about rape. I mostly thought about kidnapping or just being abducted. I just know the whole time I was thinking, I hope I'm going to be okay. Where are we

going? . . . you know . . . to myself. And meanwhile he's just
talking to me: "How old are you? Do you have a boyfriend?"
He asked about family members—different stuff like that.

She was not familiar to me, . . . wasn't someone from the
neighborhood. And I did not recognize him from days before
or from just walking around. I came to find out that he was
nineteen, but he appeared to be in his late twenties. It was really weird. 'Cause when he asked me how old I was, I said
eleven—though I was thirteen—assuming he would think,
Well, she's just a kid; I'll let her go; she's a baby. . . . You know.
But he didn't seem to care about that. I told him my name was
Donna. I saw some younger guys about my age down the
block, and they called to me. And he was like, "If you say
something, I'm going to shoot 'em." They still were yelling to
me, . . . and there were people on the street, . . . and we were
just walking along. It was really weird. It was not that he was
going to kill *me*. He said he was going to kill *them*. Then a cop
car drove by, and he told me not to say anything. I wanted to
do something, but I thought to myself, Yeah, sure, I'm going to
run down the block after a car—that would be real smart. So
we continued to walk maybe five or six blocks from where I
live, but it was still familiar neighborhood. I didn't actually *pass*
my house, but I was on the block parallel to my house.

At first he was going to take me into the park. But there
were so many people there that he decided that was not a good
place. So we *crossed* the street and there's a railroad, . . . you
know, like the SEPTA. And there was a little park outside.
There were bushes. It's a *nice* walk from my house. You might
not *want* to walk there on a real hot day, but it's walkable. So
we get to this spot in the bushes, and there's a clearing; I could
see the train tracks. We walk in, and he tells me to lie down.
Then he started pulling on my pants and all this stuff. He said,
"Take down your pants and underwear." He pulled my under-

wear down, and he left the sanitary napkin I was wearing. He wasn't violent, . . . not physically violent. I came to find out later that he wanted me to appear as I had when I left home—no marks—so that I wouldn't tell anyone. He didn't want me to appear to be damaged in any way.

So this is when I *see* the gun. He pulls it out. He has it in his hand when he begins to rape me. He put the gun in my mouth. He goes through the typical rape scenario you see in a movie: "Say you love me." . . . You know. And then during all this he's still like making small talk like, "Well, you know I have a girlfriend." . . . Really weird stuff, . . . and there were people right across the street!

I don't know *how* I stayed calm. I think it's just in my personality—who I am. Like in most situations I'm always just very laid back and *not*, I guess, what they would say "out of control." I was just very much, . . . you know, . . . my normal self. *Inside* I was scared. I think my biggest fear was that because I had my period I would get pregnant. I didn't understand the whole thing about when you could get pregnant or not. That's all I could think about. And, . . . you know, . . . Don't let him kill me. Other than that, I was very calm. I knew I had seen him, and he had a gun, so I thought, Why is he going to let me go?

When he was finished, he said, "Okay. Get dressed." It was like, "Well, was your shirt tucked in or tucked out? Was your coat buttoned up or not?" You know, . . . all this stuff to make sure I looked the same when I got home. *He* didn't undress. I didn't cry when he raped me. After it was over, he said, "Okay. Go home now." He said, "Don't run, don't tell anybody. 'Cause if you *tell*, I'm gonna kill your family. I'm going to kill everybody. And if I go to jail, I'll still find you." I thought *maybe* he might kill me, but I was going to tell anyway. I said to him, "Oh, no, of course I won't tell." I promised—whatever he

wanted to hear. If I could go *home*—yeah, *sure*, I won't tell. I'll
go home and just continue my life. And so he let me go. He
went across the street to the park, and I went home. I was walking and looking over my shoulder to see where he was, and
then I started running. He told me if I started running he
would shoot me, but I didn't really see him anymore so I just,
like, took off. I wasn't hurting, . . . not really, . . . not at that
moment anyway. It had to be after 3:00 that all this began. It
was still light when I was walking home. By the time I got
home, it was dark. Still, it could have been like 5:00 because it
was December.

When I walked in the door, I just started crying right away. I
guess all that holding in just came out. My mother was on the
telephone, and when she saw me she just hung up. I told my
mom, and she said right away, "It's *my* fault." I think she said
that because she sent me to the store. But I always went to the
store, and I always went by myself because my one sister close
to me in age never wanted to go. She said it was too far, so I
always would say, "Okay. I'll go to the store. I'll get it." I think
my mother thought she should have been worried more about
the time. But I don't think it was that long.

My mom called the cops. The cops talked to me, and they
put me in the car right then—that night. Since it had just happened, they drove me around the neighborhood to find this
guy. Of course, if I had seen him that night, I probably would
have said, "No, that's not him," 'cause he told me he was going
to kill me. I only remember the cop and myself in the car. And
I remember driving up one block, and they threw this guy up
to the window: "Is *this* him?" Thank goodness it wasn't, because
I was scared. And the guy was like apologizing to me. . . . I
guess 'cause he was a known rapist or something. I don't know
why they pulled him out of nowhere. He was like, "Oh, I'm so
sorry. I didn't do it. It wasn't me. I'm so sorry for you." I said,

"No, it's not him." So by this time the cops had *totally* scared me. When they asked me, "Which way did he go?" Of course, I said the opposite way in the park, because if they found him, what would I do? Would they lock him up? Was he going to *kill* me?

After that, the cops took me to the hospital. Most of that I blocked out. I can remember only one woman and being up on the examining table. She asked me some questions. When I said I was on my period, she said, "Oh well—then why are you here? You're *not* pregnant." I don't remember what happened after that—at all. I just remember walking in the door, and I remember that woman. That woman was just so put off by my *being* there . . . for some reason. I never understood that. The next thing I remember was being at the police station.

The police *did* catch him about a month or so later. He had raped another girl, and she reported it. She was about my same age. The police called and said, "We found the guy," and they came by and showed me his clothing. The night of the rape I did a sketch for them at the station. They had a split book, with noses, eyes, mouths so you could make a face . . . and I put one together. I'm assuming they didn't believe me 'cause later when they caught the guy, they said, "Wow! Your picture looks exactly like him!" Then the cops and the DA apologized to me. I guess they didn't believe me 'cause I was sitting there like I am sitting here now—very calm. I guess also because of my age, . . . that I could give such an accurate description. But it's always been like that. Once I see a face, I can see it again. I'll know that I've seen that person somewhere. I might not remember where.

Then things got kind of weird. At the police station they gave me the other girl's phone number who had been raped, but said, "You can't talk about the rape or what happened to you." So I thought, What am I going to talk to her about then?

I don't *know* her. Why else would I talk to this girl? They introduced us and everything. I met her at the preliminary hearing. No, actually, I met her at the lineup after I picked him out. They said, "This is the other girl." I felt, Why am I being introduced to her? I can't really talk to her about what I would want to talk to her about. It was like, "What do you guys want me to say to her? Are we supposed to become best friends over this?" *(She laughs.)* I think they were kind of put off by me not really responding to all this. I guess they felt they were doing me a favor. It was like introducing me to a stranger on the street and saying, "You should know her because she's black; so talk to her, but don't talk about being black."

I pressed charges. That was the *best* feeling in the world! I remember I went to the preliminary hearing in family court. And I remember the rapist's *mother* was there. My mom was there, my counselor from WOAR, and the other girl—she was there. For some reason they decided I should go first. I was telling what happened to me, and I started to cry. On the way out, I saw the rapist up real close to me, and he looked right at me. The judge just went off on him, like, "You don't *deserve* to be looking at her." And she was yelling at my DA, "Don't let her walk that close to that filthy animal."

I definitely felt like something had been accomplished after the trial because in my mind I had figured we'd go to court and they would slap him on the wrist and that would be all. Then he'd be out the next day and he would kill me. But he got put away. *That* was a good feeling. Like someone in the court system actually *cared* what happened to me and thought it was wrong. And after the rape, my family totally closed in around me. I was in high school, and *every day*—someone would walk me to the school bus stop—which was right around the corner from my house—and stand there with me 'til I got on the school bus. *Every* day. And when I got off the school bus, there was somebody standing there waiting to walk me—one block, maybe a block and a half—to my house. I put up with it for a while, and then I was like, "No! *Stop*. I'm fine. I've dealt with it. Go away." 'Cause even though I wasn't okay, I felt like, Look what this is doing to my family.

For a long time I would not walk by the spot where he first approached me. To get from my house to the main street, I would not take the quickest way because I had to walk by that spot. Instead I'd walk a block—over a block—up, just to go around that road. I didn't walk up and down the street anymore. And whenever I went somewhere, I'd always see where the closest police station was . . . or where there was someone I knew. I made myself aware of my surroundings, because I thought if it ever happened again and I was snatched and taken somewhere that was not familiar, I would be able to find my bearings and get to somewhere safe. So I would figure out how many houses between *this* person's house and the *next* person's, or count how many blocks to the police station, or a phone . . . or any place I could get help if I needed it. For a while I had the feeling he was lurking around somewhere, waiting to come back to get me.

My emotions that first week after the rape were mixed up . . . mostly anger. I wanted him to die. *And* I was upset with myself, . . . with what I could have done, . . . what I *should* have done. I felt afterwards that I didn't resist at all. I just sort of stood there and let him do this to me. Why didn't I run when he first approached me? Being shot would have been better than being raped. At the time I would rather have been dead. It was just too hard to deal with. I *knew* it wasn't my fault, but I thought society would think it was.

I had nightmares for a while after the rape. I don't even

know if they were really nightmares because sometimes I'd just
close my eyes during the day, and I could see everything that
happened. And then sometimes I would go to sleep and I
would see it. It didn't matter . . . daytime . . . nighttime. I
could *see* it just like it happened. No bodily reaction. Just this
very vivid picture in my head that I could never seem to push
away or get rid of. I never had any headaches or stomachaches
or pains or anything. I guess I dealt with it more internally—
you know. I sort of tried to put it in perspective for myself.
Each time I would deal with it, I told myself I would be fine. I
think one reason why my *body* didn't react to the rape adversely
is because my body is so used to me holding everything inside.
I think my tolerance is just so high. . . . I just kept everything
in for all those years. It was like, . . . "Oh, one more thing!
Okay, move over."

For a time, I pushed the rape and what happened aside
'cause I needed to get on with my life. I was going to the ninth
grade. I thought, I can't go on like this. I didn't die—I'm okay.
And so at first, I felt ashamed. Somehow all the neighbors
found out. And then all my male friends started asking me,
"What happened?"—like, "We'll protect you" type of thing.
That really irritated me. I didn't want anyone to know. I just
said, "*No*, I was not raped." I made that clear, because of the
whole stigma that goes with being raped. None of these kids
were expressing that, but in my mind it was still a stigma.

I really didn't want to talk to anybody at school about
what happened, but I started going to WOAR's counseling. I
thought it might do some good. They had a teenage group I
attended for a while. But all the rest of the girls were either survivors of acquaintance rape or incest. I just felt my situation
was so different; I felt like I didn't have anything in common
with them. But still it turned out to be great because I made a
connection with one of the counselors and one of the teenagers

who I am still friends with today. I stayed for a month or two. And while I was in the group I was able to talk about the rape and hear other people who experienced something similar. Outside of myself, I got to see how they were dealing with it and see that my feelings were okay, . . . like the nightmares and different stuff like that. That was good for me. I *wanted* to talk to somebody else about it. I think being exposed to a group therapy situation and making those good connections really helped me. The girl and I shared our stories a lot and were supportive of each other. I had my own sort of private, outside-of-family support person. I could tell her things, and I didn't feel like it was a burden. With my family, I felt, Why should I burden them with this thing? Not that *they* felt it was a burden, but to me it was. And I didn't want them to think I was upset all the time.

My family is real important to me. We stick together. I was the youngest, . . . the child that was sort of like the hope of the family. I was the one who was supposed to get married and have the kids and have that kind of lifestyle. My sisters had already made other choices that didn't work. They all have kids, and they've all been married and divorced. One of my brothers is gay—and I grew up in a household where it was accepted. The family had gotten over all its prejudices and trauma with him. My mother knew *I* was gay. She had asked me point-blank about two years before the rape. Still, in spite of the openness, I had the fear: I don't want to tell this to my family. They can't have *two* gay kids. I had no idea what to say to her at first. And then after the rape, I thought, I can't once again let the family down. I felt I was disappointing them again. But even as a kid I didn't want to get married because I looked around and I didn't see any successful marriages in my family. Why should I go through that? I thought.

I always wanted to have kids, . . . still do. I'll just be a single mom. But that's another story. But when I think about it, if this rape had to happen to somebody in my family, I was glad it happened to me, . . . out of anybody else in my family. If it had been my sisters, they might not have lived; I think they would have struggled more. All those things I "should have said" and the "things I could have done," they would have done it all. The situation could have been a lot worse.

Later on, the rape sort of made my social life difficult. I didn't date much in high school. When I got to college, I had my first real meaningful relationship, and it [the rape] did affect me. Somehow a relationship I had with this particular woman emotionally triggered something. I remember when she kissed me, I had a flashback of that night in the bushes. I guess other relationships didn't mean as much to me, so it had never affected me in that way. She and I talked about it for a long time—many weeks. Then after that, it seemed okay. I think it was sort of my body's way of telling me, "You need to tell her this." Since then, if someone asks me if I was raped, I'll tell them, but other than that, I don't really feel a need to tell anybody.

I have often wondered if the rapist did that to me because of something that was going on in his life. I never felt sorry for him, but—you know—was this just his way of taking out his frustration of what was going on in his family or whatever, or his way of expressing himself or getting love? I had those thoughts, but I always felt he got what he deserved. And shame on him! But, still, I'm not bitter about all men. I always figured that this was one guy, and everybody is himself. Why should I blame every other male or black male in the entire world? They weren't there. And just maybe if they had been, they might have helped me.

I've also thought it would be interesting to see if there are any differences between gay and straight women and their reactions to rape, since a lot of women—gay and straight—hate men after a rape or are very uncomfortable with them. It would be interesting to see if there are any correlations between the rape and the fact that they were gay. Hmmmm. But then, . . . I don't think either way would be really different. And if you have too many subdivisions you might start to build more prejudices—you know—trying to figure out how to qualify for which category. I guess racial differences are enough to deal with.

I don't think most white women I know would understand some of the things that happened with me. Like when I say how my family reacted to my rape or when I say my mom told my aunt even though I told her not to tell anybody, they ask, "Why did she do that? Isn't that betraying your trust?" The way I grew up, of course you tell your aunt or your uncle or whoever. It's a given that certain things are going to happen in the family and to the family when something like my situation happens. In that way it's good to be able to talk to someone who has a familiar base, so you don't think you're totally off the wall. Maybe we're just culturally different. As black women, I think, we are very family-oriented, and we're focused on protecting our families. I think some of our experiences are different from white women, but then some are similar as just women. If you're black and you talk to a black woman about being raped, you don't have to try to understand all of the differences in your backgrounds and then added to that try to understand what she's trying to tell you about your trauma. I just think it makes it a little easier to tell your story.

While I was in college, I felt there was a lot of ignorance and self-denial that women—black and white—had about rape and sexual violence in general. I saw a lot of women who had boyfriends who beat them up like it was an everyday occurrence. And the women didn't feel as though they should be fighting to stop this. I think we need to let each other know that this is not acceptable and that you don't have to tolerate violence—from *anybody*. That's the only way we can begin to put a stop to violence against women—especially black women—'cause you don't hear them come forward and say, "This happened to me." We need to do it because then maybe our children, our young girls, will see that "this happened to my mom or aunt or cousin or my mom's friend," and realize from a young age that they don't have to tolerate violence—sexual or otherwise. It's fine being strong, but I think we need to be strong in a way to say, "*No!*"—to not allow it—and *not* say, "Well, this guy is my friend; this is my issue; this is my family and *I'll* deal with it." We need to work together. I think by our silence, we are saying it's okay. We should stop fighting these little individual battles. We need to make it as a family of black women.

SHARING WITH JENNIFER

When she arrived that evening, I was standing on my front porch staring into the dark, with policemen rushing about collecting evidence as if I weren't there. As Bessie approached me, her arms were outstretched. She and her husband were relatively new neighbors to whom we had always waved a hand as we hurried off to our respective 9-to-5s. We kept promising ourselves that we would have them over for dessert and welcome them to the neighborhood. We were always "too busy." *This* was our welcome.

A strange greeting as I walked into her open arms saying, "They raped me." "I know," she whispered back. But how do you know? I thought, I didn't tell anyone. And then tears began to burn my eyes. Bessie stayed with me until the last policeman fled, and when the final car was about to leave for the hospital with me and David on board, she asked, "Do you want me to go with you?" I declined her invitation, saying that David was with me. At the very last minute I recanted: "Please . . . I changed my mind. Please go."

And it was Bessie who became my "dresser" for court, gently confiding that my skirts, although "quite lovely," were "just a little too short" for courtroom attire. I had no idea that one had to dress—to prepare—for the role of witness. Bessie gave me her clothes to wear. She knew exactly what to do, what to say. That's how we became friends—and family.

We all need our Bessies, Jennifer, you are right. And I hope what we are doing here—telling our stories—will enable all women to have such friends and support.

WESLYNE, MY MOTHER

Mothers are immortal. . . . Mothers never leave the children they love.

—*Hope Edelman,* Motherless Daughters

In September 1995, near the fourteenth anniversary date of the rape and burglary, I arranged a visit to Washington, D.C., specifically to talk with my mother about the rape. She was extremely nervous about the idea. Realizing the length of time that had passed between the trauma event and my impending visit, reinforced, for me, and I think for her, the profundity of the silence surrounding my rape.

After so many years of holding back, my mother's words at times spilled furiously, followed by moments of silent tears and a shake of her head as if in disbelief. Many times she was overcome with still pent-up anger and, I believe, a grief that she was never allowed to vent. At those moments, I would halt the taping session. As my mother began to tell her story, she referred to "my daughter" as if I were not present; later she began to speak directly to me. I watched her eyes as she talked; at certain moments we did not seem to be in the same place. It was as if she had returned to my aunt and uncle's home of fourteen years ago when she first saw me after the rape. From time to time, she would pause in her recollections, touch my hand, and ask if *I* was all right. Eight months passed before I was able to listen to the tape and present her story, which follows.

MY MOTHER'S TELLING

I'm the mother of a rape survivor. My daughter was raped—one evening in September 1981. The next day was Labor Day. I will never be able to outlive that memory. Every Labor Day I think about it. It should have been me rather than her, but God didn't see it that way.

I found out about the rape when you [Charlotte] called me. The morning had been going along fine, and then I heard this voice that said just "Momma! Momma!" I knew it was not something good—your voice was very strange. You said, "I've been raped! And they robbed me too!" And I said, "Oh, God, how could they *do* that to you?" I called my husband: "Something awful has happened!" After that moment I don't know what happened. I gave him the phone.

I know I ran to the bathroom and beat on the wall. I probably hit my head on the wall too. I was so hurt—so hurt. I just kept crying. Then I said to myself that I had to get myself together because "We've got to go up there to Philadelphia." I just could not believe that anyone would *do* this to my Charlotte—to you. When I came back in the room, your dad just wouldn't talk to me. I said, "Do you know what's happened?" He said, "*Yes! I know.* What are we going to do? . . . What are we going to do?" I said, "We've got to get there—

we've got to get there." He kept saying, "It's awful. . . . It's just so awful." We just kept saying the same things over and over.

Meanwhile, the phone rang and it was David's mother. She went on to tell me the same thing you [Charlotte] had told me. And she said, "We're going to get ready to go up there too." I was *still* in a daze; I just couldn't find myself—you know—and I can't remember exactly what happened. I imagine I must have packed my clothes; I don't remember packing. Naturally I wanted your dad to go with me, but David's parents talked Dad out of it. David's mother negotiated the details; his father was going to drive the three of us since we live in the same city. I wanted Dad with *me*, but being the type of person I am and you know I am, I said, "Okay." David's mother explained: "We don't all want to be in the car together. If something should happen, then they won't have *anyone* to help them." And so that's why we didn't all come together. Maybe they thought Dad was too upset to go. He *was* quite upset. I knew that as soon as we got there you were going to say, "Where's Dad?" and you did. Dad had to go on the train alone. I don't remember driving up there. It was just a *total* blank. All I could think about was getting there, finding this person and actually *killin'* him. I really did.

When I got to Philadelphia and came into the house, you were lying on the sofa. I hugged you and said, "How could he do this to you?! Where *is* he?" I knew you couldn't answer me, but that's what I said. I stayed with you a while and kissed you—hugged and squeezed you. I remember I started to holler. But everybody in the room had to see you; they were waiting their turn to come and tell you how sorry they were. You said, "I feel like they're passing me like a dead body—like I'm on view." You said that. I said, "Thank God it isn't a viewing. He has torn you up in mind only, but your body will still be all right."

I called my sister first; she was the only one in the family I really talked to about the details. I told her to call the rest of the family. I told other people when I returned. No one really could talk about it. And I guess it's just the way it is—even my *husband*, your father, your precious dad, whom I love dearly— just couldn't talk about it. And even today, fourteen years later, he will not talk about it. It hurt me real badly when you said, "I wish he [the rapist] had killed me." When you said that, I said to myself, "Now, I'm *never* going to ask her *again* about that." See that is why Mother hadn't said any more about it. Because I *knew* the way I felt about the whole thing, and because I was afraid you'd say that again. You never told me not to tell any-one. I told everybody you were raped—I didn't keep it from anyone. I just didn't talk to *you* about it.

You forbid me to come to the trial. You didn't want me to come even *after* the trial. You said, "No, Mother. I don't *want* you up here." I couldn't have gotten a gun anywhere, but I might have killed the rapist with my bare hands if I had come up there. I might have disrupted the whole place, and you knew that. I would have had to say something at the trial. So I respected you and I didn't go. I told the priest that I would have killed him—and I would have. I say this again and again to you, and I'll say it to *anyone*. I used the priest as my source of consolation. I couldn't get it from my husband 'cause he wouldn't talk to me about it. When I told my husband I would have killed the rapist, he said, "Oh Wes, don't *say* that." But I meant it. But then, . . . I didn't think he was worth me going to prison and giving up my family, . . . as much as I hated both of them [the rapists]. Even today, every now and then, it comes over me—that bitterness, . . . that need to kill him.

Later on, nobody mentioned the rape to *me*, not even my sister, even though they knew about it. We talked around it. People would say, "Well, it was so bad for Charlotte." But they never asked how you were making out later on. And they *never* asked about *me*. I had to get that on my own. My brothers never asked me either. I talked to my close friend about it, and she just said, "Everything will be all right." I guess I probably would have said the same thing to her if it had been her daughter. 'Cause you don't know until a thing hits home. It's like a person losing their mind or a person being sick. You don't feel it until it's actually in your family or it happens to someone you love. There's *no* one to talk to. That's why something like this takes such a toll. I've read books on rape, and I've filled myself with information of that type. Now I can talk to a person about you without crying.

I remember talking with David the day after it happened. I went looking for him. He was upstairs lying on the bed. When I said his name, he got up and just grabbed me, and we held each other. I can remember some of the words he was saying. He kept saying, "I should have saved her—I should have saved her." I said, "*Saved her*? You did all that you could do." He said, "Oh, I'll never forget that poor guy's face. I'll never forget as *long* as I live. If I could get to him, I would tear them apart." And his face was *bitter* and hard. He was just so . . . in pieces, and I held him in my arms. I told him, "It's all right, David. We're with you. I know how you feel—I can *imagine* how you feel. You're the husband; I'm the mother." That moment was so sad for me. I don't think I could tell anyone what it was really like. He looked like somebody lost—really lost. He told me he had tried. He said the man had the gun at his head—which we found out later. He said he wished he could have taken that gun away from him, but he couldn't. He said, "If I had done it, Mom, he probably would have killed Charlotte and all of us." I said, "Yes, he probably would have." Then he wouldn't say nothing more. He just . . . just growled . . . with anger, . . . lots of anger. That's the only time I talked with David about it. We never talked again. He never mentioned it to me; I have never mentioned it to him. But with the love he has for you, I can imagine how he felt—he was just trying to express it to me. I don't know whether his mother had been up there with him; I don't know. But I do know that he couldn't have been closer to me at that time if he had been my own son. *(She cries.)* I just felt so bad for him. I really did.

I talked to your brother that day too. We hugged and cried, and he said, "Mother, it's going to be all right." I have not spoken to him about it since that day. Sometimes we talk about people in the news being raped and we say, "Well, we know about that." . . . Or something to that effect. And, yes, we *do* know about that. But your brother and I never say any more.

You said you didn't talk to me that night after the rape. But you did. You came to me and said, "Mother, I just can't sleep. I can't sleep." I said, "I know you can't sleep. Come on up here." And I pushed the chair around, and I tried to get on the chair with you. I hugged you, and you were shaking. . . . I rocked you and said, "Charlotte, what did they do to you? Tell me. What did they do to you?" You said, "Mother, two of them raped me." And you told me other things. You said, "It hurt so bad." And then I asked you what else happened, and you said, "I can't go on. You know what happened." "No, I wasn't there," I said. Then you said, "Okay. I'll tell you in detail tomorrow." When the next day came and I asked you to talk to me, you said, "I can't tell you. I can't talk now about that." That was it. I knew then that you couldn't. The other thing I remember—you said, "They took the chain off my neck. . . . I asked them if they wanted any money. They said, *No*, they didn't want no money. They wanted *me* and they called me all kinds of names." You told me the names they called you—"bitch" or something or other like that. You also said that the man who raped you first said, "You think you're a high muckety-muck. I'm in for people like you—that's why I'm doing this to you."

I talked with my doctor, my neurologist, about the rape. I had to tell him because I was having a strange feeling in my head. I just couldn't get things together. He said it could have been because I was worrying so much about you and how you were doing. He said *some* things you can't push back. He said, "You need to come and tell me what happened." So I did. He did some tests and told me I'd had a mild seizure. Also I talked to my friend who's a psychiatrist, and she was helpful. She was the only person I talked to about the details and how I was feeling.

I know I'm not the same person I was before it happened. Only thing I say got me through these fourteen years was God and my faith. I say to mothers—to parents, "If something happens to your child, talk it over with them." I made that mistake by not talking it over with you. I was protecting you. I have not talked to *anyone* for fourteen years—not like this. But thoughts about the rape filled my mind all the time. And you know you would have done the same thing for me if it had happened to me. You would have said, "I'm not going to keep talking about it because every time I talk about it, Mother's going to cry or something like that." I didn't talk to you all these years because I thought I was protecting you. That's what happens—when you love a person.

SHARING WITH MY MOTHER

For so many years I refused—or failed—to explain all that happened to me on that evening in 1981. I could not bear the thought of your eyes filled with my pain. You are strong. You endure and triumph over so much. I trembled at the thought of telling you everything. Against giving you sorrow, I shut my eyes, my memory, my heart.

But you knew. You had always understood everything. Your face held only comfort—strong lines of a mother's unquestioning faith, a prayer that this daughter would find her voice and soar.

Our voices blend now in this survival chorus. I am grateful. I am amazed.

Look at us and know us and you will know yourselves, for we are *you,* looking back at you from the
dark mirror of our lives! [my emphasis]

—Richard Wright,

Twelve Million Black Voices

Part III

THE OTHER HALF
OF SILENCE

Men's Stories about the Women They Love
Who Have Been Raped

... You cannot aid half a people; you have to seek to assist the
men as well as the women of any oppressed group.

—JUNE JORDAN, *CIVIL WARS*

We can put to rest the rape problem in one generation if its eradi-
cation is as important to us as our cars, jobs, careers, sport-games,
beer, and quest for power.

—HAKI R. MADHUBUTI, *CLAIMING EARTH*

To date, the most obvious and long-standing label for the black
man in United States society is "perpetrator." Or as Angela
Davis asserts in *Women, Culture, and Politics*, "the most insidious
myth about rape is that it is most likely to be committed by a Black
man."* The internalized myth of black male sexual deviance, therefore, keeps us all in our respective places—blacks and whites alike.
Women become frozen in stereotypes, unable to support one anoth-

*Angela Y. Davis, *Women, Culture, and Politics* (Vintage Books, New York,
1990), p. 42.

er in the woman crisis of rape and sexual violence, irrespective of race. As a society we absorb the notion, and unwittingly pass it on, that "black men rape white women." And there seems to obtain a contradictory belief: "If black men rape white women, they surely will rape their own." Lost in the terror of this complex stereotype, we relinquish our abilities to know ourselves and to seek the humane support of real people regardless of simplistic racial, class, or gender distinctions.

Accessibility of a victim—geographic, locational proximity—is the usual theory offered for intragroup violence. The simplistic myth of only black men raping only white women is shattered by the usual reported rapes of black women by black men and of white women by white men. There is no criminal surplus in one particular "race" for crimes of sexual violence. And according to statistics from the U.S. Department of Justice, the highest percentage of all reported rapes in 1994 were perpetrated by someone known to the victim (68 percent), not a stranger.* The rapist, therefore, could be a casual male acquaintance, the young man who delivers groceries, the lover of your best friend, a boyfriend, a husband. This, of course, sends flying another popular notion that rapists are always random strangers lurking in alleys or the shadows of office buildings waiting for unsuspecting victims to pass their way—usually after dark. The fact that numbers for reported "date" and "acquaintance rape" surpass those for "stranger rape," brings under scrutiny almost every man one knows—whether he is black or white. Unfortunately human beings who live closest together are the ones who do the most injury to one another.

"Acquaintance rape" and "date rape" are two similar types highlighted in the literature on rape. When a man accused of rape is familiar to a woman as a result of casual contact, I prefer to call the

*U.S. Department of Justice, *Violence Against Women* (Bureau of Justice Statistics, Washington, D.C., 1994).

event "acquaintance rape." The victim and perpetrator, for example, may have been casually introduced at a social gathering or have exchanged little more than a passing nod upon entering a building. I use the term "date rape" when a woman is raped by someone with whom she has agreed to have a social exchange. In neither instance has the woman given prior consent to sexual contact or intercourse.

A distinction should be made between the two types of rape since the terms can be confusing and are often used interchangeably. However, from my own observation and interviews, there seem to be different and more complex aftershocks for women raped by men in an *agreed-upon* social arrangement or date. Invariably, the women in these situations feel a greater degree of responsibility for the criminal violation of their own persons: "How did *I* make this happen?" The third type of rape discussed in the literature—"stranger rape"— is the one least perpetrated, although it is the type most frequently reported to authorities and the one most susceptible to media coverage. I make these separations in type only as clarifications for the reader. In no way do I make judgments concerning relative degrees of trauma. Rape is rape.

Let us now attempt to rework the mythology of the black man as rapist. What if we considered black men as nurturers, caregivers, and loyal "significant others"—roles usually reserved for women and most assuredly reserved for black women? Traditionally, black men are not observed or acknowledged to have these capacities. We hear repeatedly, however, of white men who "stand by their women" in Take Back the Night marches, who carry banners and shout slogans in the college squares. What about black men? Are we afraid to draw attention to their presence in support of our survival lest we, the women involved, be misunderstood as dependent? Would it take away from our long-cherished "strength under adverse conditions"? Why is it that white and black students, women *and* men, cannot seem to address rape issues together on their campuses? In the arena of advocacy, voices of black men have been silenced as well as our

own—silenced in fear of the accusatory phrase accompanying criminal identification: "Yes—*he's* the one." But *all* black men are not
rapists. We must be wary of a categorical silencing.

But why should men's stories be part of a work in which women
speak of their woundings by rape? When I explained my project on
black women and rape to a group of students, I encouraged the men
to tell their women friends about my work, hoping I might get calls
that would lead to interviews. One young man waited for me after
class and inquired about getting help for his friend, a rape survivor,
who lived in another city. His concern for her was touching. Later
the same evening, I replayed in my mind my after-class encounter
with the young man and considered the possibility of including
men in my conversations on rape. From the beginning, shaping
stages of my project, I had been concerned about the possible negative responses of black men thinking they had been slandered by
black women's stories of rape. I wondered if black men would talk
honestly about their part in women's lives. Would they even come
forth? Having black men discuss their supporting roles could well
be another aspect of black women's survival, I further mused. And I
certainly saw the opportunity for telling men's stories about black
women who had been raped as a way to demonstrate that black
men, like all men, are diverse within the category of "maleness."
Some even work to change the status quo for women. And so I
called the young man and asked if *he* would consent to an interview.
"Why me?" he asked in disbelief. "Because I believe you have something to teach me," I replied. Our conversation was more than
either of us had anticipated. It was to be the first of many. Like the
women I've interviewed, these were ordinary men, and they mattered.

Once I had broken my silence with the men of my community,
once I had extended the parameters of survivorship in my project to
include black men in the "unorthodox" role of supporter, I realized
that we, the women who have endured the rape and humiliation,

must now be secure enough to allow such men to support and weep with us. As black women we must recover *all* our systems of support. Without the men of our community understanding the horror and devastation of rape, and without their acceptance of an alternative role in relation to us, we black women and men will continue (as we have been led), to fulfill society's negative prophecy of who we are and what we do.

The men profiled in this section talk about their views on rape in our black communities (I acquainted them with current rape statistics) and about their dilemmas and hardships in supporting women who are rape survivors. Each man was startled to learn that what he had done to support rape survivors was in any way extraordinary. But those who agreed to talk with me had been selected by black women as persons to whom they could disclose—in some instances for the first time. These men became unique because women who survive rape are extremely discerning in who they choose to tell—especially when that person is a man. The men who speak here seem to understand the need for collective action. They share their approaches to supporting rape survivors and attempt to explain what they feel they require and don't have in order to successfully nurture. It is important that these men and others like them know their worth. If we are ever to ameliorate the problems of sexual violence that plague our communities, black women must allow and encourage black men to be concerned about the topic and problem of rape. It is a collective conversation; it should be a community effort.

There were many supportive and caring men in my life at the time of my rape—family members and friends. They were there when others forgot or felt uncomfortable hearing repeatedly my tirades of hate, anguish, and confusion. I did not always solicit their advice or validation. I was embarrassed by what I thought was my own fragility. I was silenced by feelings of guilt. The men in my life had not been taught how to approach me or the topic of rape, and I was in no stable way able to serve as guide. Neither side knew how

to begin a conversation on rape; the topic was too sensitive, bur-
dened with layers of oppression and taboo. Some men do not know
the story of rape. We have never told them. They have not heard *our*
stories of rape—of our sisters, daughters, mothers, and grandmoth-
ers. To be excluded is heartbreaking and lonely. Not being told—
not knowing—the story of the women in their lives, in their community, must make them feel accused. We must tell them the stories and keep retelling them. Black men need the stories to map a
course of action, to become responsible, so sexual violence in our
communities might one day cease.

Men don't always know how to ask the right questions. But once
they learn, they need us to teach them how to hear the answers. And
so, black men have a place here. I have asked them to speak, however briefly. In these men's stories, we have begun a conversation
that breaks the other half of the silence.

JOSEPH, MY FATHER

. . . rape is a men's issue. Rape says much more about men than it ever has about women. Rape is a louder statement about masculinity than it is about femininity.

—*Rus Ervin Funk,* Stopping Rape: A Challenge for Men

When I asked my father for an interview, I expected a cursory refusal. He said he would *consider* the request. Months later I was able to ask the questions I had been waiting to pose for fourteen years. We were finally able to sit face to face and discuss the horror of my having been raped. This was the first time we had talked about what happened to his "little girl" so many years ago.

After the rape, I had spent a few days with my parents in their home, and my father and I took walks around the neighborhood. Mostly, *I* talked. My father remembered those walks. Since that time we both have been tentative and afraid to talk about my rape—as if not speaking about it would make it dissolve. Silence is my father's way of dealing with ugliness and trauma. For him there must be an inside reckoning, a "conversation with the Lord."

My father is seventy-four years old. Although he lives comfortably with my mother in a city not far from my own, we don't see each other as often as we both would like. Until a recent illness, which curtailed some of his activity, my father had been extremely active in church, community, and part-time employment, since retiring from a government job in the mid-1970s. In the past he and my mother visited frequently, but age and illness have slowed their pace. They have always been an integral part of my family life.

My father has always been a supporter of whatever projects, school play productions, or career ventures I entered into—from childhood to adulthood. He has always believed in me. "Why are you doing this? Why bring it all back up?" he would periodically ask, when I told him I was writing a book about black women and rape. However, when he realized I was not turning back, he began to offer support.

MY FATHER'S STORY

My greatest concern was always how you were dealing with the problem and what had happened to you. As far as talking about your rape, I elected *not* to discuss it. I knew what had happened from what you had told me. That was sufficient. I didn't know any details, and I *didn't* particularly care to know any. As long as *you're* doing okay, that's all I care about. I was very *angry* then. I'm still very *angry*.

I first found out about the rape by phone. I'm not quite sure who called. It wasn't until later, when I arrived in Philadelphia, that I learned the seriousness of the attack. We had company when the phone call came. I recall very well we were on the back porch and it was Labor Day; we were having a little get-together—just family. We told them that something had happened. I don't think either one of us [your mother or I] knew the details at that time. But I have *never*, I don't think, *ever* talked to anybody else except my two sisters about it. I guess I was trying to block it out, hoping it wasn't as bad as it turned out to be. I don't think I ever cried. *(He pauses.)* I was angry, but I didn't cry. If I had been there and had the means, I guess, I would have gotten killed. If the person who raped you had had a gun, I probably would have gotten killed. I've thought about that very seriously. If I had to name feelings, it was sorrow—sorrow for you, and anger about the situation that day. I wished it had been *me* instead of *you*. You know? But that wasn't possible. And . . . I was very hurt. *Very* hurt. . . .

When I got to Philadelphia, I remember you were upstairs and you came down, and I was standing at the end of the steps, and it was something I said to you . . . or maybe I put my hand on you or something. . . . I said something wrong or did something wrong . . . and you kind of went to pieces! You didn't exactly cry. You didn't want me to touch you. I had already touched you and you were very upset over that. And I think somebody said something like, "Don't kid her." And that's when things began to sink in for me . . . the trauma you had been through. I *never* even talked to my sister-in-law or my brother, and they were right there in the city. They were the ones who really supported you, more than anybody else. I never discussed it with them as long as my brother lived. *We* knew it. *He* knew it. It was just something that was not a conversation. I don't remember you ever talking to me about it.

I never talked to David about it. I extended to him my concern and my support, but so far as discussing in detail, going back to specifics, I didn't. And I didn't ever talk to my grandson. He never asked me anything. I listened to your mother talk about it to a certain *degree*. And then when it got to a point that I knew it was getting to me, I turned it off. Don't get me wrong. I don't go around with a chip on my shoulder. I only get angry and worked up when I begin to discuss it. Your mother and I still don't talk about it. You kinda deal with things your own way. You think about it, try not to let it take over your mind, and you block out some of it. You say, "Well, it's a situation I can't help. I cannot change it. Let's forget about it." It's through the goodness and power of God that I've been able to deal with the situation as well as I have.

After all these years, I'm still sorry that the individual who did this—and I may end up working this out with God—didn't get *life* in prison! I mean the two of them. So far as the trauma that you went through and the problems that you've had since this, and I'm sure some have been *related* to the rape, David and you have handled it very well. And there's nothing I could do differently.

I am a grandfather and knowing what I know now, I wouldn't mind bringing up the subject of rape with my young grandsons. I believe that a kid growing up in this day and age should be given a pretty good lesson in sex education and the responsibility of the male and the female. But I think a boy's father should handle it. I think as a fighter we glory in Tyson's ability to fight, but kids should be made aware of what he has been labeled as—and then convicted of. I won't go into how I feel personally about that situation, but kids should be given both sides.

The black population is more apt to keep silent about rape than whites. Because I think it's a fact—whether I'm a black man, a black female, or whatever—all white males would be more apt to say they're not going to believe me. No one cares, . . . and white people maintain that type of attitude. That's why most black people don't pursue the legal system. Being a black person, I can understand, and I *agree* in part that they would *not* listen to me as quickly as a white. That's what we are fighting for. This is what the blacks are fighting for today. We have never been put on an equal with whites. We're considered inferior. I'm seventy-four years old . . . and racism still exists. From the time I spent in the tobacco fields of North Carolina to now! It's not quite as bad. I can go more places now, but *deep* down, *deeply rooted*—racism is *there*. And it's no secret. The blacks know it. We have been oppressed. We are not taken seriously when we go to the legal authorities. And that's why the average black person does not *report* incidents like rape. They're afraid they're going to be used again. Knowing what I know now, I would talk to a group at my church about your book and about what's in it—except I'm not as good now with my thoughts as I once was. I can't conduct myself as well as I could before the stroke. I can't do the job that I could do three years ago because I get very emotional now with the least little thing.

I just can't conceive of a man—a black man, or white—committing a rape and at gunpoint. It's not within me to comprehend. I JUST DON'T UNDERSTAND THE INDIVIDUAL who can *do* that. And I hope I will never encounter one who could *rape* a woman, . . . who would *force* a woman to have sex. It's a very *serious* crime, and I just . . . I just cannot understand. I've been reading it in the papers for the last fifty years about people being raped. But not my daughter. When you *read* it . . . you know it's a story. It can't happen to your daughter.

GERALD

*When he told me that I was made for his use, made to obey his
command in every thing; that I was nothing but a slave, whose
will must and should surrender to his, never before had my puny
arm felt half so strong.*

　　　　　　　　　　　　　—*Linda Brent,* Incidents in the Life of a Slave Girl

Gerald is twenty-one and a senior in college. He is of medium
height, and wears his hair short with a neatly trimmed moustache.
In high school he played varsity soccer. Gerald is one of three brothers who grew up in a middle-class, suburban setting before coming
to college. His mother and father strongly promoted the ideals of
college, and Gerald is proud to have followed in the footsteps of his
quite successful older brother, now a corporate executive.

Gerald met Dale while they were coworkers the summer before
her graduation from high school. The summer after their meeting
they became close friends and dated. About a year later, Gerald discovered in a telephone conversation with Dale that she was a rape

survivor. He wanted to talk to me about her rape, if only to try to understand what Dale was going through.

GERALD'S STORY

So far as I know, I only have one friend who is a rape survivor. She told me last summer. She was eighteen when she was raped. I've known Dale since she was a senior in high school—about three years ago now. We were actually involved romantically the summer after I met her. During that summer we spent a lot of time together, and then during the year she just dropped off calling me for almost a year. She didn't even give me a call to say good-bye. So that kinda got me to wondering what actually had happened. After a span of about six months, I called her out west where she lives. She never returned any of my calls. I don't even know if the messages got to her. Eventually she called me; she got my number from the school office last year. We spoke a couple of times before she confided to me what exactly happened. She's fine now. She's active on her campus politically; she's very outspoken.

It was a date rape. She was seeing a fellow who lived around in her neighborhood. Then there was another guy she was talking to at the same time. He was supposedly still very interested in her, but she didn't want to have anything to do with him [romantically]. They were still friends. He was the one who raped her. She just went on a platonic date with him, . . . or at least that's what she thought. And the words that she used were, "I was just taken advantage of." The word "rape" never came out in *any* of our conversations. But I know that's what it was. I just knew. I believe we spoke about the incident just that once. She maybe hinted at it in another conversation. It was very uncomfortable. She said she didn't know what to do. There was *no* support mechanism for her there in her town. She was not able to deal with it all, so she just up and left right after it happened and went West.

I did not use the word "rape" with her. But, like I said, I know that's what it was. I knew it was a sensitive issue, and I was not familiar with how to handle the situation. I didn't want to just straight up say, "So he raped you?" or "How are you dealing with your rape situation?" or something like that. I just asked her a couple of things after she told me [about the incident]: "How are you doing?" "How are you holding up?"

Dale had had a somewhat rough life. Her father leaving her . . . and her mother with several children and some of them at home. I know Dale's a very intelligent person. She had some bad things thrown her way that made her into a stronger person. So when she broke down and told me about being "taken advantage of," I knew it had to be serious. That's why I made the connection about rape. She would not have been so upset if it had been something less than rape. I don't know if there are any varying degrees, but for me rape is rape. So that's why I immediately came to you when I heard you were doing a project on rape. It just kinda clicked in my mind.

Dale is doing all right now. My first reaction when she told me was silence. Complete silence. I think we sat on the phone for about thirty seconds just completely silent. I heard tears in her voice, and it was something way in the back of my mind saying, "Could she have been raped?" At that time she was building up to what happened or to what was going on. Finally she came out and said, . . . you know, . . . "And then he just took advantage of me." I don't know what happened after that. Thirty seconds is a long time when you're just sitting on the phone. I didn't know what words to have come out. I didn't know whether to say, "I'm sorry" or "How are you feeling?" or

"Where is he now?" or "Who have you told?" I mean, all those questions eventually came out, but I didn't know which ones first to say or how to say them. Should I be comforting? What do I *say* to be comforting? Should I be more demanding—like, "Let me go get this guy"? What does she *want* me to do? I just didn't know. I guess I handled it okay.

I think I was the first person she told. She is not close with her mother, and her friends and family are pretty much one big blurred group of people that don't really do much for her. She might have ended up telling her aunt 'cause I think they're close. But I'm not sure of that either. I asked her how well she knew the guy. She had known him for a few years. After the rape I'm not sure if she got help physically. Later on, down the line, I think she got psychological help. I think it was after she started college. But all this happened to her about two years before she went to college. We used to speak a lot . . . maybe once every month. I haven't spoken to her since the end of last semester. I haven't *seen* her since we talked on the phone and she told me about the rape.

I know rape is taking advantage of someone without consent. But to me that means like *any* sort of roughhousing or sexual play without consent. One person is the forcer and the other is the forced. It doesn't necessarily have to be rough as in bruises and stuff, just something where someone is not definitely down with the situation. I don't know exactly if it has to involve penetration. I would say probably in the legal sort of matter, *yes*. But there have been situations where I wouldn't exactly call it rape, but people have been fondled and caressed and kissed and they didn't want it. I call that a *kind* of rape.

I know someone who has raped. He's older than I am. He's in his midtwenties now, . . . somewhere around twenty-six or twenty-seven. I know him because I know the person he raped.

And I don't know if it's a one-time deal with him. I know that it seems like it might be in his character to be like that. But I don't want to go that far to make an accusation. I don't really know him. And I don't know if he still does that sort of thing. I don't know of any particular cases of rape on this campus. But the more I speak with the women on campus, the more I hear that there is a lot more in this community that black women don't speak about. One topic is lesbianism and the other is rape. I have a lot of female friends, and I've been trying to spend a lot of time with them. In some of my conversations with them they've said, "You wouldn't believe how many people have been raped." They just don't want to talk about it. Rape by family members, rape by peers, rape by professors . . . And I have no idea who these people are. But these women who are my friends *do* know. But I didn't ask them to disclose the names.

Knowing all that scares me. It scares me that it hasn't been brought to the forefront so that somebody can help. I don't even know if these women have just not brought it out in public, or have dealt with it on their own, or if they're just completely bottling it up. It alarms me that the number they are hinting at is as large as it is. I guess with rape, self-esteem is involved. I mean, I haven't been raped so I wouldn't know for sure, but I can just estimate how hard it must be for someone *not* to think, "Was this my fault? Did I lead him on?" And if they think that it was all their fault, and they bring it into the public's eye and come out with it to someone they don't know, . . . then I guess they'd *really* start to judge themselves. "Is that person gonna think I'm a bad person?" It's a self-image, self-conscious, self-esteem type of situation. At least in my personal experience, black women are very self-conscious about themselves, the way they look and the way they want to present themselves—not necessarily more or less than white females, but that's just been my experience. And for them to bring a rape to the forefront, that would really start to hurt them.

If I was still interested in Dale in a romantic way, the rape would not keep me from being close to her, . . . seeing her again. Definitely not. But at first I would really want to make sure that she is all right. I would just make sure that she is psychologically and physically all right with herself, as well as against any other standards before wanting to delve into a relationship with her. But I think I'm in the minority of men who would feel this way. For one, I've always had, . . . ever since I've known, . . . more female friends than male friends. My whole family brought my brothers and me up to be very sensitive. So I've been able to listen a lot more to women and hear what they're talking about than the traditional macho image of a man and how he relates to a woman. I've found myself to be in the minority in a lot of different situations because of that. You *might* be able to have conversations with lots of other guys on campus, but I don't know how candid they would be or how often you would hear someone say, "Someone confided in me about being raped, and I handled it like X-Y-Z." You know?

I belong to a fraternity, and we've had date-rape forums. Every year we have hosted a forum with another campus organization. We've had some pretty good discussions. One time we had a large turnout, and the conversation was very candid. We had some role playing where the women and men would act a certain way and then the group was asked, "How would you react in this situation?" "Was she raped?" "Was he in the right, or was she in the right?" "Who was wrong?" It was a good situation. I think one of the most prevalent issues among black males—this is *my* opinion—I never want to speak for the black male race or anything like that—has been that there's always been a gray area about what exactly is "consent." That's really what the black males speak up the most about—settings where

the woman will say yes and then act a certain way that's contradictory. You know? How do you read it? How do you judge it?
And then it's kind of like a gamble. If you stop, and start to
walk away, and she pulls you back as she's saying, "No, I don't
want this to happen," and she's pulling you forward and hug-
ging you more and more, . . . then that's when the males are
like, "Well, why then are we at fault? Why are we the ones that
are getting bashed here? She's acting one way and saying something else. Or she's saying yes but pushing me away." That's
what's always been the most argued point about date rape with
males. *My* one point is communication. It's so important. In
the fraternity, we have talked about communication with
women, but not about rape itself or how to handle those contradictory situations. Romance is nice, but believe me romance
has become very mechanical and chemical . . . you know? You
really have to be so straightforward. It's hard to be smooth
nowadays.

For me the first step to try to stop rape in the African
American community would be to go the churches. That's
where I feel that I would get the best cooperation and the most
interest from black males. At least within *my* church—it's
Baptist—we have a number of black male leaders who are in
the business world and the larger community. I see the church
as the meeting point—the first place to find people that are
trying to take action or at least trying to speak up. At least I
would know that they would be in the right mind-set to go out
and help others. At the campus level, I guess I'd start to encourage people to set up a specific counseling service for rape victims—a specific service for the black community so that black
women and men feel comfortable going to them. So that
they're not calling up on some 1-800 hotline for the university
and speaking with a random operator about these intimate sexual details. So that they can go to someone they know or go to

someone they can at least relate to on an African American vibe and relate what's happened.

There's a lot of gossiping that goes around within the small black family—in the black community at the university. It's so tight, and everybody after a while starts to know everybody else's business, or at least they know what's going on. It's not the same with the white community on campus; there's more of them [whites]. I think there are some differences in how we act on dates and what we expect. I think on this campus there is more alcohol involved with whites when they date. If communication is the biggest problem, we need to set some sort of forum in place that can facilitate, that can ease these communications on campus—between black females and males and between blacks and whites.

When I think of black men and women and rape, a couple of things flash through my mind. The first one is the image of the black man's fantasy of the white woman that everybody has about us. If that were true, then you would think that there would be more of a tendency for stranger rape, a black man with a white woman. The other image that comes to mind is the idea of how promiscuous the black male supposedly is. I see now more of a responsibility on the black male to start to understand the statistics about rape and see that this is happening in the community. There should be more communication. Black men need to take action against stereotypes and against rape. We should not leave it completely upon the women's lib movements to say, "We've been raped." We need to say, let's fix this whole anomaly. *We* understand what's going on. We're trying to work amongst ourselves here to bring changes as well.

AMOS

In the history of the United States, fraudulent rape charge stands
out as one of the most formidable artifices invented by racism. The
myth of the Black rapist has been methodically conjured up when-
ever recurrent waves of violence and terror against the Black com-
munity have required convincing justifications.

—*Angela Y. Davis,* Women, Race, and Class

Amos is a tall, slender, assertive twenty-two year old, with a contagious sense of humor. He grew up in a household of women. Early
on he became comfortable being the only male in the house and has
always felt particularly protective of his two sisters. When he interviewed with me, he was a senior in college—the first in his family
to attend a university. He was very active in campus organizations
and was determined to make changes in his own family and for the
"generations to come." Amos "talked big," but I had the impression
that under it all was a fear of what would be expected of him later,
after college.

Amos's relationship with Mae was a platonic one. They spent
hours talking about their shared campus experiences as well as the
inner-city neighborhoods in which they had learned their first

lessons. Amos was devastated when Mae disclosed to him her sexual assault; he tried to provide support. As he talked with me about her continuing ordeal, it became apparent that he was disturbed not only by *her* pain, but about his own inability to make a difference. Mae was twenty-two years old when she disclosed to Amos a rape that had occurred when she was eight. Perhaps Mae was like the sisters he'd left at home.

AMOS'S STORY

I talk to women as women and individuals—as a friend first and foremost. And although my intentions may be to get involved romantically, that's the first objective for me—to get to know that *person*. At the time Mae told me about herself, we were taking a class together and we were talking about things in general. I asked her if she would help me with a class project about "defining sexuality." She was by far my closest female friend at college, and I felt comfortable talking to her about sexuality and stuff. During the course of my interview with her for the class, she told me about the rape. I don't know why. Actually she's pretty comfortable I think with her experience, . . . in accepting it, . . . because she said, "I thought I had told you." But she hadn't. And I think I probably overreacted when she did tell me.

My reaction was total disbelief! I was probably more emotional than what she thought I should be, . . . but she was just a little *girl* when it happened. She said, "It's been such a long time. Why are you reacting like this? I'm fine! And everything's okay." Of course, I kept on probing: "How are you? How does this affect your relationships?" She kept saying, "It's *okay!* I'm fine!" I felt helpless. I didn't know what to do, what to say. But, you know, no one has a scarlet letter on their clothes, and you can't tell that someone has been raped or molested. I just really felt sad for her. I also felt very proud of her because she had been able to work this thing out and get over it, and, you know, she's getting on with daily life.

At the time, Mae was going through a transition. I guess, a lot of introspection. Trying to figure out things in her life spiritually. I always thought she was a strong woman. I think when you look at Mae, you can't help but see a pillar of strength just by her size alone. But she also gives this impression by her presence and the way she carries herself. So if anything changed after she told me of the rape, I had a greater sense of respect for her strength as a person. To have gone through something like that, been a survivor, and still have managed to have healthy relationships with men, or relatively healthy relationships, is something to be proud of.

When Mae told me about the rape, I saw it as an extension of her arms, I guess to bring me in closer to her by sharing that experience with me. By sharing an experience like that you can't help but become closer to another person. Perhaps that was some of the reasoning behind her telling me. I guess she really believed in our friendship, and I felt it was very important for her to divulge this information in order for me as a friend to understand some of the things she had gone through. Mae and I have a very affectionate relationship. And in my experience in handling traumatic situations, I think sometimes it's best just not to say anything. That was pretty much the way I handled it. I didn't say anything at first. I did touch her, so there was contact between us. I squeezed her hand. But verbally I wasn't saying anything. I was just sort of there to listen. And she knew that. But there really wasn't *much* silence—primarily because it had been more than ten years after this rape had occurred. After she told me, I asked her how she felt about it. She said she felt a sense of justice had occurred because this guy was caught and put in jail. Then she had to deal with her own scars, her own emotional scars after that. But at least knowing that her perpetrator had been found and put behind bars really made her feel good.

We are both in an organization that tries to actively come to some sort of solutions or some sort of understanding about how we relate to the opposite sex based on individual experiences. She is definitely working through lots of issues. Because not only was she raped, but she didn't have any strong male figures in her family at all—during her whole upbringing. And the men that *were* in her life were nonproductive. There was the classic case of the matriarch in her family; all the women were taking care of everything. That's what Mae's accustomed to. So in her relationships with men she pretty much wants to exert a lot of influence, a lot of power, and she's trying to work through that. That can scare a man off. No matter what, I intend to remain friends with Mae. . . . Absolutely!

I must have been about eight or nine when I first heard the word "rape" used. A lot of the public schools, at least in my city, give these films about not going with strangers and not accepting candy. It was one of those films, I think. So I guess my earliest thoughts on rape involved molestation of children and it really wasn't that specific. It was someone more or less being taken advantage of. Rape became something to do with girls my own age around seventh or eighth grade. There was a lot of explanation about younger women that are twelve or thirteen years old talking to older guys—about sixteen or seventeen—and the whole idea of "taking" sex as opposed to an exchange. We called it "jailbait." It was pretty much an older guy having no business being with a younger woman. And I knew that you could be charged with rape. But it was a term that was used almost in jest, I think. No one really took it literally.

College was the real awakening for me about this whole rape issue. For the most part, the masses haven't had an opportunity to go to college and learn about some of these issues. They are only learning it through television via talk-show hosts or [ABC's] *20/20* or what have you. We really don't have a handle on what this whole rape issue is. But the rude awakening— "becoming sexually accountable" is the term I would use—was in college. As a sixteen or seventeen year old in high school, there's a certain level of irresponsibility that you're sort of granted in a lot of arenas, not only sexual. It's not necessarily *given* by parents or the establishment, but you give it to yourself. A sixteen year old, even a fourteen year old, can be a rapist. But you say, it's okay *because* I'm young and naive to act irresponsibly, and so you do some wild and crazy things 'cause you think nothing really is going to happen to you. But once you turn eighteen, you're *sexually accountable* for your actions, and there are consequences for your actions as well!

Within the fraternities there are men who have a great deal of respect for women and treat them accordingly. *Also* there are men in the fraternal system who *don't* have a great deal of respect for women and treat them accordingly. And what happens unfortunately is that you don't have enough men joining these fraternal organizations with a firm sense of who *they* are and how they're going to react and respond to women before they get involved. It's a lot easier for them to be swayed toward the negative as opposed to the positive, and that's probably what's happening. That's what people see when they look at fraternities—black or white.

I would not say that the fraternal system is "pro-woman." For the most part, I think women are objectified. But I see it as a two-way situation because unfortunately there are *women* out there who are turned on, . . . I don't know how you want to really phrase it, . . . by men who are a part of fraternities.

Because of the Greek letters you sport across your chest, you're given some sort of absolute respect or admiration for the things that you've gone through to get those letters. And women help to perpetuate this attitude. I think it's just insane. It's not just a one-sided story. It's definitely a two-way street. The reason men view women as objects has to do with the sexual arena. There is no other way of looking at it. You're at a fraternity party, and everyone's drinking, having a good time, dancing and doing their thing. I'm not faulting anyone who chooses to have a one-night stand or to sleep with someone after a party or whatever, but until women decide not to sleep with a man so soon, it's always I think going to continue to happen—the objectification.

Women would like to *think* that men don't view them in that way, but that they're just becoming more liberated sexually and they're going for theirs. Unfortunately, I don't think women who do that have a positive impact on the liberation of women. The way I see it, there are percentage-wise *very few* women who are truly liberated sexually. The vast majority *want* to be liberated sexually. They have these concepts of what a liberated woman should be about, but they get involved in situations that they find themselves not being able to control. When they get into a situation, they might think it's fine. "All I really want to do is screw this guy. He really turns me on. We have a really great time in the bedroom." Then what happens is . . . the term is "catching feelings,"* . . . the women start catching feelings for this guy. Unfortunately, there are many more women than men who view love and sex as synonymous. The women get caught, the guys leave, and that's generally what happens. Nowadays there just isn't much talking going on with sex.

I know a guy who is now viewed by a lot of black women on

---

*Generational jargon meaning "an arousal of sexual interest and emotional attachment."

campus as a rapist. He's still a friend of mine. I don't trust him particularly, but he made a practice of getting women drunk either by playing games or having them smoke marijuana with him, then getting them high or drunk and trying to screw them. That was his strategy for getting women. I don't know if *he* thinks of it as rape. We don't discuss it. He's a pretty forceful guy, you know, pretty determined to get whatever he wants. I haven't spoken to anyone firsthand who has accused him of raping them. This is just something I heard from a female friend of mine about him. But I wasn't surprised either, just because of the things I had seen when I was around him.

To be truthful, I don't think that women and rape—black women and rape—has even been discussed in *one* conversation I've had with any of my male friends. Guys would think I was weird if I brought up the topic. My fraternity hosted a workshop on date rape, and we got a pretty good turnout. I don't know why there is no other talk about it. I think most black women credit themselves with being more intelligent and more wise than white women about sexual situations. But this is *my* perspective on it. I hear black women saying things like: "I don't understand white women. They do some of the most stupid, insane things. I would *never* have done that. Not that she asked for anything, but she put herself in a very precarious situation that really got out of hand. *I*—on the other hand—would *never* have gotten into that situation to begin with." I think, primarily, black people don't see rape as *our problem*. It *is* our problem.

Sometimes black women *do* look down on black women who get raped . . . maybe who get raped by strangers. But a lot of black women I've spoken to about the subject say that their friends—or *they*—were victims of incest. An uncle or father or cousin. It's almost like, I don't want to say "acceptable," but it's like they feel it's easier to understand how they could have been

vulnerable in that familiar, family-like situation. I think that a
woman who is forced to do something—anything—that she
doesn't want to do sexually, that's rape! And I think she has to
say no. A guy wants to hear "*No*." Most of the guys I know are
not trying to risk rape, or being accused of rape. Being *accused*
is enough to question your integrity. It doesn't have to be
proven.

Unfortunately, I think a lot of black men have reverted to
utilizing their penises to exert their manhood. So that may very
well be some sort of reason, if you will, for rape. Some sort of
power that black men are trying to exert, that they don't have.
The definitions of manhood in America are very Eurocentric
viewpoints—that is, the man should be the sole provider for his
family financially. As black people we really don't have an eco-
nomic base, so it's very tough for a man to provide that for his
family. So for the black man who wants to define manhood in
just financial terms, he's going to be disappointed. I think in
their battle to try to secure some sort of dignity—some sort of
manhood in this society—this is what black men maybe are
resorting to, . . . raping and using the phallus as a tool of
power. Unfortunately, it shouldn't be power over our own
women—or over *any* woman. It should be power over something else. I was sad when I heard the statistics for black-on-
black rape—that black men would put black women through
that kind of pain and that kind of horror.

The community starts with the family. And that family starts
with a partnership between the man and the woman, working
together. That means if the woman is a better provider than the
man, then she provides; and if the man is a better nurturer for
the kids than the woman, then he nurtures. It's a collective; it's
a union. We have to view the family as the cornerstone to
building our nation, and we gotta operate together to give back.
We gotta live for our kids. In America, we have a very narrow

definition of what family is all about. It has to shift. Because our families don't always have two partners, two kids, a garage, a dog, a lawn, and two weeks' vacation.

Education—getting down to the grassroots level and helping people understand we can't operate individually and excel—is the answer to changing things. Until we start operating collectively and cooperating, the negative situation regarding rape, and everything else for black people, is going to persist. Wherever I am, I'm going to do whatever I can. I want to be able to give something positive back. And that's going to be a part of me and the way *I* operate.

ZACHARY

*. . . old ideas die slowly, especially the notion of sexual provocation
and false accusation, and in the prosecution of a rape case, the
defense attorney typcially attempts to impeach the victim's
credibility by addressing rape as a crime of passion, implying that
the victim has aroused such desire.*

—A. Nicholas Groth,
Men Who Rape: The Psychology of the Offender

Zachary is about 5'10", athletically built, and intense. As we spoke,
he nervously pushed his wire-rimmed glasses back on his nose. He
is a forty-four-year-old high school teacher, married with two children. We met at a conference where participants spent the day discussing their teaching and current work projects. When I told him
I was writing a book on black women and rape, Zachary disclosed
that years ago he had been involved with a woman who was a rape
survivor. We continued our conversations during the course of the
three-day conference, and on the last day, Zachary gave me permission to use his story. Even though the experience for Zachary was
many years past, it is one that remains vivid in his memory. He says

it is a "moment in my life I will always remember" for the things it taught him about himself and about a woman for whom he still cares.

ZACHARY'S STORY

At the time I was about thirty-one or thirty-two, and Alice was twenty-four. I was single. Although Alice told me during the first period we dated that she had been raped, I had not remembered it. She told me again when we started dating a second time. She was upset that I had not remembered: "But I *told* you!" she said—as if I should have remembered. She had so much faith and trust in me, so my not understanding—my forgetting about her disclosure of rape—meant to her that I was unable to deal with who she had become.

Alice never got therapy after her rape. She had been on a date with her boyfriend. She was eighteen and at college. Someone hijacked them on the road in the small town where she was living. The man told her boyfriend to get in the trunk of the car. She said she would have fought him, but he threatened to kill her boyfriend if she didn't give him what he wanted. She doesn't remember how long they were out there in the woods. After he raped her, he let them go. She did not go to the hospital, but went back to the dorm. She told someone at the dorm; I don't know who. But I do know that there were no charges. *And* I know that the rapist came back looking for her. It was a small town and a small school. She said, "He came back for me!" She has brothers and she never told them or her parents.

The rape had a lot to do with our relationship. It got in the way. I think it's one of the main reasons our relationship did not work. She did not want to touch or be touched. We slept together but we had no sex. I couldn't fulfill her notion of what a partner should be. Then the time came when I *did* want to have sex and she didn't. It changed the nature of the relationship. It was strange, but our sense of closeness had to do with our reluctance to talk about the rape. But still I kept going back and forth—we were a long distance apart—to see her even though we didn't sleep together. We had lots of common interests, and we still had a real sense of closeness. I think she felt safe with me because I had just separated from my long-time girlfriend; I didn't want or need to get involved sexually, and Alice didn't want to either—for different reasons. The fact that she had been raped had a lot to do with it. We looked good on paper, but the relationship didn't work.

When I first met Alice, I was pretty down on women and cynical since my girlfriend and I had just split up. I was in and out of dating relationships. Alice was probably the one person with whom a relationship was comfortable. We didn't expect anything of one another. And I found out very quickly with Alice that I had to tell and *do* the truth. I definitely couldn't play games with her. I had to be serious about what I said and did. What was uncomfortable was that I found out that *I* could fail her, and her other men couldn't. She was looking for success from me. Soon after we started seeing each other, I found out that she had invested so much in me, and she was expecting a return on the investment. I was just looking at the two of us as equals. She was sharing secrets with me. I was very special to her, but I didn't see it. When I realized it, it blew me away. The highs and lows of her—the unpredictability—I didn't understand. That I could fail her really didn't come to me 'til years later.

After Alice told me of her rape, she became sacred to me. I could adore her. I could love her. I could not touch. She pushed me further away, even though I grew closer to *her*. It was an unsettling duality. I felt I was in the position of therapist. We'd talk for hours. She'd say, "Zach, I've shared *everything* with you, things no one else knows. I've been spiritually and mentally intimate with you. I can say anything to you, and you should be able to do the same with me." At first I couldn't give anything back. She placed a crown on my head, and it was too heavy to bear. I didn't want to be another man, another person to disappoint and fail her.

Then there came a period in her life when she would sleep with anyone—one-night stands—it didn't matter. She would say, "Fucking is one thing and intimacy is another. What I have with you is intimacy. I feel much closer to you than to the men I fucked. Making love is one thing, but being close to you is more special." That bothered me a great deal. I wondered if we *had* been physical if I would be someone she just "fucked." So we never had sex. That "specialness" has been preserved.

Her rape—violation—affected her, and I wanted to "minister" to her. I wanted to be the one to make it all better. Her call for "space" or for "closeness" was never clear. She didn't always know either. The more we got to know one another, the worse it got. Here was someone I loved, someone with whom I could be fulfilled. But because of the rape, she didn't want kids, and she didn't want to be married. Because of *those* two things, I didn't want to stay with her.

There was consistently more tenderness on my side, even when she *seemed* not to want it. Maybe it was all a mask. It was so confusing. She would say, "You should have said this; you should have done that." I couldn't seem to get it right for her. So I decided to keep a distance. That's what she *seemed* to need. I thought, I'll try to treat her more special, more sacred. She was not like other women. It was like she wanted me to treat her special and at the same time treat her like everybody else. So I began to settle in my own comfort zone where she was concerned. Instead of going toward the pain, I pulled away. I didn't know whether I could pay the price.

We still talk a few times a year. We found that we could still be friends. When we talk, I can still feel the pain, the anger, the bitterness. She still has never told anyone [else], and she swore me to silence. She's working now and going to school. I guess I thought I had handled the issue of her being raped by being celibate, but I've learned over the years that sexuality and rape are separate. I thought they were the same.

Alice has changed how I regard women in general. I see her as being courageous and strong. The frightened woman—the scared, wounded woman in back of the courageous warrior woman—has made me much more sensitive to other women. I had Alice pegged a certain way, but as the layers fell away, I learned more and more about her. When I have a son, as soon as he learns language, I will start teaching him about women and how to be soft. The macho ethic of the black community works against us. I have two nephews and someone told one of them, "You're crying like a girl." That's not good. Women are seen as victims, and men are not supposed to cry. And so we have women acting like victims, and men who are afraid to show their feelings. Without a doubt, knowing Alice has changed my life.

DAVID

Sassafrass looked around to see if there was something else she could make to make them feel more like loving each other and hitting sunrise with hope. . . .

— *Ntozake Shange,* Sassafrass, Cypress, and Indigo

David is my husband. At the time of the interview, he was fifty-two years of age. David began his story strong of voice, with conviction. He did not seem to understand his own courage during our mutual ordeal or his stolid perseverance through the years after my rapes.

But quickly he returned to that evening long ago. His voice changed. He filled with the emotions of that distant moment. Throughout his nonstop narration, he referred to me only as "my wife." It was as if I were not there—as if the "me," a healing and articulate "interviewer," did not exist. Obviously, David was a speaker who had never told, to anyone, this *particular* story of his soul. He was a man silenced, now invited to speak. Hours passed. His voice grew weary, mirroring the dead slump of his body. Light changed in the room where we sat. With few interruptions or questions from me, finally, David stopped talking. "Are we done?" I asked. He nodded, "Yes."

David's voice is heard now—without interruption.

DAVID'S STORY

The rape took place fourteen years ago, in 1981, and it occurred in our house. I was in our house with my wife and our son, nine years old. Someone broke into our house at gunpoint. There were two men, young and black. They both raped my wife.

When we heard the crash, it never occurred to me or my wife that someone had broken into our house—was actually *in* our house. I went downstairs to investigate. I went into the living room—I didn't turn on lights. I went into the dining room, picked up a vase for a weapon. As I got to the door leading from the dining room to the kitchen, I was confronted by a young black man with a gun. And from that point, events unfolded horribly and fast. He told me to put the vase down and get on my knees. I did it. He asked how many people were in the house and who they were. Then he told me to stand up. He marched me with the gun at my head into the front hall, where he told me to call my wife to come downstairs. I *did* that. And I told her not to *do* anything because there was a man with a gun and we were being robbed. I don't remember if he said, "Get down here, bitch," but something like that. The language that began when he came in the house was all "bitches," "niggers," "fuck this," "damn," and "shut the fuck up." I know he said something to her.

When she got downstairs, he held me and put the gun to her head and told her to turn off the alarm. "And if this alarm goes off, I'll blow your head off. I'll kill you," he said. Neither one of us knew why he wanted the door open. We thought he was going *out*. But as soon as the door was unlocked, it was like a gush of violence came rushing in—although it was awfully quiet . . . everywhere, . . . a strange kind of quietness. On the street and in the house—everything sort of went to that moment. Another person—very *big*, it seemed, and more violent and rough—rushed into the house. Then, there was pushing and shoving, confusion, noise. . . . I don't remember who said what, then.

The next thing I knew, our son was coming down the stairs in his pajamas. At first, I wasn't sure why or how he was coming down the stairs. Then, I remembered: the first man had gone upstairs. He was coming back down with our son. By this time my wife and I were both on the floor, face down, in the front hall. I kept saying, "Please don't hurt my family. Take whatever you want. Just don't hurt my family." I kept saying that. When I did, the second black man kicked me in my face. He said, "Shut the fuck up." I remember my wife telling our son not to be afraid and holding him.

Then, the men said they were going to take me upstairs. I remember the person who was speaking did not seem brutal to me at that moment. But still it made no sense for me to be upstairs. Now, though, I suppose it was to avoid resistance on my part. His almost niceness threw me off guard. And I was still saying, "Don't hurt my family." They were insistent that I had to go.

One man stayed downstairs. That was strange to me. The other one took me upstairs. He pushed me onto the bed in mine and my wife's bedroom, tied me up, with my hands and feet behind my back. He put the spread on the bed over my head. I could hear him going through drawers in our bedroom. I lost track of time. I heard my wife cry. I asked: "Where's my wife?" "She's in the next room," he said. I kept asking. The next thing I knew, my son was beside me, tied, scared, under the spread. I couldn't see who brought him. I told him not to be afraid. I kept talking to him. After what seemed like forever, my wife was there too.

I don't remember *seeing* her! Maybe it was the way we were lying, the way we were tied. I told her not to be afraid. She said she was all right. We had to breathe—like we were running—to keep from screaming. There was pulling, jerking—the opening of closets, drawers—suitcases zipping, unzipping. I thought we were going to be killed.

But there was still quiet all around us. The street was quiet. Except for the noise *they* were making, our house was quiet. I don't even remember the humming of appliances, creaking of floors. After we listened to them going in and out the front door so many times, we finally heard a car engine start, and I said, "They're gone!"

It wasn't until we were outside, on the porch, that my wife told me about the rape. I think she said, "I've been raped" or "He raped me." I don't remember. I said, "Which one?" And she answered, "Both of them." She was shivering. Her face was broken—like she had come in from falling in a pond that was frozen. . . . I realized the porch light was on. And then everything seemed to "come up"! Things began to happen—like in a movie script—life all of a sudden just started. I went to get our neighbor and brought her back to the house. My wife had been saying over and over, "I need to talk to somebody. Can you get Bessie?" And I had kept saying, "We don't need anybody. I need to stay here. We can't go now." I finally realized why she was saying that.

Detectives and police were all over the house. Lots of bustling. Lots of questions. I was so *angry!* I remember punching the wall—breaking the wood in the front hall. And I don't

know where our son was during that time! I don't know if he
went next door, or if he was around in the house. I don't
remember where my wife was. I was lost. But my wife told me
that out on the porch I had told her I loved her and would
always love her. I don't remember it. People were everywhere in
our space. Then it was time to go to the hospital.

Bessie, our neighbor, went with us. In the car, my wife was
sitting in the middle. It was such a rough ride.

I didn't know where I was. I'd never seen these streets before.
They were all very dark. My knuckles were swelling where I had
hit the wall. But that was good. The pain was something I
could put my mind on, so I wouldn't lose my mind. Riding in
that car—the only thing I could think of was getting rid of her
being raped. It was like the hospital would *do* that. Because it
was a medical place. It was like she had an infection, or a bad
cut. It was like we were going to an emergency room after
something has happened and left you hurt.

When we got there, I *knew* that emergency room. It was
familiar. It was a Sunday, so the place was not crowded. There
didn't seem to be any people *anywhere* in the world for some
reason that night. It was the small hours of the morning by
then—about two or three o'clock.

I remember a man came into the emergency room wearing a
kind of orderly shirt, blue or green. He said something about
"I'm going to help you. . . ." It was emergency-room-nursing
language. He called my wife, "Hon"! He did *not* look like help
to me. But I felt pretty helpless, so I didn't really know what
help looked like. My wife said, "Could I please have a woman
nurse?" He was *not* pleased. He got huffy and seemed insulted.
But we got a woman nurse, and she was very solicitous. I don't
remember a doctor. There must have been one, since I now
know somebody had to get a "rape kit." I do remember my wife

getting an injection. But I don't think I was in the room; maybe Bessie was. My wife screamed so loud, . . . so loud.

We must have thought to bring clothes with us—or maybe Bessie told us to. My wife asked if she could take a shower after all the medical business was over. They led us to a room nearby.

I can still see that shower in slow motion. She got in with her clothes on. And it was like every piece of her clothing came off with pain—like a burn victim being debrided. The look on her face was just so blank, weary. And I still thought that the medicine, the hospital would make it better after the shower. But people had already done what they were going to do. She had become so fragile, like—will-less.

I don't know what happened to the other clothes my wife wore to the hospital. I guess we threw them away—or maybe they were evidence. I don't remember having *anything* when we left, cause I *didn't* have anything. I didn't have a wallet; I didn't have ID; I don't remember keys. I *must* have had *keys*. I felt naked.

Then we went to the police roundhouse. There was a room, a desk, a typewriter. I don't think they wanted me there with my wife, but I wasn't going to leave her. They could have been trying to protect me—so I wouldn't hear what she had to say. But I couldn't leave my wife. I listened to her tell what happened to her. She was detailed and chronological and sequential. Her story seemed to go on forever. Her voice was fragile, but it was not broken. She did not cry. I now realize she was in shock. I must have been in shock too. I don't remember being tired. I don't remember thinking about bed or sleep. I certainly had no idea of a plan.

We left the roundhouse at dawn—the daylight was there! I never thought I'd see day.

The night of the rapes and robbery—I was so angry. . . . I felt like I wanted to kill the people who had done this to my wife. And I felt really really sorry for her. I felt guilt that I could not—*did* not—stop that rape from happening. I felt like a weak coward . . . and, I didn't feel anything was dirty or evil about *her* . . . that she had been *ruined*, or even soiled.

I felt that she had been hurt, and I wanted to destroy the people who had hurt her. I didn't think about whether it would make *her* feel better. I felt it would make *me* feel better. Maybe it was a male code of honor. Maybe I felt I *owed* that to her. There was a sense of wanting revenge, vengeance. I *never* hated black men who are called "black underclass males" before that moment. But, at that moment, I hated *all* of them. I would have been glad to take a flamethrower and wipe out the entire United States population of them—their music and their clothes, their hair, their eyes—without blinking an eye! . . . I know there's a self-hatred in that. But that's how I felt.

A very slow process of locating one of the perpetrators of the crime helped to change my feelings. My wife prosecuted. One of the men was caught, the first one who came into our house. At a bank machine, where he used the PIN number, there was a camera. It took a picture of him. He was found guilty and put in prison. That was cathartic. The trial and prosecution, resulting in conviction and a heavy sentencing, made the blame more specific. But I still hated "them."

After all the trial business was over, there was still the aftermath of the rapes. I felt rage, sorrow, frustration, . . . aversion toward my wife, . . . and the urge to leave my marriage.

I think I grew very angry with my wife because we could not be intimate like we had been. Touching could not be done. Before all that happened . . . I could touch her spontaneously and without thought. But our sex life became a nightmare, or nonexistent. Everything had to be programmed. My firm conviction was that she could not enjoy sex . . . with *me*. Not because there was no desire, but because she could not separate the act of sex—even with me who loved her and who she loved—from the trauma of the rape. . . . She was afraid at every sound. We were on twenty-four-hour, every-second alert against the unknown. And as a man who enjoys sex and who had enjoyed a healthy, active, satisfying sex life with my wife—and she with me—I felt horrible. . . . I had fantasies of this *never* having happened. Or, of simply saying I can't deal with this anymore. My fantasy was of moving to another place—in the country, in the United States, or abroad—and finding a normal, *free*, spontaneous, nonraped woman. Put the past behind me, completely. It sounds horrible, . . . but that is how I felt.

I equated the horror of rape with an illness. With an illness, the *patient* has specific physical things to concentrate on—even mental things to work with, to get beyond. But the person who *attends* the patient, or a wife or loved one who has been raped—has all his everyday life obligations to satisfy, whatever they may be. He has to concentrate on being normal. The caregiver, the "protector," is not *supposed* to be sick—not supposed to miss a single beat of time.

So, he is expected to go on with work and social life and keep the household running, and at the same time be the perfect guardian, helpmate, nurse. The caring is so unrelieved! Even nurses have *shifts*! And because the patient *is* the patient—or the rape survivor—she is completely focused in her emotions, feelings, realizations of pain. She becomes totally and silently absorbed in her trauma. The person who is the helper and the intimate "other"—who's *supposed* to be intimate—is really just a *body*, viewed and seen—and maybe not even that, since sometimes he's not even sure he is always seen. Nobody comes to the hospital to see how the *nurses* are doing! I was very much alone, . . . or at least I felt that way. I didn't have the *words* to explain what I felt or what we were going through.

I tried therapy once. It was a complete disaster. The person I chose was wrong. Or maybe I wasn't ready for therapy. But then, about a year and a half later, I entered a counseling program. It was extremely helpful. But I don't think the therapist had a *clue* about rape or rape surviving. I think what he realized was he had a *guilty* man on his hands—a man who was frustrated and longing for escape. I really think if my wife and I had gotten therapy together—if we had been able to find someone—we might not have had such a difficult time. But she didn't trust anybody; and I guess I didn't much either. The truth of the matter is we were career people, workaholics, type A. We had not even investigated the possibility that we needed marriage counseling *together*. We thought we could take care of anything *ourselves!* Our relationship had always been very private. Even our parents weren't privy to even the *remotely* intimate parts of our life. I think if we had done therapy together, it would have made a difference. But within our marriage—and our family of three—there was complete silence. I was complicitous, totally, in the silence. It would, somehow . . . just get better.

The marriage and our family continued by sheer force of will. I was determined that they would go on, that we would be sheltered, fed, clothed. That our son would be protected, educated, made to feel, as much as possible, that my wife and I were living *together*. But we really weren't. We were sleeping in the same bed, occupying the same house, but were not living— period. Certainly, we were not living together. We had a very good masquerade—a mask of normalcy. This went on for four or five years. In many ways, it was a prison term—maximum security. We abandoned friends—to some extent, family. I never thought to ask how she felt about the marriage—whether she wanted to stay or not. I didn't ask because I was acting—or so I thought—*for* her. She had counseling, but she still could not walk down the street by herself, in broad daylight. She certainly couldn't go to the door of our house by herself. I didn't know about counseling, so I couldn't tell whether her counseling—or mine—was good or not. We were together almost all the time; I never thought any of it was abnormal. I thought things would have to get better with time. I *willed* it to get better.

The turning point came when my wife began to work again. She was able to get herself back up and running on the work front. She was in graduate school. After a few years she even finished a degree! But we left the city for a year—almost exactly one year after the rapes and robbery had occurred. It was a different place and a different house, but unfortunately it was not a *safe* house. We were just as vigilant in that house as we had been—if not as frightened—in the house where we were robbed and brutalized and had moved back into.

Staying in that same house where the horror happened to us—living there for a long year—had something to do with the great difficulty we experienced. My wife never wanted to go back there, but I forced her to do it. Our son wanted her to do it. He wanted it as "his" house. But then, he didn't know all that had happened. Maybe it was a bad decision to go back in. But I don't think it would have mattered where we were living. My wife would not have been able to move on her own without the protective presence I provided. And there was no one else who could provide it, because she didn't trust anybody. So a different space in 1981 would not have made a difference—unless we had moved out of the country—and that was not possible.

I stayed. Made everything work the best I could. I've only ever deeply loved—to the point of the complete obliteration of every other thing or consideration—two people in my life. One is my wife, and the other is my son. So it was self-interested love—if that's not a contradiction in terms. Only if *she* got better would she, the best person, be able to help our son grow up. He was one of the most joyful occasions in our life together. And then, too, I'm pretty stubborn. When I make up my mind to do something, I try to get it done. . . .

But this thing will never be over. I know that now . . . and I feel sad.

A year later, David presented me with the following gift:

After All that Happened
(For my wife, who survived rape.)

You have come back to me
Through legends, rumors, wars of the self, analysis, tears,
And real blood, the agony of operations incalculable,
The severing of heads and tearing of flesh,
The mightiness of your suffering is beyond question or
Doubt.
When they pushed you farther than the mind could bear
    and
You took residence outside your skin to behold their sick
Violence, I was bound hand and foot beneath
Ashes of despair.
I heard your tears but could not move.
The sun the next morning rose as though nothing was
    wrong.
But your blood was a screen across it.
My eyes were the color of milk.
You touched my forehead, but
Cringed when I reached for your face. You knew it was no longer
There.

And now you have come back to me through caverns of
   despair.
You are not afraid of man monsters who
Walk midnight streets with their flags waving, killing women
And children across the old city's moons.
You have come back across deserts of loneliness and
   depressions
Set in stone.
You are moving across gleaming mirrors,
Your image rejoined to solid flesh.
Your mind is in a flowering garden now.
And I love you more than ever,
And I love you more, more,
More than ever before
All that happened.

. . . to go on living [we] have to tell stories, . . .
stories are the one sure way [we] know to touch the
heart and change the world.

—Dorothy Allison,

Two or Three Things I Know for Sure

CODA

As I Am Now*

Everybody's got . . . somethin' broken. . . . The way I figure these days,
the less broken have to take care of the more broken.

—THE FILM *ANGIE*

Fourteen years ago, on the "morning after" my rapes, I was still
in shock. I knew then that I was broken and needed fixing. I had
no idea how long the repair would take, but I thought, even in that
numbing instant, there would be a beginning and an end to the
pain of memory. In fact, only the intensity of those memories has
diminished. Pain, physical as well as psychic, carves deep and curious crevices into our minds and bodies. The conscious control of
memory keeps psychic pain at bay just as the intravenous drip of
morphine allays physical anguish. I hadn't realized that flashbacks

*This title was inspired by May Sarton's *As We Are Now* (W. W. Norton, New
York, 1973).

267

would return; that ancient, thought-buried fears would once again haunt the night. I thought I was finished with all that. Whole again. I thought. Not entirely. To refer to Toni Morrison's term in the novel *Beloved*, "re-memory" would make itself a felt process of daily living. Wholeness, I would learn, is a forever journey.

For years after the rape, I was unable to rest comfortably alone in a hotel room. I either stayed awake all night or slept in fitful starts until daybreak—always listening and watching. I railed against the night. I had to relearn previously second-nature behaviors as one learns to reuse a hand or an arm that has been traumatized. Now I am a better traveler. But still I am relearning. What was once simple is no longer so. I must plan life and action in great detail. I must know always where I am going. An excursion abroad always requires planning, but for me so does a trip across my own city. Days can be burdensome simply because they involve new situations, people, or emotions. Without warning, old and painful feelings reemerge. I now prefer lighted rooms to darkened ones. I like to feel in control of my physical surroundings. I need to know I can leave a place when I choose.

Not all women react to rape trauma like me. Some pick up the pieces of their lives, remarkably and efficiently move on. And there are others who get unmercifully locked into victim behavior and never share with another the fact of their trauma. They do not speak words of acknowledgment that begin to unlock the silent pain. I know from my research on disease and trauma that there are levels of attack and severity, idiosyncratic responses, and varying modes of patient-coping behavior that accompany any physical illness. Now, after all these years, I know that such variations accompany wounds to the spirit. We are each different in our experiential lives as black women. With our common historical fears, we bring a diversity of strengths and vulnerabilities to our rape trauma and recovery.

Even now, after writing my book, when my spirit is ever stronger, I am still stunned when I hear the word "rape." When I see it unexpectedly, it catches and redirects my attention, tenses the muscles of my body. I read newspapers to scan for interesting articles and important headlines, and I become easily distracted when I see the word "rape." I clip and file the article, as though a compendium of "incidents" will ward off further attacks. It is compulsive behavior. I would like to think that one day I will no longer need to clip and file or, better still, not have to resolve to correct the habit, because there will simply be fewer and fewer articles to clip. I keep my therapist handy like a pocket dictionary—accessible whenever I need her.

I am now able to walk down crowded streets in bustling cities and look black men in the face without fearing I will see the image of my rapists. And although always aware, I no longer move about with my hand on pocket-concealed sharp, deadly objects. I am no longer afraid of a caring touch from black men. I can once again savor the joy of making love. I no longer worry irrationally that young black men will somehow feel they have been insensibly doomed to the realm of "rape suspect" because America has instilled a fear of black men in all women, black and white. I breathe a sigh of relief that I no longer feel compelled to call black men acquaintances my "brothers" when I would just as soon not do so. But it still disconcerts me that even in a well-lit, well-appointed restaurant, I look at tidy, well-shaven black men and wonder if ever they have raped a date, or their wives with whom they are being so publicly and appropriately intimate. I look at presexual, kneesocked girls on buses and wonder how many of them live with secrets of rape and incest. When I pass through black communities and see day-care centers and school yards filled with black and brown and a few white children running and pushing in play, a sadness sweeps over me as I realize that many of them don't have a vocabulary for the atrocities already performed on their unknowing, unwilling bodies. Then again, anger nearly overwhelms me. I know that only we can save ourselves:

For Sethe it was as though the Clearing had come to her with all its heat and simmering leaves, where the voices of women searched for the right combination, the key, the code, the sound that broke the back of words. Building voice upon voice until they found it, and when they did it was a wave of sound wide enough to sound deep water and knock the pods off chestnut trees. It broke over Sethe and she trembled like the baptized in its wash.*

I am now able to articulate without fear, guilt, or shame that I am a black woman who has survived rape. I have survived my own silences. I am forever changed, and this realization no longer paralyzes me. Each day brings new revelations. Finding my place in a chorus of sound, I mean to knock pods off chestnut trees and bring the guilty to justice, the indifferent to attention, and the needful to safe harbor. As Joy Harjo says in her poem "The Creation Story":

> I'm not afraid of love
> or its consequence of light.
>
> It's not easy to say this
> or anything when my entrails
> dangle between paradise
> and fear.†

. . . .

The way out is to tell: speak the acts perpetrated upon us, speak the atrocities, speak the injustices, speak the personal violations of the soul. Someone will listen, someone will believe our stories, someone will join us. And until there are more who will bear witness to our truths as black women, we will do it for one another.

For now, that is enough.

*Toni Morrison, *Beloved* (Alfred A. Knopf, New York, 1987), p. 261.
†Joy Harjo, "The Creation Story," in *The Woman Who Fell from the Sky* (W. W. Norton, New York, 1994), p. 3.

ACKNOWLEDGMENTS

My gratitude begins and ends in my spiritual grounding, which has made this journey a possibility and its outcome a reality. Then I offer my appreciation to the vast number of people who have helped bring *Surviving the Silence* into existence. Thank you, each and every one. I am well aware that I did not write this book alone. I wrote the first line and then the rest moved in its own time.

A special and profound thank-you goes to all the women with whom I have spoken who assisted in ways directly and indirectly to turn my personal tragedy into a chorus of voices. Even though all the stories I heard and "translated" were not reproduced, please know that your courage and strength carried me through the very difficult periods of worrying this manuscript into a book. I know your faces, your gestures, your lives. Without the efforts of *all* of you there would be no book. My appreciation is extended also to the men—those voices present and those absent—who were brave enough to speak their minds on a topic rife with anxiety and confusion.

To my Temple University faculty and colleagues—Hank, Gary, Tony, Lori, Don (in memoriam), Terry, and Kermit—who kept my eyes on the prize of the Ph.D., I send my thanks. I extend appreciation to my former colleagues at the Germantown Friends School, Philadelphia, and to my glorious students there, who unknowingly sustained me during the early and harsh times of my rape recovery. Through your example in our Thursday morning Meetings for Worship, I learned to face myself, to speak with courage, and to accept my pain. To my generous colleagues in the College of General Studies (CGS) at the University of Pennsylvania, thank you for your genuine interest in my writing project and for rallying me onward whenever I flagged. Special thanks go to the director of CGS, my caring colleague, Richard Hendrix, whose generosity of spirit and confidence in my work made possible my leave time from the university to complete this book.

To my students and the African American Arts Alliance at the University of Pennsylvania who helped me "break silence" I send a special thank-you. To my student research assistants—Athena Chang, Soroya Webb, Hayley Thomas, Erme Maule, and Salamishah Tillet—the importance of your work is beyond measure. Your extraordinary research talents, ease with the Internet, and general tips at various stages of the project were enormously helpful. Thank you for your friendships.

To my colleagues and friends who generously read portions of the manuscript in progress and who graciously gave of their critical reading time, I offer my heartfelt thanks. A special line of thanks goes to my writer buddies and sisters-in-the-struggle who seemed never to tire of listening to me talk about "my project." My love to all of you.

I send my deepest appreciation and love to an assortment of family, friends, and extended family who initially walked me through the flames and later assisted in various ways to help me keep my hand in the fire as I wrote: Melvin (in memoriam) and Amy Pierce; Webster Smith (in memoriam); Sara and Larry; Ellen, Laurie, and Bill; Bessie and Sandy; Flora, Mike, Mertol (in memoriam), and the other neighbors of Phil-Ellena; Rinna and Gary; Pat and Don; Betty-Ann and family; Bettina and Gino; Regina and Manthia; Lori Jo and Karen; Joe and Sue; Tama, Paul, and family; John and Eleanor; Bill and Pat; Jim and Teri; Bill J.; W. D. (Bill)

Ehrhart; Marjorie L.; and finally, Aileen Christianson, who came from Scotland just to hold my hand and listen to my story weeks after the trial. Thank you, Ellen Lehman Dohmen, Adele Magner, Patricia Del Rio, Amy Rogers, Emy Rouse, Michele Rubin, Kurt Schlesinger, Margie Strosser, and Kalí Tal, for continuously listening without judgment to my many starts and stops, offering advice and love, and nodding me on.

My appreciation goes to Philadelphia's Women Organized Against Rape (WOAR) and all the dedicated women who work there, present and past, for allowing me to train in their volunteer programs long before they knew I was a rape survivor. And thank you, subsequently, for wholeheartedly supporting my personal struggles and my work on rape and black women. Assorted thank-you notes: to my wary transcriptionist, whose work on this emotionally grueling and precise task was inordinately appreciated; to Ed Rendell and the Sex Crimes Unit of the Philadelphia Police Department; to Mark Lipowicz, my "Perry Mason," for his kindness and professional acumen; to Joe Britt and Gil Mathis, whose astute detective skills made a trial possible; to my very special friends and advocates Bessie Jordan Byrd and Sara Bergstresser for being my guardian angels—in court and out.

Thank you, Jane Dystel, for being the agent extraordinaire, and for understanding the importance of my manuscript and the voices within. My appreciation goes to the Jane Dystel Literary Agency staff, who always treated me with respect. Thank you, Jill Bialosky, for your expertise and exquisite editorial care in suggesting revisions in a difficult and delicate manuscript. You were careful always not to bruise my ego, and sought to preserve my voice and integrity. You gave *Surviving the Silence* a home. Thank you, Eve Grubin and Susan Middleton, for your roles in bringing my manuscript to book form. Thank you, Deborah Morton Hoyt, for capturing the spirit of my work in your artistic design.

I will always be indebted to Geraldine DePaula, M.D., who remained a resource and a touchstone as I uncovered my wounds, excavated my traumas, and strove to articulate the rape traumas of others. And a simple thank-you does not seem sufficient for "Uncle" and Amy, who gave us their home and their arms for comfort in our darkest hour. I offer my deepest appreciation to my father-in-law (in memoriam) and mother-in-law, who have always loved and nourished me as one of their own.

Like chocolates, I always save the very best for last. To my parents, Weslyne and Joseph, for whom adequate words of gratitude are impossible, I salute your courage in breaking your silences—my love and respect to you always. To my son, I would proffer the world if I could harness it, for his forever believing in me and my power to do what *he* thought was "the best." Your words on reading a first draft more than once spurred me on and inspired my creativity. To my husband—colleague, confidant, nurturer, lover, and friend—who knew that in telling my story I would, per force, "tell" his: I extend an unending string of gratitudes. Whenever I had doubts, you never ceased believing that I would begin and that I could finish. Your words of encouragement followed me each line, each page, each day: "I loved you before, I love you now, I'll love you forever."

To those whose names do not appear here, forgive my oversight. Know that I have thanked you a million times in my heart.

SELECTED READINGS

The following titles offer suggested readings of novels, autobiographies, and non-fiction pertaining to rape and issues of survival. The listing is by no means exhaustive. These titles are preeminently works that resonate with my own project and spirit of survival.

Allison, Dorothy. *Bastard Out of Carolina*. Dutton Book/Penguin Group, New York, 1992.

————. *Two or Three Things I Know for Sure*. Dutton Book/Penguin Group, New York, 1995.

Allison, Julie A., and Lawrence S. Wrightsman. *Rape: The Misunderstood Crime*. SAGE Publications, Newberry Park, Calif., 1993.

Angelou, Maya. *I Know Why the Caged Bird Sings*. Random House, New York, 1970.

Bart, Pauline B., and Patricia H. O'Brien. *Stopping Rape: Successful*

Survival Strategies. Athene Series, Teachers College Press, New York, 1993.

Blume, E. Sue. *Secret Survivors: Uncovering Incest and Its Aftereffects in Women*. Ballantine Books, New York, 1990. (Blume is the creator of the Incest Survivors' Aftereffects Checklist.)

Boumil, Marcia Mobilia, Joel Friedman, and Barbara Ewert Taylor. *Date Rape: The Secret Epidemic*. Health Communications, Deerfield, Fla., 1993.

Brent, Linda. *Incidents in the Life of a Slave Girl*, ed. L. Maria Child. Harcourt Brace Jovanovich, New York, 1973.

Brownmiller, Susan. *Against Our Will: Men, Women, and Rape*. Copyright 1975. Fawcett Columbine/Ballantine Books, New York, 1993.

Buchwald, Emilie, Pamela R. Fletcher, and Martha Roth, eds. *Transforming a Rape Culture*. Milkweed Editions, Minneapolis, 1993.

Caignon, Denise, and Gail Groves. *Her Wits about Her: Self-Defense Success Stories by Women*. Perennial Library/Harper & Row, New York, 1987. (Authors are founders of Women Who Resist: The Success Story Project.)

Cary, Lorene. *Black Ice*. Alfred A. Knopf, New York, 1991.

Conroy, Pat. *The Prince of Tides*. Houghton Mifflin, New York, 1986.

Estrich, Susan. *Real Rape: How the Legal System Victimizes Women Who Say No*. Harvard University Press, Cambridge, 1987.

Eyman, Joy Satterwhite. *How to Convict a Rapist*. Copyright 1980. Scarborough House, Lanham, Md., 1994.

Fairstein, Linda A. *Sexual Violence: Our War Against Rape*. William Morrow, New York, 1993.

Finkelhor, David, and Kersti Yllo. *License to Rape: Sexual Abuse of Wives*. Free Press/Macmillan, New York, 1985.

Fraser, Sylvia. *My Father's House: A Memoir of Incest and of Healing*. Reprint. HarperCollins, New York, 1989.

Funk, Rus Ervin. *Stopping Rape: A Challenge for Men*. New Society Publishers, Philadelphia, 1993.

Gardner, Debbie. *Survive: Don't Be a Victim*. Warner Books, New York, 1984.

Gates, Henry Louis, Jr., ed. *Reading Black, Reading Feminist.* Meridian/Penguin Group, New York, 1990.

Goodman, James. *Stories of Scottsboro.* Vintage/Random House, New York, 1994.

Groth, A. Nicholas, with H. Jean Birnbaum. *Men Who Rape: The Psychology of the Offender.* Plenum Press, New York, 1979.

Guy-Sheftall, Beverly. *Words of Fire: An Anthology of African-American Feminist Thought.* New Press, New York, 1995.

Herman, Judith Lewis. *Trauma and Recovery: The Aftermath of Violence from Domestic Abuse to Political Terror.* BasicBooks/ HarperCollins, New York, 1992.

Herron, Carolivia. *Thereafter Johnnie.* Vintage Contemporaries/ Random House, New York, 1992.

hooks, bell. *Ain't I a Woman? Black Women and Feminism.* South End Press, Boston, 1992.

Horos, Carol V. *RAPE.* Tobey Publishing, New Canaan, Conn., 1974. (Includes a nationwide directory of U.S. rape crisis centers.)

Johnson, Kathryn M. *If You Are Raped: What Every Woman Needs to Know.* Learning Publications, Holmes Beach, Fla., 1985.

Jones, Gayl. *Corregidora.* Random House, New York, 1975.

Jordan, June. *Technical Difficulties.* Vintage/Random House, New York, 1992.

Katz, Judith H. *No Fairy Godmothers, No Magic Wands: The Healing Process after Rape.* Revised Edition. R&E Publishers, San Jose, Calif., 1984.

Kelly, Liz. *Surviving Sexual Violence.* Polity Press, Oxford, England, 1988.

Lefkowitz, Bernard. *Our Guys: The Glen Ridge Rape and the Secret Life of the Perfect Surburb.* University of California Press, Berkeley, 1997.

Lena, Dan, and Marie Howard. *Defend: Preventing Rape and Other Sexual Assaults.* SPI Books/Shapolsky Publishers, New York, 1992.

Levy, Barrie, ed. *Dating Violence: Young Women in Danger.* Seal Press, Seattle, 1991.

London Rape Crisis Centre. *Sexual Violence: The Reality for Women.* Women's Press, London, 1984.

Lorde, Audre. *Sister Outsider.* Crossing Press, Freedom, Calif., 1984.

————. *Zami: A New Spelling of My Name.* Crossing Press, Freedom, Calif., 1982.

Madhubuti, Haki R. *Claiming Earth: Race, Rage, Rape, Redemption.* Third World Press, Chicago, 1994.

McEvoy, Alan W., and Jeff B. Brookings. *If She Is Raped: A Book for Husbands, Fathers and Male Friends.* 2nd ed. Learning Publications, Holmes Beach, Fla., 1990.

McLennan, Karen J., ed. *Nature's Ban: Women's Incest Literature.* Northeastern University Press, Boston, 1996.

Morrison, Toni. *Beloved.* Alfred A. Knopf, New York, 1987.

————. *The Bluest Eye.* Holt, Rinehart & Winston, New York, 1970.

Naylor, Gloria. *The Women of Brewster Place.* Viking Press, New York, 1982.

Parrot, Andrea. *Coping with Date Rape and Acquaintance Rape.* The Rosen Publishing Group, New York, 1988.

Rhodes, Jewell Parker. *Magic City.* HarperCollins, New York, 1997.

Roiphe, Katie. *The Morning After: Sex, Fear, and Feminism.* Back Bay Books/Little, Brown, Boston, 1993.

Russell, Diana E. H. *The Politics of Rape: The Victim's Perspective.* Stein & Day Publishers, New York, 1984.

Sanday, Peggy Reeves. *Fraternity Gang Rape: Sex, Brotherhood, and Privilege on Campus.* New York University Press, New York, 1990.

————. *A Woman Scorned: Acquaintance Rape on Trial.* Doubleday, New York, 1996.

Scott, Kesho Yvonne. *The Habit of Surviving.* One World/Ballantine Books, New York, 1991.

Searles, Patricia, and Ronald J. Berger, eds. *Rape and Society: Readings on the Problem of Sexual Assault.* Westview Press, Boulder, Colo., 1995.

Spring, Jacqueline. *Cry Hard and Swim: The Story of an Incest Survivor.* Virago Press, London, 1987.

Steinem, Gloria. *Outrageous Acts and Everyday Rebellions.* Signet/ Penguin Group, New York, 1986.

Tal, Kalí. *Worlds of Hurt: Reading the Literatures of Trauma.* Cambridge University Press, New York, 1996.

Thomas, T. *Men Surviving Incest: A Male Survivor Shares the Process of Recovery.* Launch Press, Walnut Creek, Calif., 1989.

Thompson, Becky W. *A Hunger So Wide and So Deep: American Women*

Speak Out on Eating Problems. University of Minnesota Press, Minneapolis, 1994.

Vachss, Alice. *Sex Crimes*. Random House, New York, 1993.

Walker, Alice. *The Color Purple*. Harcourt Brace Jovanovich, New York, 1982.

———. *In Search of Our Mothers' Gardens*. Harcourt Brace Jovanovich, New York, 1983.

Walker, Rebecca. *To Be Real: Telling the Truth and Changing the Face of Feminism*. Anchor/Doubleday, New York, 1995.

Wallace, Michele. *Black Macho and the Myth of the Superwoman*. Copyright 1978. Verso Press, New York, 1990.

Warshaw, Robin. *I Never Called It Rape: The Ms. Report on Recognizing, Fighting and Surviving Date Rape*. HarperCollins, New York, 1994.

White, Evelyn C. *The Black Women's Health Book: Speaking for Ourselves*. Seal Press, Seattle, 1990.

Wolf, Naomi. *Fire with Fire: The New Female Power and How to Use It*. Fawcett/Ballantine Books, New York, 1993.

I suggest, as well, the following poets, who were inspirations for me: Margaret Atwood, Houston Baker, Gwendolyn Brooks, Toi Derricotte, Rita Dove, Joy Harjo, June Jordan, Ethelbert Miller, Adrienne Rich, Sonia Sanchez, and Alice Walker.

RESOURCES, NATIONAL AND LOCAL

RAINN: RAPE, ABUSE, AND INCEST NATIONAL NETWORK*

1-800-656-HOPE / 1-800-656-4673
HOTLINE

The Rape, Abuse, and Incest National Network (RAINN) was established in 1994. It is a free, twenty-four-hour hotline for survivors of sexual assault. Anyone anywhere in the United States can pick up a phone and call 1-800-656-HOPE to be in touch with a crisis center near them. All calls to RAINN's 800 number are completely confidential.

Source: Information from the Internet (http://www.rainn.org) and from E. Maule, Women's Center, University of Pennsylvania.

When a call is made, the caller will first hear a voice-mail recording: "Hello. You have reached RAINN, the Rape, Abuse, and Incest National Network Hotline. To speak with a counselor, please press 1 now. To join RAINN, make a donation, etc., press 2 now. . . ." The caller may then press 1 and the phone rings. The caller is then connected to the closest crisis center for help.

RAINN, founded by singer/songwriter Tori Amos, is funded by several sources. The original funders—Warner Music Group and Atlantic Records—are committed to RAINN's survival. Other funders include MCI, Westwood One, the Ryka Rose Foundation, and the Jacobs Family Foundation. RAINN receives no funds from any government entity. There is no cost for a crisis center to participate.

To reach the RAINN business office, call the hotline, and select the appropriate number code. The mailing address below is for business only. *A counselor can only be reached through the 800 hotline number above.*

RAINN
252 Tenth Street, N.E.
Washington, D.C. 20002
(202) 544-1034 (phone)
(202) 544-1401 (fax)
E-mail: RAINNmail@aol.com

PHILADELPHIA RESOURCES*

Abused Women
739-9999

Addiction Hotline
(610) 645-3610

American Red Cross
299-4000

Amulis (Self-Defense)
224-1573

AWARE (Self-Defense)
727-1218

Center City Crime Victim Services
665-9680

Child Abuse
(800) 932-0313

DA's Office Child Abuse Unit
686-8084

Eliza Shirley Shelter for Women
568-5111

Gay and Lesbian Counseling Services
732-8255

HUP Psychiatry Referral Line
3600 Spruce Street, 19104
349-5220

Linea Dierecta
(Hotline for battered
Latinas)
235-9992

Mental Health Advocate
(Mobile emergency team)
685-6440

Philadelphia AIDS Hotline
985-AIDS

Philadelphia Lesbian & Gay Task Force
(Violence/Discrimination Hotline)
772-2005

Philadlephia Sexual Abuse Project
842-9987

Runaway Hotline
(800) 621-4000

Suicide and Crisis Intervention
686-4420

Teen Hotline
1233 Locust Street, 3rd floor, 19107
731-TEEN (Staffed by teens to educate teens)

Voyage House (Teen counseling and runaways)
545-2910

*Source: E. Maule, Women's Center, University of Pennsylvania.

Women Against Abuse Hotline (and
    shelter)
    386-7777

Women in Transition (for battered
    and/or substance-abusing
    women)
    751-1111

Women's Therapy Center
    567-1111

Youth Crisis Line
    (800) 448-4663

Women Organized Against Rape (WOAR)
1233 Locust Street, 19107
985-3333
(24-hour hotline)
counseling, education, advocacy—*FREE*

Sex Crimes Unit of
Philadelphia Police
685-1180
685-1181
685-1182

DA's Office Rape Unit
686-8084

There is a balm in Gilead
To make the wounded whole. . . .

—Traditional African American Spiritual

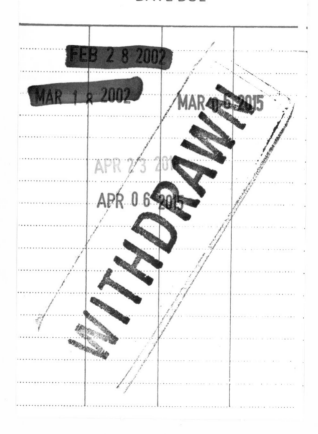